4th RaPID Workshop: Resources and ProcessIng of linguistic, para-linguistic and extra-linguistic Data from people with various forms of cognitive/psychiatric/developmental impairments

Held at LREC 2022

Marseille, France
20 - 25 June 2022

Editors:

Dimitrios Kokkinakis
Charalambos K. Themistocleous
Kristina Lundholm Fors
Athanasios Tsanas
Kathleen C. Fraser

ISBN: 978-1-7138-6112-6

Printed from e-media with permission by:

Curran Associates, Inc.
57 Morehouse Lane
Red Hook, NY 12571

CURRAN ASSOCIATES INC. proceedings.com

Some format issues inherent in the e-media version may also appear in this print version.

Association for Computational Linguistics
209 N. Eighth Street
Stroudsburg, Pennsylvania 18360

Phone: 1-570-476-8006
Fax: 1-570-476-0860

acl@aclweb.org

Additional copies of this publication are available from:

Curran Associates, Inc.
57 Morehouse Lane
Red Hook, NY 12571 USA
Phone: 845-758-0400
Fax: 845-758-2633
Email: curran@proceedings.com
Web: www.proceedings.com

LREC 2022
Language Resources and Evaluation Conference
20-25 June 2022

PROCEEDINGS

The 4th RaPID Workshop: Resources and ProcessIng of linguistic, para-linguistic and extra-linguistic Data from people with various forms of cognitive/psychiatric/developmental impairments

Editors:
Dimitrios Kokkinakis,
Charalambos K. Themistocleous,
Kristina Lundholm Fors,
Athanasios Tsanas,
Kathleen C. Fraser

Proceedings of the LREC 2022 workshop on: Resources and ProcessIng of linguistic, para-linguistic and extra-linguistic Data from people with various forms of cognitive/psychiatric/developmental impairments (RaPID-4 2022)

Edited by:
Dimitrios Kokkinakis,
Charalambos K. Themistocleous,
Kristina Lundholm Fors,
Athanasios Tsanas,
Kathleen C. Fraser

EAN: 9791095546771

For more information:
European Language Resources Association (ELRA)
9 rue des Cordelières
75013, Paris
France
http://www.elra.info
Email: lrec@elda.org

Message from the General Chair

Welcome to the LREC2022 Workshop on *"Resources and ProcessIng of linguistic, para-linguistic and extra-linguistic Data from people with various forms of cognitive/psychiatric/developmental impairments" (RaPID-4).* This volume documents the Proceedings of the RaPID-4 Workshop held on Saturday, June 25th, 2022, as part of the 13th edition of the LREC 2022 conference (International Conference on Language Resources and Evaluation). In this version of RaPID we also had the opportunity to incorporate the PSST share task on *"Post-Stroke Speech Transcription"* (task: *"Automated Phoneme Recognition of Anomic Speech"*, see here https://psst.study for more details and below for an outline).

RaPID-4 aims to be an interdisciplinary forum for researchers to share information, findings, methods, models and experience on the collection and processing of data produced by people with various forms of mental, cognitive, neuropsychiatric, or neurodegenerative impairments, such as aphasia, dementia, autism, bipolar disorder, Parkinson's disease or schizophrenia. Particularly, the workshop's focus is on creation, processing and application of data resources from individuals at various stages of these impairments and with varying degrees of severity. Creation of resources includes e.g. annotation, description, analysis and interpretation of linguistic, paralinguistc and extra-linguistic data (such as spontaneous spoken language, transcripts, eyetracking measurements, wearable and sensor data, etc). Processing is done to identify, extract, correlate, evaluate and disseminate various linguistic or multimodal phenotypes and measurements, which then can be applied to aid diagnosis, monitor the progression or predict individuals at risk.

A central aim of the workshop is to facilitate the study of the relationships among various levels of linguistic, paralinguistic and extra-linguistic observations (e.g., acoustic measures; phonological, syntactic and semantic features; eye tracking measurements; sensors, signs and multimodal signals). Submission of papers are invited in all of the aforementioned areas, particularly emphasizing multidisciplinary aspects of processing such data and the interplay between clinical/nursing/medical sciences, language technology, computational linguistics, natural language processing (NLP) and computer science. Processing of such data can be used to identify, extract, correlate, evaluate and disseminate various linguistic or multimodal phenotypes and measurements, which then can be applied to aid diagnosis, monitor the progression or predict individuals at risk. The workshop will act as a stimulus for the discussion of several ongoing research questions driving current and future research by bringing together researchers from various research communities.

The workshop solicited papers describing original research; and preferably describing substantial and completed work, but also focused on a contribution, a negative result, an interesting application nugget, a software package, a small, or work in progress. The workshop acted as a stimulus for the discussion of several ongoing research questions driving current and future research and challenges by bringing together researchers from various research communities. We are grateful to our Program Committee members for their hard work in reading and evaluating all submissions. At the end, each submission received between 3 to 5 reviews, which helped the authors revise and improve their papers accordingly.

There were 12 contributions accepted for the workshop. Keynote speakers were: Dr. Athanasios Tsanas, the Usher Institute, University of Edinburgh, UK, and Associate Professor Visar Berisha, Arizona State University, USA.

Workshop URL: https://spraakbanken.gu.se/en/rapid-2022.

The PSST Challenge

The PSST Challenge is a collaboration between Oregon Health and Science University (OHSU) and Portland State University (PSU). A project supported via a grant from the National Institute on Deafness and Other Communication Disorders NIH (R01-DC015999-04S1), the purpose of which is to promote the use of clinical datasets of aphasic speech by the mainstream machine learning community. The original dataset comes via the AphasiaBank project (https://aphasia.talkbank.org, R01-DC008524), and access to the data is governed by the AphasiaBank project's protocols.

Anomia, or word-finding difficulty, is one of the most prominent cognitive sequelae of stroke, affecting 2.5-4 million stroke survivors in the US alone. Its ensuing communication difficulties can have a major impact on the ability of a person to produce words and can affect their daily activities and health-related quality of life. Existing diagnostic and assessment tools are laborious to administer, and efforts to automate their administration often require detailed phonemic transcription by clinical staff, limiting their use in practice.

Historically, automated speech recognition (ASR) technologies have struggled to adequately handle disordered speech of the form produced by individuals with anomia. Furthermore, the most clinically-interesting features of speech mispronunciations, neologisms, etc. are precisely those that ASR finds the most challenging. Recent years, have seen major advances in the state of the art in ASR, with architectures such as wav2vec 2.0 achieving notable decreases in phoneme error rate; however, these results have been on speech from individuals without neurologic impairment.

The PSST Challenge will engage the ASR community in translating the latest computational techniques to the task of high-accuracy automated phoneme recognition in disordered speech, which has applications in many different clinical domains. Participants, after completing a data use agreement, will have access to a unique dataset for phonemic ASR, consisting of a set of audio recordings of English-speaking individuals with anomia undergoing assessments, as well as a new set of high-quality annotations including phonemic transcriptions.

The primary task will be high-accuracy automated phoneme recognition of disordered speech, with a second task focused on classifying audio samples into clinically-relevant categories. No clinical background is necessary, and we encourage participation by people with all levels of computational expertise.

Contacts for the task: Steven Bedrick (bedricks@ohsu.edu) or Gerasimos Fergadiotis (gf3@pdx.edu). Shared Task URL: https://psst.study.

Topics of Interest

The topics of interest for the workshop session include but are not limited to:

- Infrastructure for the domain: building, adapting and availability of linguistic resources, data sets and tools
- Methods and protocols for data collection
- Acquisition and combination of novel data samples; including digital biomarkers, continuous streaming, monitoring and aggregation of measurements; as well as self-reported behavioral and/or physiological and activity data
- Guidelines, protocols, annotation schemas, annotation tools
- Addressing the challenges of representation, including dealing with data sparsity and dimensionality issues, feature combination from different sources and modalities
- Domain adaptation of NLP/AI tools
- Acoustic/phonetic/phonologic, syntactic, semantic, pragmatic and discourse analysis of data; including modeling of perception (e.g. eye-movement measures of reading) and production processes (e.g. recording of the writing process by means of digital pens, keystroke logging etc.); use of gestures accompanying speech and non-linguistic behavior
- Use of wearable, vision, and ambient sensors or their fusion for detection of cognitive disabilities or decline
- (Novel) Modeling and deep / machine learning approaches for early diagnostics, prediction, monitoring, classification etc. of various cognitive, psychiatric and/or developmental impairments
- Evaluation of the significance of features for screening and diagnostics
- Evaluation of tools, systems, components, metrics, applications and technologies including methodologies making use of NLP; e.g. for predicting clinical scores from (linguistic) features
- Digital platforms/technologies for cognitive assessment and brain training
- Evaluation, comparison and critical assessment of resources
- Involvement of medical/clinical professionals and patients
- Ethical, gender bias and legal questions in research with human data in the domain, and how they can be handled
- Deployment, assessment platforms and services as well as innovative mining approaches that can be translated to practical/clinical applications
- Experiences, lessons learned and the future of NLP/AI in the area

Organizers

Dimitrios Kokkinakis – University of Gothenburg – Sweden
Charalambos K. Themistocleous – Johns Hopkins University – USA
Kristina Lundholm Fors – Lund University – Sweden
Athanasios Tsanas – The University of Edinburgh – UK
Kathleen C. Fraser – National Research Council – Canada

PSST Organizers

Steven Bedrick – Oregon Health & Science University – USA
Gerasimos Fergadiotis – Portland State University – USA
Robert Gale – Oregon Health & Science University – USA
Mikala Fleegle – Portland State University – USA

Program Committee:

Visar Berisha, Arizona State University (USA)
Gaël Dias, University of Caen Normandie (FRANCE)
Jon Andoni Duñabeitia, Universidad Nebrija and the Arctic University (SPAIN/NORWAY)
Davida Fromm, Carnegie Mellon University (USA)
Valantis Fyndanis, University of Technology, Cyprus and University of Oslo (NORWAY)
Gloria Gagliardi, University of Bologna (ITALY)
Kallirroi Georgila, University of Southern California (USA)
Leontios Hadjileontiadis, Khalifa University (UNITED ARAB EMIRATES)
Christine Howes, University of Gothenburg (SWEDEN)
Alexandra König, University Côte d'azur and INRIA (FRANCE)
Saturnino Luz, The University of Edinburgh (UK)
Christina Manouilidou, University of Ljubljana (SLOVENIA)
Jeanette Melin, RI.SE (SWEDEN)
Ricardo Muñoz Sánchez, University of Gothenburg (SWEDEN)
Emily Prud'hommeaux, Boston College (USA)
Angus Roberts, King's College (UK)
Masoud Rouhizadeh, University of Florida (USA)
Roozbeh Sadeghian, Harrisburg University (USA)
Kairit Sirts, University of Tartu (ESTONIA)
Spyridoula Varlokosta, University of Athens (GREECE)
Yasunori Yamada, IBM Research (JAPAN)
Åsa Wengelin, University of Gothenburg (SWEDEN)

Table of Contents

RaPID-4 Workshop Program

Saturday, June 25, 2022

09:00–13:00 Session 1

09:00–09:10 Welcome and Introduction

09:10–09:40 Invited Speaker 1: Associate Professor Visar Berisha - Developing speech-based clinical machine learning models that work: should we believe reported accuracies in the academic literature?

09:40–10:05 *The Effect of eHealth Training on Dysarthric Speech*
Chiara Pesenti, Loes Van Bemmel, Roeland van Hout and Helmer Strik

10:10–10:30 *Generating Synthetic Clinical Speech Data through Simulated ASR Deletion Error*
Hali Lindsay, Johannes Tröger, Mario Magued Mina, Philipp Müller, Nicklas Linz, Jan Alexandersson and Inez Ramakers

10:30–11:00 *Morning Coffee Break*

11:05–11:30 *A Novel Metrological Approach to a More Consistent Way of Defining and Analyzing Memory Task Difficulty in Word Learning List Tests with Repeated Trials*
Jeanette Melin and Leslie Pendrill

11:35–12:00 *Extraction and Classification of Acoustic Features from Italian Speaking Children with Autism Spectrum Disorders.*
Federica Beccaria, Gloria Gagliardi and Dimitrios Kokkinakis

12:05–12:30 *Classification of German Jungian Extraversion and Introversion Texts with Assessment of Changes During the COVID-19 Pandemic*
Dirk Johannßen, Chris Biemann and David Scheffer

13:00–14:00 *Lunch*

Saturday, June 25, 2022 (continued)

14:00–16:00 Session 2: PSST Challenge

14:00–14:20 *The Post-Stroke Speech Transcription (PSST) Challenge*
Robert C. Gale, Mikala Fleegle, Gerasimos Fergadiotis and Steven Bedrick

14:20–14:40 *Post-Stroke Speech Transcription Challenge (Task B): Correctness Detection in Anomia Diagnosis with Imperfect Transcripts*
Trang Tran

14:45–15:05 *Speech Data Augmentation for Improving Phoneme Transcriptions of Aphasic Speech Using Wav2Vec 2.0 for the PSST Challenge*
Birger Moell, Jim O'Regan, Shivam Mehta, Ambika Kirkland, Harm Lameris, joakim gustafson and Jonas Beskow

15:10–15:30 *Data Augmentation for the Post-Stroke Speech Transcription (PSST) Challenge: Sometimes Less Is More*
Jiahong Yuan, Xingyu Cai and Kenneth Church

15:30–15:50 Open Forum Discussion

15:50–16:30 *Afternoon Coffee Break*

16:30–18:10 Session 3

16:30–17:00 Invited Speaker 2: Dr Athanasios Tsanas - Harnessing voice signals using signal processing and statistical machine learning: applications in mental health and other biomedical and life sciences applications.

17:05–17:20 *CorEDs: A Corpus on Eating Disorders*
Melissa Donati and Carlo Strapparava

17:25–17:40 *A Database of Multimodal Data to Construct a Simulated Dialogue Partner with Varying Degrees of Cognitive Health*
Ruihao Pan, Ziming Liu, Fengpei Yuan, Maryam Zare, Xiaopeng Zhao and Rebecca Jane Passonneau

17:45–18:00 *Segmentation of the Speech Flow for the Evaluation of Spontaneous Productions in Pathologies Affecting the Language Capacity. 4 Case Studies of Schizophrenia*
Valentina Saccone and Simona Trillocco

18:00–18:10 Closing remarks from the RaPID-4 and PSST organizers

Proceedings of the RaPID-4 @LREC 2022, pages 1–8
Marseille, 25 June 2022

The effect of eHealth training on dysarthric speech

Chiara Pesenti[1], Loes van Bemmel[2,3], Roeland van Hout[4], Helmer Strik[4,5,6]
Department of Humanities, Department of Artificial Intelligence,
Institute for Computing and Information Sciences, Centre for Language Studies,
Centre for Language and Speech Technology, Donders Institute for Brain, Cognition and Behaviour
University of Turin
Radboud University Nijmegen
chiara.pesenti@edu.unito.it, {loes.vanbemmel, roeland.vanhout, helmer.strik}@ru.nl

Abstract

In the current study on dysarthric speech, we investigate the effect of web-based treatment, and whether there is a difference between content and function words. Since the goal of the treatment is to speak louder, without raising pitch, we focus on acoustic-phonetic features related to loudness, intensity, and pitch. We analyse dysarthric read speech from eight speakers at word level. We also investigate whether there are differences between content words and function words, and whether the treatment has a different impact on these two classes of words. Linear Mixed-Effects models show that there are differences before and after treatment, that for some speakers the treatment has the desired effect, but not for all speakers, and that the effect of the treatment on words for the two categories does not seem to be different. To a large extent, our results are in line with the results of a previous study in which the same data were analyzed in a different way, i.e. by studying intelligibility scores.

Keywords: eHealth, Parkinson's Disease, dysarthric speech, POS tagging, function and content words

1. Introduction

The automatic acoustic-phonetic analysis of atypical speech is a promising pathway in pathological speech assessment. Automatically identifying the most relevant characteristics of pathological speech could lead to a reliable, accurate and non-invasive assessment method, able to distinguish typical speech from atypical speech, as well as measuring the extent of speech problems and diagnosing different types of atypical speech.

We focus in this study on dysarthria caused by Parkinson's disease (PD). PD is a chronic and progressive neurodegenerative disorder that significantly affects the use and cost of societal resources. More than 90% of patients with PD suffer from speech disorders (De Swart et al., 2003), collectively referred as dysarthria. Such disorders are typically characterized by increased acoustic noise, reduced voice intensity, harsh and breathy voice quality, lack of emotional expression and tonal changes, disturbances of speech rate, imprecise articulation of consonants, involuntary introduction of pauses, rapid repetitions of words and syllables, and sudden deceleration or acceleration in speech (Yang et al., 2020). These symptoms often have serious repercussions on speech intelligibility and daily communication. Moreover, some of them, such as the lack of emotional expression, characterize dysarthria caused by PD, and do not arise in other types of dysarthria.

Speech training with a serious game was given to eight PD patients. Especially focusing on acoustic features related to loudness, intensity and pitch, the game aimed to improve the intelligibility of people with dysarthric speech. Ganzeboom et al. (2022) collected human ratings of the speakers' intelligibility scores of utterances in a pre and post test and concluded that there was a significant speaker-specific improvement. Furthermore, the positive effect of a web-based treatment is thoroughly investigated and confirmed in Ganzeboom et al. (2022). We aimed to investigate its positive effects on acoustic-phonetic features related to loudness, intensity, and pitch.

In this study, we investigated whether this improvement is directly reflected in the acoustic features of loudness, intensity and pitch at the word level, using NLP parsing tools. We also wanted to explore the differences of these three types of acoustic features among two global word categories, namely content words and function words.

2. Background

2.1. *Treasure Hunters*: a web-based treatment

The serious speech training game Treasure Hunters was developed in the project CHASING: 'CHAllenging Speech training In Neurological patients by interactive Gaming'. Additional information about CHASING project is given in (Ganzeboom et al., 2022) (`http://waag.org/project/chasing`, `http://hstrik.ruhosting.nl/CHASING`).

The Treasure Hunters game is based on the Pitch Limiting Voice Treatment (PLVT), where the goal is to improve speech intelligibility by speaking louder, without raising the pitch. Treasure Hunters gives automatic feedback on the users' voice loudness and pitch, encouraging them to speak loud and low.

The target group for the Treasure Hunters game are older patients suffering from dysarthria due to PD. Previous studies by Ganzeboom et al. (Ganzeboom et al.,

2018) (Ganzeboom et al., 2022) showed that the effect of the game on intelligibility varied between speakers. For some speakers the game seemed to have to desired effect, while for others this is not the case.

2.2. Loudness, intensity and pitch

PLVT is the standard treatment in dysarthria therapy in the Netherlands (Kalf et al., 2011). In this treatment, patients are encouraged to speak 'loud and low', implying that they should try to increase voice intensity, while avoiding to raise their pitch, which easily happens when intensity increases. Increasing voice intensity often also results in better articulation. The purpose of avoiding the side effect of pitch increase distinguishes PLVT from Lee Silverman Voice Treatment (LSVT) (Ramig et al., 1995), which focuses only on increasing intensity. Therefore, in the current study, we focus on loudness, intensity, and pitch.

To study the effects of this therapy, we selected features from eGeMAPS (Eyben et al., 2015) and features extracted with our own Praat script that are related to loudness, intensity, and pitch. Note that the entire set of acoustic features was already analyzed at the utterance level by van Bemmel et al. (2021) for the same dysarthric speakers. Several individual features related to loudness and pitch were found to be relevant in classifying before and after treatment recordings. Here, instead of at utterance level, we want to analyse those features at word level. Moreover, we want to identify more general factors or components in the many features related to intensity, loudness, and pitch.

2.3. Content and function words

One of the aims of this study is to investigate whether there are meaningful acoustic-phonetic features for the distinction between content words and function words. These two classes of words are based on syntactic-semantic criteria. Content words are members of open word classes with a clear lexical meaning, such as names, nouns, lexical verbs, adverbs or adjectives. They are phonologically and morphologically independent. Function words belong to closed word classes that do not carry a full lexical meaning, and determine the grammatical relations between content words. They are often phonologically and morphologically dependent, have reduced scrambling possibilities, and usually have a shorter length and high frequency of occurrence.

Importantly, content and function words have been studied in relation to atypical speech. Several studies on stuttering (Howell et al., 1999), aphasic speech (Bird et al., 2002), and amyotrophic lateral sclerosis (Turner and Tjaden, 2000), observed differences in the production and perception of these two word classes. In particular, Turner and Tjaden (2000) focused on acoustic differences between content and function words, finding no statistical difference between healthy and pathological speech for vowels acoustic features of formants, space area and duration. Their work also highlights that these features values were generally larger for content words and that the difference of vowel space area for content and function words, although not statistically relevant, tended to be smaller in pathological speech than healthy speech. Bird et al. (2002) instead, studied the production and the comprehension of these two categories of words, finding discrepancies between content and function words only for reading tasks, but not when the imageability was controlled.

To determine how Dutch parts of speech are distributed among these two categories, a literature study on Dutch content and function words was carried in order to classify Dutch POS tags into the two word categories, as explained in section 3.3.

2.4. Research Questions

1. Does the web-based gaming treatment have an impact at word level with respect to loudness, intensity, and pitch?

2. (a) Is the impact general or dependent on the speaker involved, and (b), if speaker dependent, do loudness, intensity, and pitch values improve in line with the intelligibility score improvements found in Ganzeboom et al. (Ganzeboom et al., 2022)?

3. Does the treatment have the same impact on content and function words?

3. Material and methods

3.1. Data and Participants

The speech data were recorded from eight native Dutch speakers with Parkinson's Disease (PD) who underwent web-based treatment with the "Treasure Hunters" serious game for speech training (Ganzeboom et al., 2022). During the four weeks of training the speakers were instructed to speak loud and low, following the concept of Pitch Limiting Voice Treatment used in the Treasure Hunters game. Each speaker was recorded twice, pre-treatment (T2) and four weeks after continuous treatment (T3). During both times, each speaker was asked to read seven Dutch sentences out loud after reading it silently for themselves.

We selected all 32 read sentences from the phonetically balanced story "Papa en Marloes" (11 sentences; (Van de Weijer and Slis, 1991)) and the text of apple pie recipes (21 sentences), both used by Ganzeboom et al. (2022). These sentences vary between 4 and 14 words with a total of 251 words (143 content words, 108 function words).

Table 1 shows general information about the speakers.

3.2. Extracting and POS tagging OTs

Part-of-speech (POS) tags were created for each word in the orthographic transcriptions (OTs) using Alpino (Bouma et al., 2000), a dependency parser for Dutch. The OTs were obtained for each recording through manual transcription by students at Radboud University. The differences between the standard written text

Table 1: *Speakers' general data*

Speaker	Gender	Age (years)	Time since diagnosis (years)
01	M	73	4.5
02	M	56	8.0
03	M	60	4.5
04	M	63	5.5
05	F	53	9.0
06	M	75	2.0
07	F	67	3.0
08	F	62	3.0

of the prompts and uttered words of the OTs are due to the intrinsic nature of the read speech. Indeed, read speech has a syntactic structure rather consistent and not fragmented, similarly to written language, but at the same time shares some typical elements of spontaneous speech such as stuttering, repetitions, fragmented words, filled pauses, elongated vowels and no punctuation.

By comparing the POS tags of the prompts with the POS tags of the OTs, it turned out that the absence of punctuation marks prevented the correct functioning of Alpino for the OTs. Therefore, a Python code was created with the aim of locating and identifying the punctuation of the prompts and reinserting it into the OTs. To avoid errors, the spot of insertion of the punctuation was determined by the first three words preceding and the first three words following the prompt punctuation. In order to predict the accuracy of the OTs POS tagging, all POS tags of the prompts were manually checked, and it turned out that out of a total of 252 words, 24 were incorrectly tagged by Alpino. Only four of these errors concerned the tagging of a content words instead of a function words or vice versa, while the others were wrong tags assigned to words belonging to the same word category.

3.3. Words labelling into content words and function words

The ultimate goal of POS tagging was to label all uttered words as content words and function words. All POS tags used by Alpino have been matched with an additional tag indicating the membership to one of the two global word classes. This step was accomplished through a Python script.

According to the literature research on Dutch content words and function words, a model of tags matching between Alpino POS tags and the two words categories was created. The matching model, shown in Tables 2 and 3, was designed with the aim of making the matches compatible with both the POS tags available and the outcomes of the literature studies.

3.4. Acoustic features, outliers detection, data normalization

A total of 103 acoustic features were automatically extracted using Praat (Boersma and Weenik, 2020)

Table 2: *Matching model for content words*

POS tags	Content words
N, SPEC	nouns (+ proper nouns)
WW	main verbs
ADJ	adjectives
BW	adverbs with semantic meaning

Table 3: *Matching model for function words.*
*: + 300 adverbs (adverbial grammatical function)

POS tags	Function words
LID	determiners (articles, prenominal pronouns)
VNW	pronouns
VG	conjunctions
VG	subordinate conjunctions
TSW	interjections
VZ	adpositions
TW	(cardinal) numerals
WW	auxiliary and copula verbs
BW	conjunctive adverbs*

and openSMILE (Eyben et al., 2010). The 15 features extracted by Praat are duration, the four formants, pitch variance, gravity center and the mean, minimum, maximum and standard deviation of pitch and intensity. Using the python package openSMILE, the 88 extended Geneva Minimalistic Acoustic Parameter Set (eGeMAPS) (Eyben et al., 2016) features were extracted. These 103 features were extracted on word-level after the speech was force aligned using an in-house forced aligner (`http://webservices.cls.ru.nl`). Note that in (van Bemmel et al., 2021) the same features were extracted with the same method at phoneme, word and utterance level.

Afterwards, outlier detection was carried out among the values of the extracted feature. Thus, a percentage of outliers of about 20% was detected. It turned out that most outliers were due to a worse quality of the audio at the end and beginning of recordings.

A further pre-processing step was the data normalization. Our data were standardized calculating the z-scores. Since there were multiple recordings per speakers, it was possible to calculate z-scores per speaker, thus minimizing the inter-speaker differences and the identify-confounding (Chaibub Neto et al., 2019).

3.5. Features reduction

From the 103 acoustic features, 24 features relating to loudness, intensity, and pitch were selected for further dimensionality reduction with Principal Component Analysis (PCA) (Pearson, 1901). Based on the Eigenvalue being larger than one, six principal components were formed, as shown in Table 4. Three of the principal components were related to loudness and intensity features (*li1, li2, li3*), and the other three were related to formant and pitch features from Praat (*F0.1, F0.2, Ppitch*). Inspecting the subset of features grouped in each of the six components and the component loadings, it was possible to notice that some components were more representative for loudness, intensity and pitch than others. Among the principal components related to loudness and intensity, *li1* grouped mean and higher values of loudness and intensity, *li2* grouped lower values, whereas *li3* grouped values expressing the variation in loudness. Among the principal components related to pitch, *F0.1* grouped static values of pitch obtained with eGeMAPS, *F0.2* grouped pitch dynamic values and range obtained with eGeMAPS, and *Ppitch* grouped pitch range and variation obtained with Praat.

Note that interpretation of principal components is not as straightforward as interpretation of acoustic features, as components are a combination of features. However, we can state that *li1* and *F0.1* seem to be the most complete and exhaustive components for the representation of loudness and intensity and pitch respectively. For this reason, although we have analyzed and reported the values obtained with all six components, we focused more on *li1* and *F0.1*.

3.6. Statistical analysis: Linear Mixed Regression Models

Linear Mixed-Effects Models (lmer; package lme4 (Bates et al., 2007)) in R (R Core Team, 2020) was used for the statistical analysis, in combination with the packages lmerTest and SjPlot. The analysis contained two fixed variables, Time (pre vs. post treatment) and Wordclass (function vs. content words), plus their interaction. We included three random effects: Speaker, Word, and Speaker-by-Time. The last effect is a random slope that enables the analysis to capture speaker specific treatment effects. The criterion variables in these analyses were the scores on the six PCA components.

Table 4: *PCA groupings obtained with Praat and eGeMAPS features related to intensity, loudness and pitch*

PC1: li1
loudness_sma3_percentile80.0
loudness_sma3_amean
intensity_max
intensity_mean
loudness_sma3_pctlrange0-2
loudness_sma3_percentile50.0
loudness_sma3_meanRisingSlope

PC2: F0.1
F0semitoneFrom27.5Hz_sma3nz_percentile20.0
F0semitoneFrom27.5Hz_sma3nz_percentile50.0
F0semitoneFrom27.5Hz_sma3nz_amean
F0semitoneFrom27.5Hz_sma3nz_percentile80.0
HNRdBACF_sma3nz_ameanpitch_minpitch_mean
pitch_min
pitch_mean

PC3: li2
loudness_sma3_amean
loudness_sma3_pctlrange0-2
loudness_sma3_percentile50.0
intensity_min
loudness_sma3_percentile20.0

PC4: F0.2
F0semitoneFrom27.5Hz_sma3nz_amean
F0semitoneFrom27.5Hz_sma3nz_percentile80.0
HNRdBACF_sma3nz_amean
F0semitoneFrom27.5Hz_sma3nz_pctlrange0-2
F0semitoneFrom27.5Hz_sma3nz_meanRisingSlope
F0semitoneFrom27.5Hz_sma3nz_meanFallingSlope
jitterLocal_sma3nz_amean

PC5: Ppitch
pitch_min
pitch_maxpitch_var
pitch_mean

PC6: li3
loudness_sma3_meanRisingSlope
loudnessPeaksPerSec
loudness_sma3_meanFallingSlope
jitterLocal_sma3nz_amean

4. Results

4.1. The fixed effects

No significant effects (p<.05) were found for Time or its interaction with Wordclass for any of the six PCA components.

The variable Wordclass has a significant effect on the values of *li1, li2, F0.2* and *li3*. As the boxplots for these components show, *li1* and *F0.2* are lower for function words, while *li2* and *li3* are larger for function words. Given the absence of significant interactions between Wordclass and Time, speakers thus show similar differences between content and function words in pre- and post-treatment.

The boxplots 3 and 2 show the normalized values of content and function words recorded for the eight speakers for the components *li1* and *F0.1*.

4.2. The random effects related to Speaker

Inspecting the plots of the random effects, the observation was made that the component values shown by the speaker intercepts may differ between speakers. More interesting are the slopes of Speaker-by-Time.

The slope values of *li3* and *Ppitch* do not deviate from 0 for any speaker, indicating that there is no significant difference between pre- and post-treatment for any speaker. The speaker results of the random slopes of the other four components can be seen in Table 5. The "-" symbol indicates a negative slope, meaning that the value of this component decreased from T2 to T3 for

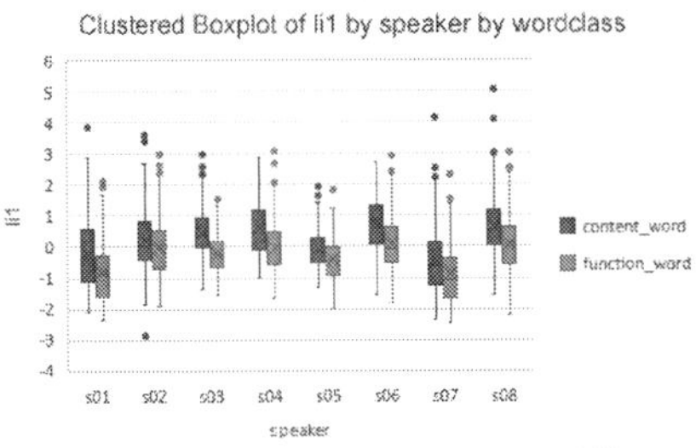

Figure 1: Boxplots of the normalized component *li1* (relating to loudness and intensity) per Speaker per WordClass.

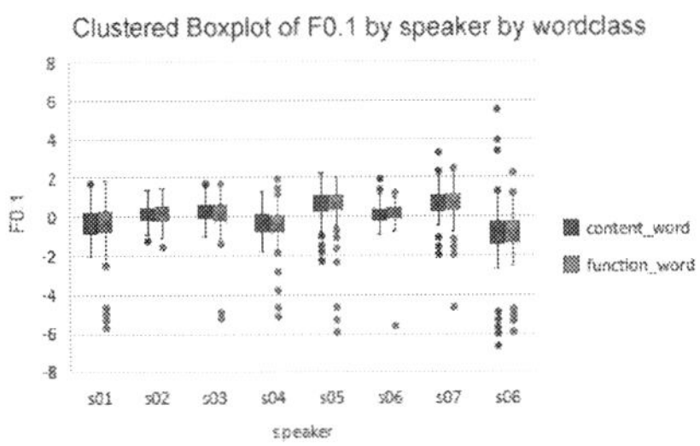

Figure 2: Boxplots of the normalized component ıF0.1 (relating to formants) per Speaker per WordClass.

that particular speaker. The "+" indicates a positive slope, meaning an increase in component value instead. The confidence interval of specific slopes did not cross the 0, and those slopes are therefore considered significant. These slopes are marked in the Table 5 with *s. Other slopes were too small to be considered significant.

Given their component loadings, the *li1* and *F0.1* components are most closely linked to the mean values of loudness, intensity and pitch. The other principal components are related to, e.g., lower values [minimum, 20-percentile] and variation in the feature values. Interpreting the outcome of the statistical analyses for these components is thus more complex, but also less relevant for the current research. We therefore focus on the *li1* and *F0.1* components.

Figures 3 and 5 show the normalized values for the components ıli1 and *F0.1* before (T2) and after (T3) treatment per speaker. Even if the p values of the intercept and the variable Time are not $< .05$, speaker 03, 05 and 07 show a clear increase for the *li1* component and decrease or keep approximately stable for the *F0.1* component. Figures 4 and 6 show the slopes of the random effects (intercept) speaker and Time for the components *li1* and *F0.1*, respectively. Note that the left part of Figures 3 and 5 shows the speaker intercept, indicating the between-speaker variance of the component values, whereas the right part of the figure shows the speaker slope indicating the treatment effect, i.e. the difference between the pre and post test per speaker.

Speakers 01, 02, and 06, had a negative slope for both *li1* and *F0.1*. For speakers 04, 05, and 07, a positive slope was found for both *li1* and *F0.1*. Speaker 03 had a positive slope for *li1* but a negative slope for *F0.1*, while speaker 08 had the opposite.

Table 5: Random effects on Time(T3). Symbols - and + indicate a negative or positive slope. *: |value| > 0.5, **: |value| > 1, ***: |value| > 1.5.
li3 and *Ppitch* components are not included since their values do not deviate from zero.

Speaker	F0.1	F0.2	li1	li2
01	-	-	-***	-*
02	-	-	-	-
03	-	-	+	+
04	+	-	+	+
05	+	+	+	+
06	-	+	-	-
07	+	+	+**	+
08	+	-	-	+

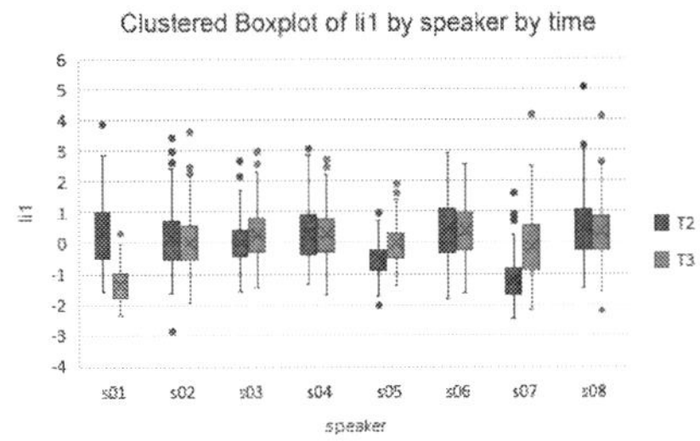

Figure 3: Boxplot of the normalized component *li1* (relating to loudness and intensity) per speaker per time point.

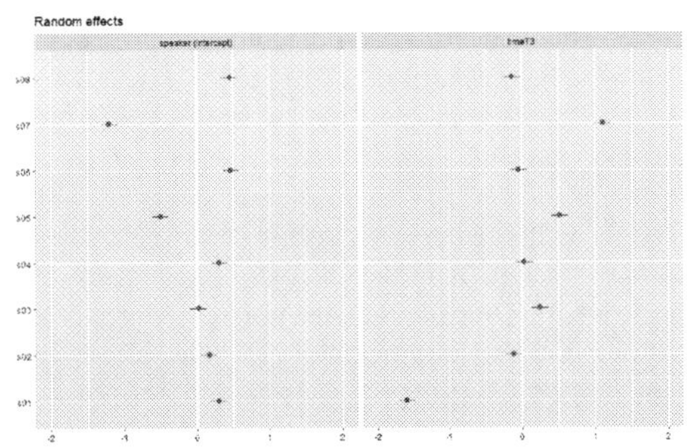

Figure 4: The random effects plot of the component *li1* (relating to loudness and intensity) shown for both intercept (speaker) and time

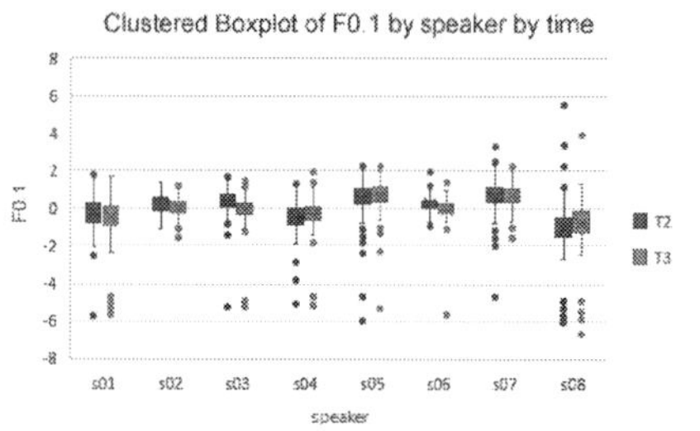

Figure 5: Boxplots of the normalized component *F0.1* (relating to formant features) per speaker per time.

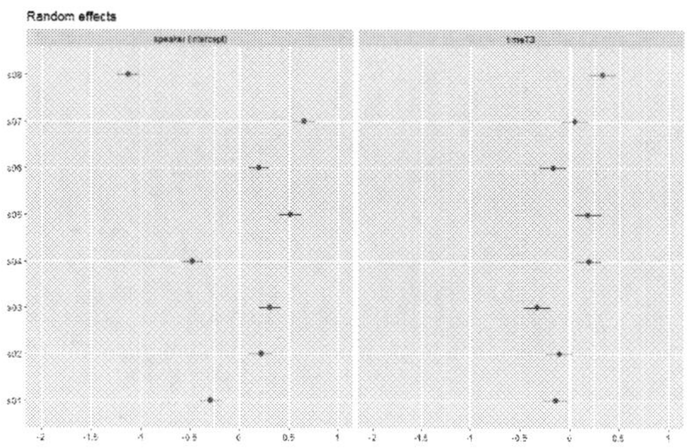

Figure 6: The random effects plot of the component *F0.1* (relating to formant features) shown for both Speaker intercept and Speaker by Time intercept

5. Discussion

5.1. Trend of loudness, intensity, and pitch compared with intelligibility scores

Our findings are mostly in line with Ganzeboom et al. (2022)'s results, especially with regards to loudness and intensity. Indeed, speakers 03, 04, 05 and 07, who increase in intelligibility scores after the treatment in Ganzeboom et al., show an evident increase of loudness and intensity after the treatment in our research. On the other hand, speaker 08, seemingly in contradiction with their increase in intelligibility score, does not show an increase in loudness and intensity after treatment in our results.

With regards to the pitch, no speaker shows an evident change for the component relating to the Praat pitch features. However, for the other two components relating to pitch (*F0.1* and *F0.2*), the differences per speaker between pre and post treatment recordings also vary. For speakers 03 and 06, who both improved, *F0.1* indeed goes down after treatment. However, for speakers 04, 05, 07 and 08, who also improved, the *F0.1* seems to increase after treatment. Speaker 01 and 2, who did not improve in intelligibility, also show a decrease in *F0.1* and *F0.2* scores after treatment. It seems that pitch is less relevant in the eventual intelligibility scoring than intensity, and even with some increase in pitch, a speaker can still be evaluated as more intelligible after treatment.

The fact that there seem to be multiple significant speaker results but not for the factor Time could be the consequence of our small sample size. With only eight speakers, there are undoubtedly between-speaker effects that interfere with the Time effect. Additionally, not all speakers profit from the treatment, something that came out in inspecting the interaction between speakers and Time.

5.2. Treatment impact on words categories

The two words categories show a clear difference in intensity as well among each other. Both in T2 and T3, speakers use greater intensity when pronouncing content words, according to component *li1*. Component *li2* gives us an unexpected result, showing larger values for function words. This is probably due to the aforementioned nature of the two different components. *Li2* indeed, is less representative of the loudness and intensity compared to *li1*, since it groups five acoustic features that mainly indicate low values of loudness and intensity, while *li1* groups features carrying mean and higher values. Even the pitch is slightly higher in the content words according to *F0.2*, while for *F0.1* the pitch of content and function words is approximately the same.

However, according to our data, there is no particular difference between the treatmen change shown by the content words treatment and the treatment change shown by the function words. Therefore, the web-based treatment seems to impact the two groups of words equally. Since all speakers show significant differences between the two word classes (function and content) in four out of six components, these natural variations between pronunciation of function and content words seems to be unchanged by treatment. Indeed, speech that does not present any tonal variance results is in fact monotonous and unnatural. The fact that the treatment does not flatten the acoustic differences between the two word categories is a positive effect and contributes to corroborate Ganzeboom's intelligibility scores, since some speakers manage both to increase loudness and intensity without changing the pitch, and to keep speech spontaneous and natural even after the treatment.

It is interesting, however, to notice that Turner and Tjaden (2000), comparing healthy speech with speech from speakers with mild to moderate dysarthria associated with amyotrophic lateralsclerosis, did not find any statistically significant difference between the patients and controls, but noticed different trends between function and content words with respect to the two groups of speakers.

5.3. Limitations

One of the limitations of our research is its focus on a reduced number of features compared to those available. This choice was dictated by the need to make the large number of acoustic features extracted for each word compatible with a valid statistical analysis. Therefore, the advantage of avoiding the curse of multidimensionality inevitably has the consequence of sacrificing information.

Additionally, the principal components obtained with PCA are less easily interpretable than the acoustic features they are created with. The components are some combination of groups of features with specific component loadings, making it difficult to draw clear conclusions out of increases or decreases of these components.

However, many of the initial 103 features are highly correlated with each other. In fact, we carried out the PCA with the aim to consider the greatest number of features that were linked to the loudness, intensity, and pitch, not limiting the research by selecting a single feature that most represented each of these three traits. Nevertheless, there is a large number of features related to the acoustic spectrum, to the four formants, and to temporal characteristics, which for the aforementioned reasons have been excluded from the research. It would be interesting to study those features in future studies.

Furthermore, we must take into consideration that the extraction of the acoustic features was done at word-level, and that different results perhaps would have come out with an analysis at utterance level as regards loudness, intensity, and pitch. In their work for instance, van Bemmel et al. (2021) detects the most relevant features of the same data used in this research analysing the features at phoneme, words and utterance level. Yet, only a word level analysis would have allowed a distinction between content and function words.

It would be appropriate to interpret our findings also in the light of the type of speech that has been analyzed, that is read speech. The nature of this type of speech has very different characteristics from those of spontaneous speech, and these differences could certainly have repercussions on a phonetic, lexical or syntactic level.

Finally, as regards the method used, we have partially adopted procedures that can only work for small corpora, such as the automatic insertion of punctuation. Also the labeling of words into content words and function words, based on Dutch POS tags, could turn problematic with words as POS tagging does not differentiate sufficiently for a classification in content and function words.

6. Conclusions

Using six principle components based on 24 acoustic features related to loudness, intensity, and pitch extracted from speech recordings with Praat and eGeMAPS, we found that some of these components reflect the changes in intelligibility after treatment with a serious game for Parkinson's Disease patients.

While no significant effect was found for the fixed factor Time, providing no proof for treatment impacting loudness, intensity, and pitch that is consistent in all speakers (answering question 1), it was found that the treatment effects differ per speaker.

Li2 and *F0.2*, components relating to loudness and intensity and eGeMAPS features of pitch respectively, were found to have significant differences between speakers for these two component values. Random effect plots of the intercept also show differences between speakers for other components (answering question 2a).

Random effect plots show the differences between speaker slopes, where the link with previous research into intelligibility improvement after treatment can be made. For the components *li3* and *Ppitch* relating to eGeMAPS features of loudness and jitter and Praat features of pitch respectively, none of the speakers had a significant slope, indicating no difference after treatment for these component values. This is in line with Pitch Limiting Voice Treatment (PLVT), where the pitch is not supposed to increase and loudness does.

The other components (two relating to loudness and intensity and two relating to eGeMAPS features of pitch) and their respective slopes differ per speaker, again showing the speaker-dependent results. Speaker 01 and 02 did not improve in intelligibility, and all four of the other components decreased as well, implying a decrease in articulation quality with the loss of loudness in line with PLVT. Speaker 03 had a large improvement in intelligibility after finishing treatment, and did indeed show an increase in loudness and intensity components while showing a decrease in pitch components, perfectly following the PLVT. Speaker 04 and 06 both had a slight increase in intelligibility and a mix of increase and decrease for both loudness and intensity and pitch. Speaker 05 and 07 both had a large improvement in intelligibility and all four components increased, implying that it is possible that speech is considered more intelligible if both loudness and intensity and pitch are increased. Speaker 08 had a large intelligibility score but a mix of increase and decrease in the four component values (answering question 2b).

Given that there is no significant effect of the interaction between WordClass and Time, we can conclude that the treatment with the Treasure Hunters game has the same (namely, no) impact on content and function words and any variation between these two groups is consistent pre and post treatment (answering question 3).

Looking at this variation between content and function words, it was found that four out of six components (*li1, li2, li3, F0.2*) had a significant difference between content and function words (answering question 2).

Overall, our research answered some questions and raised many others. Among the topics that would be more interesting to investigate in future studies, there is certainly the cause of such an evident speaker-dependent result. Many critical aspects of our method could also be further explored, such as the inclusion of more acoustic features or resolving the problems related to the POS tagging of read speech. Lastly, it would be interesting to do a similar analysis with spontaneous speech, focusing in particular on the fact that one of the symptoms of speech disorders in patients with dysarthria is also the lack of emotional expression and tonal changes.

7. Acknowledgements

We would like to thank our colleagues Mario Ganzeboom, Marjoke Bakker, Lilian Beijer, and Toni Rietveld, who were involved in acquiring the data within the CHASING project.

8. Bibliographical References

Bates, D., Sarkar, D., Bates, M. D., and Matrix, L. (2007). The lme4 package. *R package version*, 2(1):74.

Bird, H., Franklin, S., and Howard, D. (2002). 'Little words'—not really: function and content words in normal and aphasic speech. *Journal of Neurolinguistics*, 15(3-5):209–237.

Boersma, P. and Weenik, D. (2020). Praat: doing phonetics by computer (version 6.1.22). `http://www.praat.org`.

Bouma, G., van Noord, G., and Malouf, R. (2000). Alpino: Wide-coverage computational analysis of Dutch. volume 37, pages 45–59, 01.

Chaibub Neto, E., Pratap, A., Perumal, T. M., Tummalacherla, M., Snyder, P., Bot, B. M., Trister, A. D., Friend, S. H., Mangravite, L., and Omberg, L. (2019). Detecting the impact of subject characteristics on machine learning-based diagnostic applications. *NPJ digital medicine*, 2(1):1–6.

De Swart, B. J., Willemse, S., Maassen, B., and Horstink, M. (2003). Improvement of voicing in patients with Parkinson's disease by speech therapy. *Neurology*, 60(3):498–500.

Eyben, F., Wöllmer, M., and Schuller, B. (2010). Opensmile: the munich versatile and fast open-source audio feature extractor. In *Proceedings of the 18th ACM international conference on Multimedia*, pages 1459–1462.

Eyben, F., Scherer, K. R., Schuller, B. W., Sundberg, J., André, E., Busso, C., Devillers, L. Y., Epps, J., Laukka, P., Narayanan, S. S., et al. (2015). The geneva minimalistic acoustic parameter set (gemaps) for voice research and affective computing. *IEEE transactions on affective computing*, 7(2):190–202.

Eyben, F., Scherer, K. R., Schuller, B. W., Sundberg, J., André, E., Busso, C., Devillers, L. Y., Epps, J., Laukka, P., Narayanan, S. S., and Truong, K. P. (2016). The Geneva Minimalistic Acoustic Parameter Set (GeMAPS) for voice research and affective computing. *IEEE Transactions on Affective Computing*, 7(2):190–202.

Ganzeboom, M., Bakker, M., Beijer, L., Rietveld, T., and Strik, H. (2018). Speech training for neurological patients using a serious game. *British Journal of Educational Technology*, 49(4):761–774.

Ganzeboom, M., Bakker, M., Beijer, L., Strik, H., and Rietveld, T. (2022). A serious game for speech training in dysarthric speakers with Parkinson's disease: Exploring therapeutic efficacy and patient satisfaction. *International Journal of Language & Communication Disorders*.

Howell, P., Au-Yeung, J., and Sackin, S. (1999). Exchange of stuttering from function words to content words with age. *Journal of Speech, Language, and Hearing Research*, 42(2):345–354.

Kalf, J., de Swart, B., Bonnier, M., Hofman, M., Kanters, J., Kocken, J., Miltenburg, M., Bloem, B., and Munneke, M. (2011). Guidelines for speech-language therapy in Parkinson's disease. *Nijmegen, The Netherlands/Miami, FL: ParkinsonNet/NPF*.

Pearson, K. (1901). LIII. On lines and planes of closest fit to systems of points in space. *The London, Edinburgh, and Dublin Philosophical Magazine and Journal of Science*, 2(11):559–572.

R Core Team, (2020). *R: A Language and Environment for Statistical Computing*. R Foundation for Statistical Computing, Vienna, Austria.

Ramig, L. O., Countryman, S., Thompson, L. L., and Horii, Y. (1995). Comparison of two forms of intensive speech treatment for parkinson disease. *Journal of Speech, Language, and Hearing Research*, 38(6):1232–1251.

Turner, G. S. and Tjaden, K. (2000). Acoustic differences between content and function words in amyotrophic lateral sclerosis. *Journal of Speech, Language, and Hearing Research*, 43(3):769–781.

van Bemmel, L., Cucchiarini, C., and Strik, H. (2021). Using feature selection to evaluate pathological speech after training with a serious game. *ExLing 2021*, page 245.

Van de Weijer, J. and Slis, I. (1991). Nasaliteitsmeting met de nasometer. *Logopedie en Foniatrie*, 63(97.101).

Yang, S., Wang, F., Yang, L., Xu, F., Luo, M., Chen, X., Feng, X., and Zou, X. (2020). The physical significance of acoustic parameters and its clinical significance of dysarthria in Parkinson's disease. *Scientific Reports*, 10(1):1–9.

Proceedings of the RaPID-4 @LREC 2022, pages 9–16
Marseille, 25 June 2022

Generating Synthetic Clinical Speech Data Through Simulated ASR Deletion Error

Hali Lindsay[1], Johannes Tröger[2], Mario Mina[2], Nicklas Linz[2], Philipp Müller[1], Jan Alexandersson[1], Inez Ramakers[3]
[1]German Research Center for Artificial Intelligence (DFKI) Stuhlsatzenhausweg 3, Saarbrücken, Germany, 66125
[2]ki:elements, Am Holzbrunnen, Saarbrücken,Germany, 66121
[3]Maastricht University Medical Center (MUMC+)
{Hali.Lindsay, Philipp.Mueller, Jan.Alexandersson}@dfki.de, {Johannes.Troeger, Mario.Mina, Nicklas.Linz}@ki-elements.de, i.ramakers@maastrichtuniversity.nl

Abstract

Training classification models on clinical speech is a time-saving and effective solution for many healthcare challenges, such as screening for Alzheimer's Disease over the phone. One of the primary limiting factors of the success of artificial intelligence (AI) solutions is the amount of relevant data available. Clinical data is expensive to collect, not sufficient for large-scale machine learning or neural methods, and often not shareable between institutions due to data protection laws. With the increasing demand for AI in health systems, generating synthetic clinical data that maintains the nuance of underlying patient pathology is the next pressing task. Previous work has shown that automated evaluation of clinical speech tasks via automatic speech recognition (ASR) is comparable to manually annotated results in diagnostic scenarios even though ASR systems produce errors during the transcription process. In this work, we propose to generate synthetic clinical data by simulating ASR deletion errors on the transcript to produce additional data. We compare the synthetic data to the real data with traditional machine learning methods to test the feasibility of the proposed method. Using a dataset of 50 cognitively impaired and 50 control Dutch speakers, ten additional data points are synthetically generated for each subject, increasing the training size for 100 to 1000 training points. We find consistent and comparable performance of models trained on only synthetic data (AUC=0.77) to real data (AUC=0.77) in a variety of traditional machine learning scenarios. Additionally, linear models are not able to distinguish between real and synthetic data.

Keywords: Data Augmentation, Synthetic Data, Clinical Speech, Mild Cognitive Impairment, Automatic Speech Recognition, Machine Learning

1. Introduction

Analysing clinical speech by means of natural language processing (NLP) techniques is a low-cost and effective approach for many healthcare challenges, such as screening for early signs of Alzheimer's Disease from clinical speech tasks. One of the primary limiting factors of the success of artificial intelligence (AI) solutions in health is the amount of relevant data available to train models. Clinical speech data is expensive and invasive to collect and the quantity is not sufficient for large-scale machine learning or even simple neural methods. In addition, collected data is difficult—if not impossible—to share between clinical and research institutions due to concerns for patient privacy. With the increasing demand for digital AI-driven solutions in health systems, generating synthetic clinical data that can be scaled-up and performs on-par with real data is the next challenge.

Previous work has shown that automated evaluation of clinical speech tasks via automatic speech recognition (ASR) is comparable to manually annotated results in diagnostic scenarios even though ASR systems produce errors during the transcription process, namely deletion (König et al., 2018; Konig et al., 2019). While the ASR-related loss of data in such a setting is typically seen as one of the major limitations of those approaches, this natural limitation can be harnessed to naturally generate synthetic data. The concept is similar to a technique used for synthetic data augmentation in computer vision, where random parts of an image are erased in order to generate multiple training examples from a single image (Zhong et al., 2017). We propose a novel technique for synthetic data augmentation by exploiting the already occurring ASR error to randomly delete portions of the transcribed clinical speech.

In this paper, we investigate if the technique of randomly erasing speech transcripts—a result which is already seen when using ASR systems as part of an automatic pipeline—can be applied to clinical speech to generate synthetic training data. This is done using 100 older Dutch speakers where 50 show signs of mild cognitive impairment. Ten synthetic files are generated per participant for a total of 1000 data points. This paper is scoped to consider if the synthetically generated data has comparable results to authentic data in traditional machine learning scenarios. Through a series of downstream machine learning classification experiments, the synthetic data is compared to the traditional scenario as a baseline. Overall, we find that random erasing can be used to generate synthetic clinical data that performs as well as the real data. Based on the foundation of these findings, future work should investigate if more complex neural methods benefit from the addition of synthetic data as well as if the proposed method is transferable to other clinical tasks.

2. Background

In this section, background is provided to further motivate the argumentation of the paper. First, the automatic pipeline for evaluating clinical speech is described. Next, focusing on going from speech to text portion of the automatic evaluation pipeline, an explanation of how the quality of the transcription is estimated if provided . Finally, drawing from data augmentation techniques in computer vision, parallels are drawn between the technique of random erasing and the role of deletion during the transcription process.

2.1. Automatic Evaluation of the Semantic Verbal Fluency task (SVF)

The semantic verbal fluency task is a timed clinical speech test where a person is asked to name as many words as they can pertaining to a given semantic category (e.g. Name as many animals as you can in one minute). This task has been shown to be sensitive for screening for mild cognitive impairment (MCI) from typical ageing in older adults (McDonnell et al., 2020; Clark et al., 2009; Vaughan et al., 2016). The automatic pipeline for evaluating this speech task starts with recording a person during the task. Next, this speech is passed through an automatic speech recognition (ASR) model to obtain a text transcript. Once this automatic transcript has been generated multiple methods of feature extraction and analysis have been proposed for evaluating the SVF task based on relevant cognitive clinical literature. Previous work has investigated using semantically motivated measures, such as semantic word embeddings, to consider semantic clustering strategies (Troyer et al., 1997; Pakhomov and Hemmy, 2014). Other methods have considered temporal measures for clustering (Tröger et al., 2019) or investigating the task on a finer time resolution (Linz et al., 2019a).

2.2. Word Error rate (WER)

One of the first elements of an automatic pipeline for evaluating the SVF, is to automatically transcribe the speech task using automatic speech recognition. As with any automatic method, there is always some form of error. To evaluate automatic speech recognition, word error rate is used. Word error rate (WER) is the number of insertions, substitutions, and deletions that occur during the automatic transcription process divided by the number of words in the manual transcript. (Errattahi et al., 2018)

$$WER = \frac{Substitutions + Deletions + Insertions}{WordCount_{manualtranscript}}$$

The most common form of error found when automatically transcribing the SVF task is deletion. In addition, before extracting clinically relevant features from the task, the text is preprocessed, removing words outside the task domain. Therefore substitutions and insertions that are not in the semantic category (e.g. animals) would also be seen as deletions.

The effect of the automatic speech pipeline on this clinical task has been investigated previously by comparing manual versus automatic evaluation methods. Konig and colleagues found that both methods yielded comparable results when screening for dementia over the phone using the SVF (König et al., 2018).

2.3. Generating Synthetic Data

Drawing from computer vision, one of the common methods is to alter images in the training set by cropping, flipping, rotating, or randomly erasing part of the image. By perturbing the original image in some way, many versions of a single image can be created. Random erasing is a data augmentation technique where additional training data is created by erasing a random portion of an image in varying amounts. Although the idea is simple, it was previously proposed to reduce overfitting in deep learning image recognition models (Shorten and Khoshgoftaar, 2019; Zhong et al., 2017). This idea lends itself easily to the clinical speech application when combined with the WER caused by the automatic transcription process. Since the deletion caused by the WER does not affect the downstream application of detecting cognitive impairment from the speech recording, it should be possible to randomly delete portions of manual transcripts at the same rate as the WER. This can be done in many variations and combinations, yielding synthetically augmented data.

3. Data

100 older Dutch speakers completed a battery of cognitive tests including a one minute semantic verbal fluency on the subject of animals with a clinician from Maastricht University Clinic, Netherlands. Of the 100 participants, 50 are healthy controls (HC) and 50 present with mild cognitive impairment (MCI). The demographic data for the sample population is given in table 1.

	HC	MCI
N	50	50
Sex (M/F)	18/32	19/31
Age (years)	70.66 (8.96)	65.94 (7.80)
Word Error Rate (%)	20.29	23.13
MMSE (max 30)	28.68(1.27)	26.92 (2.07)

Table 1: Demographic information for the Dutch participants. The Mini-Mental State Exam (MMSE) is a test to measure cognitive function (Max score 30). Means are given with standard deviation in parentheses.

To complete the SVF task, participants are instructed to name as many animals as they can in one minute. The response is recorded and transcribed twice; once manually by trained clinicians via an iPad application. The second time the data is transcribed automatically via Google translation services. In both cases, the responses are automatically pre-processed to remove any additional sounds, such as 'uhh' or 'ahh'. The final response result is a time-aligned list of animals. For example, a transcript could look like "dog, cat, lions, tiger, bear, blue whale, dolphin".

4. Methods

4.1. Data Augmentation by Random Erasing with WER (REWER)

First, the word error rate is calculated for each participant between the manually annotated and automatically generated transcript. The, number of words to be deleted from the transcript is determined given the WER percentage. Because the goal is to simulate the naturally occurring error in the ASR transcript, the WER produced by the ASR is applied to the manual SVF transcript. An exhaustive list is created of every possible variation of the SVF with the determined number of missing words from the manual transcript. From this list, a random number generator is used to randomly select ten newly generated, synthetically augmented SVF texts per manual transcript. These files are then saved for the next step of explicit feature extraction.

4.2. Data Augmentation by Random Erasing with Constant Deletion (REWCD)

One of the limiting factors of the REWER method is that it requires manual transcription of the SVF task in order to calculate the WER. To investigate additional random erasing methods that do not require manual annotation, a constant rate of deletion is considered. Instead of a variable per participant deletion rate based on the WER determined by ASR, a constant deletion rate is considered for all transcripts. The same procedure is applied as describe in Section 4.1 where the rate of deletion is 10% and 20%. These rates are chosen to be below the average WER for the sample population given in Table 1.

4.3. Feature Extraction

A comprehensive feature set is extracted from the automatic and augmented transcripts based on recent approaches for automatically evaluating the SVF task. Previous literature has proposed investigating the underlying strategy for completing the SVF task by looking for clusters of semantically related words in the task (Troyer et al., 1997; Farzanfar et al., 2018). This process was previously automated and Four features are extracted for semantic clustering and switching based on Linz et al., 2017 using pre-trained Dutch semantic word embeddings from Fasttext (Bojanowski et al., 2016). Beyond semantics, temporal methods have also been proposed for extracting five clustering and switching metrics in SVF based on (Tröger et al., 2018). In addition, another temporal method has been investigated by breaking the sixty second task into six ten-second bins (Linz et al., 2019b; Lindsay et al., 2021). For more detailed feature explanations, short descriptions of each feature are given in Table 2

5. Experiments

Statistical Analysis is done in R Studio (R Core Team, 2017). All coding experiments are implemented using python 3.7.

5.1. Machine learning Classification Scenarios

To test the feasibility of the proposed data augmentation technique, multiple machine learning experiments are conducted.

5.1.1. Augmentation Approach with REWER and REWCD

This train-test setup is applied to the three synthetic data sets that are created as well as the combination of all of them: the WER set (WER), the 10% constant rate (C_10%), the 20% constant rate (C_20%), and the combination of all three synthetic datasets (ALL SYNTH). Since the idea of this paper is to produce synthetic data that performs similarly to the real data, we propose to train on the synthetically generated data and test on the real ASR data. To keep the models comparable to training and testing on the real ASR data, leave one out cross validation(LOOCV) is also used in this scenario. In this case, the one participant that is in the test set has all their synthetic data removed from the training set. For a concrete example, this means of the 1000 generated files, 990 synthetic data points are in the training set and 1 real data point is in the test set. The 10 data points that are removed are the files generated by the one being tested. This is done to prevent inflating model results.

5.1.2. Classic Approach

To compare the newly proposed technique to traditional methods, model performance is considered when training on the real ASR data (REAL ASR) using LOOCV.

5.1.3. Machine learning Classification Specifications

The classification models are created using the scikit-learn library[1] (Pedregosa et al., 2011).
For the feasibility of this method, binary classification is done to distinguish between the MCI and control group. Three classification algorithms are considered; Logistic Regression (LR), Random Forest (RF), and Support Vector Machine (SVC). Features are normalized using the standard scalar. Grid search is used to optimize model parameters in the training fold. In addition, univariate feature selection is done to test how increasing the number of features increases as the data increases. To gauge and compare model performance, accuracy and area under the receiver operator curve (AUC) are calculated.

[1] sklearn version==0.24.0 for python 3.7

Feature Name	Description
Word Count	The total number of animal words said in one minute, excluding repetitions
Semantic Clustering Measures	
Mean Cluster Size	Average number of animals in an semantic cluster over the entire sample
Number of Switches	the number of times switched to a different semantic cluster
Mean Intercluster Similarity	On average, how semantically related are the semantic clusters
Temporal Clustering Measures	
Mean Transition Time	Mean time (in seconds) between consecutive words
Mean Cluster Size	Average number of animals in a temporal cluster over the entire sample
Number of Switches	the number of times switched to a different temporal cluster
Mean Intercluster Similarity	On average, how semantically related are the temporal clusters
Bin Measures	
Word Count by Bin	The number of words per 10 second bin
Transition Length by Bin	The average transition time in seconds between the end of one word and the onset of the next word by 10 second bin
Semantic Similarity by Bin	On average, how semantically related the words are by 10 second bin

Table 2: Features extracted from the SVF task produced by the participants with description.

5.2. Additional Experiments

A few other experiments are considered to examine the synthetically generated data. A random baseline is generated using the permutation test to see if the synthetic data can be distinguished from the real ASR data. In addition, incremental experiments are considered to see how the amount of synthetic data used in training effects the binary diagnostic classification experiment.

5.2.1. Permutation Test

To test if we can tell the difference between the synthetic and authentic data, permutation test is computed. A permutation test consists of obtaining a randomised baseline by training a linear model a series of times while permuting the target labels in question each time, removing any dependence between the input features and the mentioned target label. In this case, the target label is authentic or synthetic. The p-value represents the probability of obtaining the model accuracies we observe, assuming the that the null hypothesis is true. For this experiment, the null hypothesis is that there is no difference between the synthetic and authentic data. To test this, authentic and synthetic labels are randomly assigned to the transcripts. A linear model is trained and tested with the randomly assigned labels. Accuracy is used to determine model performance. This is permuted 1000 times for comparison. An empirical p-value is calculated by computing how many of the random models have a higher accuracy than the model trained on the true labels. The empirical p-value is calculated by taking the number of times performance falls within the random model score distribution divided by the total number of permutations. The p-value, in this case, represents how many of the random models have superior or comparable performance to the one trained on the actual experimental scenario. We report the p-value with statistical significance set to 0.05.

5.2.2. Incremental Experiments

In addition, the amount of synthetic data used to train a model is tested where the training amount is increased incrementally. A model where one synthetic data point per participant is trained, then a model where two synthetic data points per participants is trained and so on, until all ten points per participant are used. In this scenario, the machine learning scenario is simplified. A simple logistic regression using all extracted features is created with no hyperparameter optimization. As stated previously, LOOCV is used where the synthetic data is used to train and real ASR data is used to test and no data from the test participant is seen during training.

6. Results

6.1. Machine Learning Results

Model	N	Accuracy	AUC	Method
		BEST ACC		
LR	13	0.74	0.76	REWER
SVC	22	0.75	0.76	REWER
RF	11	0.73	0.76	ASR
		BEST AUC		
LR	13	0.69	0.77	ASR
SVC	22	0.69	0.77	ALL SYNTH
RF	11	0.73	0.76	ASR

Table 3: Best result for feasibility experiments for each classifier. N is the number of features. Method is which training data had the best score. The upper table is based on highest accuracy. The lower tables is based on highest AUC.

Results for the machine learning experiments explained in Section 5.1 are visualized in Figure 1. In addition

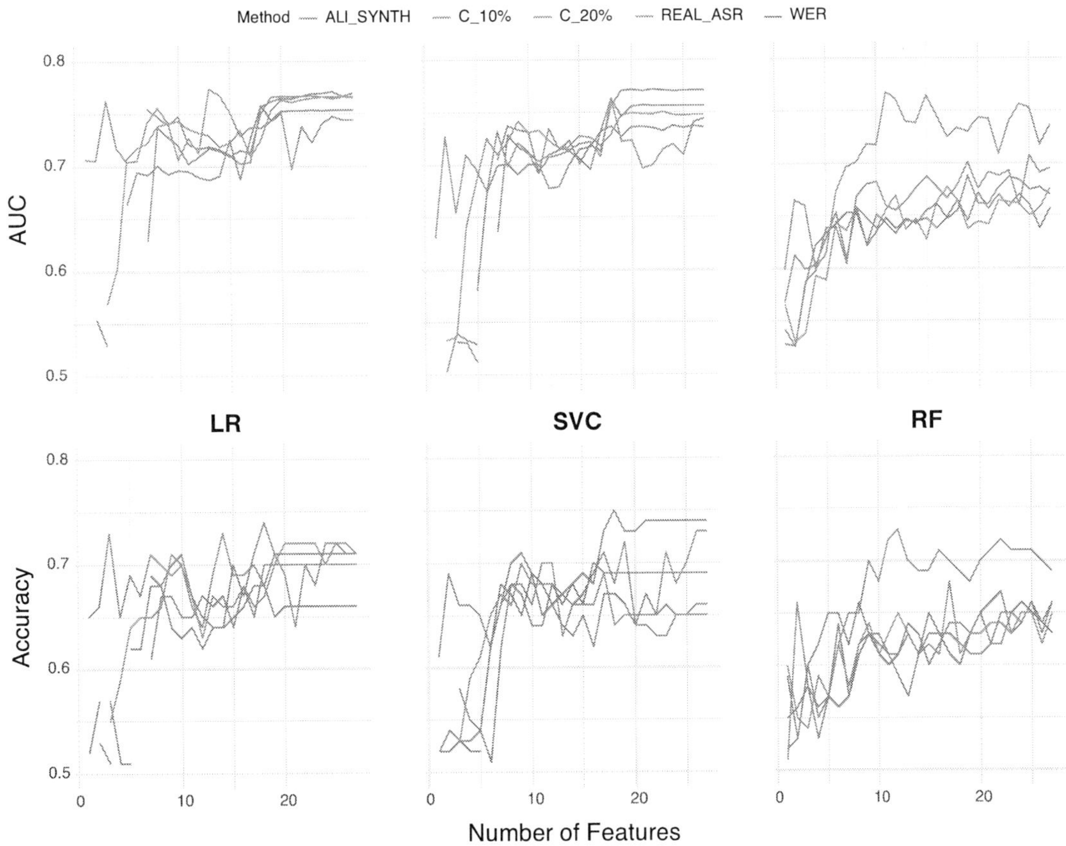

Figure 1: Visualization of results from the machine learning experiments. The number of features used to traain the modedl is represented on x-axis. Logistic Regression(LR). Support Vector Machine(SVC), Random Forest(RF). Area Under Curve (AUC).

the best accuracy and AUC score for each algorithm are displayed in Table 3.

From the results, comparable performance is seen between both the REWER and REWCD methods to the classic approach. Overall, the synthetic data improves in performance with the number of features. Looking at the best accuracy by classifier, for the logistic regression and support vector machine, the WER method produces the max result. For AUC, the support vector machine best result is achieved using the combined synthetic data sets. However, real data yields better AUC performance in general. There is also appears to be some dependence on classifier type the random forest classifier consistently performs better in both accuracy and AUC with real data.

6.2. Permutation Test Results

For the random baseline from the permutation tests, No significant p-values are reported. Values range from 0.44 to 0.56 with the average significance value being 0.51. Therefore, the alternate hypothesis is rejected and the null hypothesis is accepted. This can be interpreted as the linear model not being able to distinguish between the synthetic and authentic transcripts.

6.3. Incremental Experiments

Results for the incremental experiments are visualized in Figure 2. In addition, Table 4 summarizes the results by averaging AUC and accuracy scores by the number of synthetic data points used during training per participant.

As the amount of data increases, consistent AUC values are reported ranging from 0.74 to 077, and consistently averaging to 0.76. The accuracy presents with a mild downward slope 71% with one data to 69% accuracy at nine synthetic points per person. The slight decrease in accuracy could be to the lack of optimization during training as higher accuracy (74%) is reported for the logistic regression with ten data points per person.

7. Discussion

Of the synthetic methods considered, WER had the best accuracy. This result is expected based on the train-test setup used. The REWER method generates training data closest to the ASR test data. However, the constant deletion had comparable results to the WER and

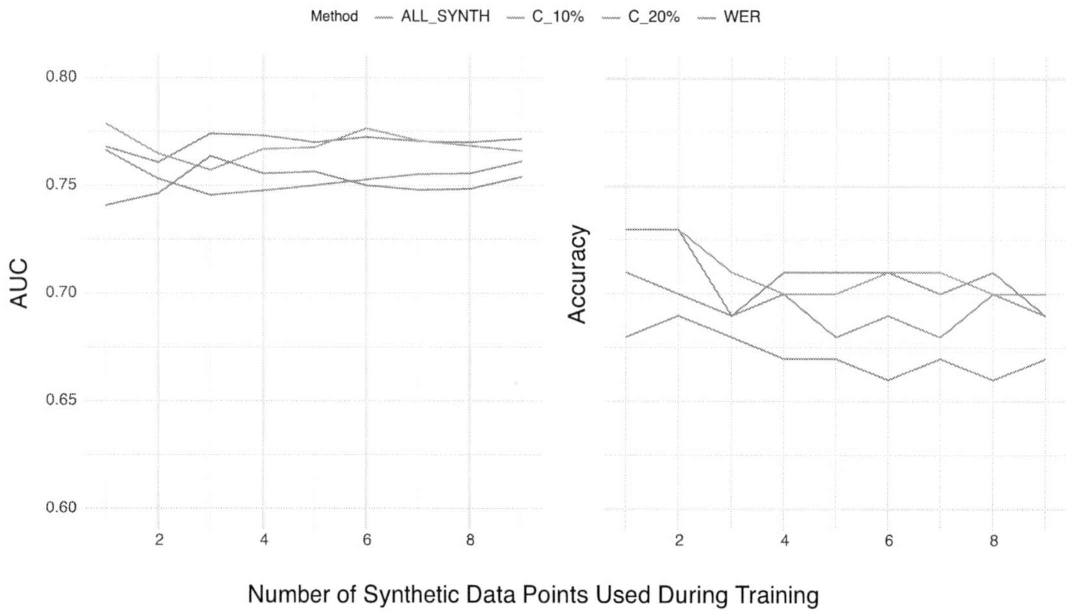

Figure 2: Visualization for the incremental synthetic data experiments. The number of synthatic data points used for training per participant is given on the x-axis. Area Under Curve (AUC).

N	AUC	Accuracy
1	0.76	0.71
2	0.76	0.71
3	0.76	0.69
4	0.76	0.70
5	0.76	0.69
6	0.76	0.69
7	0.76	0.69
8	0.76	0.69
9	0.76	0.69

Table 4: Summarization of incremental experiment results. N is the number of synthetic data points per participant used during training. AUC and accuracy are averaged over the augmentation method.

real data. One of the downsides to using WER is the need for expensive and time-consuming manual annotation. However, this can be bypassed with the constant rate method. In addition, constant deletion rates could be blended, similarly to what has been done with the ALL SYNTH method that achieved the highest AUC score for the SVM. Additional experiments determined that a linear model was not able to distinguish between the synthetic and real data based on the permutation test. Furthermore, as the amount of synthetic data used for training is increased consistent performance is reported that is comparable to the real data scenario.

One benefit of using random erasing to generate synthetic transcripts—rather than just simulating feature values from a distribution—is that the data is still explainable. There are synthetic transcripts that can be viewed and investigated. This is something that is highly sought after in clinical settings as medical professionals prefer tangible and explainable solutions.

These findings have an impact on future work. The ability to generate additional synthetic clinical data could open the door to training deep learning models and neural approaches. As well as, the raw data could be used for new solutions that are now possible due to increased amounts of data. For example, the sequence of words could be used as an input for an LSTM.

However, there are still some unknown factors of what this method has on data in other domains. For instance, this paper is scoped to a single clinical task that is focused on assessing cognition. It is unknown if this methodology would work on free speech clinical tasks, such as the picture description task or story telling task, where cognition and language abilities interact more heavily (Themistocleous et al., 2020). Future work would need to investigate the transference of this technique to other domains.

8. Conclusion

This paper proposed to generate synthetic data by simulating ASR error already found in automatic evaluation pipelines. Random erasing by either WER or constant deletion is a low cost and simple solution that effectively delivers machine learning performance that is on par with current real data methods. These findings present impactful solutions for future work to investigate how much data can be generated and achieving better performance using deep learning and neural approaches.

9. Acknowledgements

This research was funded by MEPHESTO project Q10 (BMBF Grant Number 01IS20075).

10. Bibliography

Bojanowski, P., Grave, E., Joulin, A., and Mikolov, T. (2016). Enriching word vectors with subword information. *arXiv preprint arXiv:1607.04606*.

Clark, L., Gatz, M., Zheng, L., Chen, Y.-L., McCleary, C., and Mack, W. (2009). Longitudinal verbal fluency in normal aging, preclinical, and prevalent alzheimer's disease. *American journal of Alzheimer's disease and other dementias*, 24:461–8, 09.

Errattahi, R., El Hannani, A., and Ouahmane, H. (2018). Automatic speech recognition errors detection and correction: A review. *Procedia Computer Science*, 128:32–37. 1st International Conference on Natural Language and Speech Processing.

Farzanfar, D., Statucka, M., and Cohn, M. (2018). Automated indices of clustering and switching of semantic verbal fluency in parkinson's disease. *J Int Neuropsychol Soc*, 24(10):1047–1056, Nov.

König, A., Linz, N., Tröger, J., Wolters, M., Alexandersson, J., and Robert, P. (2018). Fully automatic speech-based analysis of the semantic verbal fluency task. *Dementia and Geriatric Cognitive Disorders*, 45(3-4):198–209.

Konig, A., Lindsay, H., Tröger, J., and Ramakers, I. H. (2019). The use of artificial intelligence and automatic speech and image analysis for remote cognitive testing. In *Alzheimer Europe Conference, 23-25th October, The Hague, Netherlands.*, The Hague, Netherlands, October.

Lindsay, H., Müller, P., Linz, N., Zeghari, R., Magued Mina, M., Konig, A., and Tröger, J. (2021). Dissociating semantic and phonemic search strategies in the phonemic verbal fluency task in early dementia. In *Proceedings of the Seventh Workshop on Computational Linguistics and Clinical Psychology: Improving Access*, pages 32–44, Online, June. Association for Computational Linguistics.

Linz, N., Lundholm Fors, K., Lindsay, H., Eckerström, M., Alexandersson, J., and Kokkinakis, D. (2019a). Temporal analysis of the semantic verbal fluency task in persons with subjective and mild cognitive impairment. In *Proceedings of the Sixth Workshop on Computational Linguistics and Clinical Psychology*, pages 103–113, Minneapolis, Minnesota, June. Association for Computational Linguistics.

Linz, N., Lundholm Fors, K., Lindsay, H., Eckerström, M., Alexandersson, J., and Kokkinakis, D. (2019b). Temporal analysis of the semantic verbal fluency task in persons with subjective and mild cognitive impairment. In *Proceedings of the Sixth Workshop on Computational Linguistics and Clinical Psychology*, pages 103–113, Minneapolis, Minnesota, June. Association for Computational Linguistics.

McDonnell, M., Dill, L., Panos, S., Amano, S., Brown, W., Giurgius, S., Small, G., and Miller, K. (2020). Verbal fluency as a screening tool for mild cognitive impairment. *Int Psychogeriatr*, 32(9):1055–1062, Sep.

Pakhomov, S. and Hemmy, L. (2014). A computational linguistic measure of clustering behavior on semantic verbal fluency task predicts risk of future dementia in the nun study. *Cortex*, 55(1):97–106, June. Funding Information: The work on this study was supported in part by the National Institutes of Health National Library of Medicine Grant [LM00962301 – S.P.] and the Nun Study data collection was supported by a grant from the National Institute of Aging (R01AG09862). The authors also wish to thank Heather Hoecker for helping with digitization of the SVF samples.

Pedregosa, F., Varoquaux, G., Gramfort, A., Michel, V., Thirion, B., Grisel, O., Blondel, M., Prettenhofer, P., Weiss, R., Dubourg, V., Vanderplas, J., Passos, A., Cournapeau, D., Brucher, M., Perrot, M., and Duchesnay, E. (2011). Scikit-learn: Machine learning in Python. *Journal of Machine Learning Research*, 12:2825–2830.

R Core Team, (2017). *R: A Language and Environment for Statistical Computing*. R Foundation for Statistical Computing, Vienna, Austria.

Shorten, C. and Khoshgoftaar, T. M. (2019). A survey on image data augmentation for deep learning. *Journal of Big Data*, 6(1):60.

Themistocleous, C., Eckerström, M., and Kokkinakis, D. (2020). Voice quality and speech fluency distinguish individuals with mild cognitive impairment from healthy controls. *Plos one*, 15(7):e0236009.

Tröger, J., Linz, N., König, A., Robert, P., and Alexandersson, J. (2018). Telephone-based dementia screening i: Automated semantic verbal fluency assessment. In *Proceedings of the 12th EAI International Conference on Pervasive Computing Technologies for Healthcare*, PervasiveHealth '18, page 59–66, New York, NY, USA. Association for Computing Machinery.

Troyer, A. K., Moscovitch, M., and Winocur, G. (1997). Clustering and Switching as Two Components of Verbal Fluency: Evidence From Younger and Older Healthy Adults. *Neuropsychology*, 11(1):138–146.

Tröger, J., Linz, N., König, A., Robert, P., Alexandersson, J., Peter, J., and Kray, J. (2019). Exploitation vs. exploration—computational temporal and semantic analysis explains semantic verbal fluency impairment in alzheimer's disease. *Neuropsychologia*, 131:53–61.

Vaughan, R., Coen, R., Kenny, R., and Lawlor, B. (2016). Preservation of the semantic verbal fluency advantage in a large population-based sample: Normative data from the tilda study. *Journal of the International Neuropsychological Society*, -1:1–7, 04.

Zhong, Z., Zheng, L., Kang, G., Li, S., and Yang, Y. (2017). Random erasing data augmentation. *CoRR*, abs/1708.04896.

Proceedings of the RaPID-4 @LREC 2022, pages 17–21
Marseille, 25 June 2022

A Novel Metrological Approach to a More Consistent Way of Defining and Analyzing Memory Task Difficulty in Word Learning List Tests with Repeated Trials

Melin J [1], Pendrill L [1]
[1] RISE Research Institutes of Sweden, Division Safety and transport, Department Measurement Science and Technology
Jeanette.melin@ri.se, Leslie.pendrill@ri.se

Abstract

New candidate diagnostics for cognitive decline and dementia have recently been proposed based on effects such as primacy and recency in word learning memory list tests. The diagnostic value is, however, currently limited by the multiple ways in which raw scores, and in particular these serial position effects (SPE), have been defined and analyzed to date. In this work, we build on previous analyses taking a metrological approach to the 10-item word learning list. We show i) how the variation in task difficulty reduces successively for trials 2 and 3, ii) how SPE change with repeated trials as predicted with our entropy-based theory, and iii) how possibilities to separate cohort members according to cognitive health status are limited. These findings mainly depend on the test design itself: A test with only 10 words, where SPE do not dominate over trials, requires more challenging words to increase the variation in task difficulty, and in turn to challenge the test persons. The work is novel and also contributes to the endeavour to develop for more consistent ways of defining and analyzing memory task difficulty, and in turn opens up for more practical and accurate measurement in clinical practice, research and trials.

Keywords: Cognition, Word recall, Item response theory, Entropy, Metrology

1. Introduction

Measurement of the memory ability of persons has a long tradition in neuropsychological assessment. Tests used to measure a person's memory ability typically include language- and cultural-free blocks and digits recall as well as more complex word recalling sequences. Recently, improved diagnostics for cognitive decline and dementia, particularly when including serial position effects (SPE), have been sought when measuring memory abilities based on word learning lists (see summary by Weitzner & Calamia (2020)).

SPE address the relationship between the ordering of symbols (in the present case, words) in a list and the likelihood of them being recalled. Specifically, when a test person is asked to freely recall as many words as possible from a word list, SPE mean that the first (primacy region, *Pr*) and the last (recency region, *Rr*) words are easier to remember than items in the middle (middle region, *Mr*) (Murdock, 1962). In a recent review, Weitzner & Calamia (2020) conclude that: '*The analysis of SPE has demonstrated some utility as a marker of cognitive impairment associated with MCI, AD, and other dementias; however, research is limited by the multiple ways in which SPE are defined and analyzed.*' Despite the limitations, they found that individuals with MCI and AD showed reduced primacy and intact recency, with primacy being more reduced in AD.

In line with that, there are, to our best knowledge, few studies which properly handle the ordinal response of a test person taking a word learning list test, making any claim of a new diagnostic questionable. Our previous analyses of the *Rey's Auditor Verbal Learning List Test* (RAVLT) trial 1/immediate recall (IR) have challenged previous claims of disease-related changes in serial positions effects (SPE), in particular putting those claimed changes in relation to measurement uncertainty (Melin, et al., 2021a; Pendrill et al., 2021). Our analyses of word learning list tests so far have focused on the first trial, while the present work extends our study to include more trials repeated directly after each other, including learning effects, as well as delayed recall (DR).

An important part of ensuring construct validity and predictability is to explain how the difficulty of recalling is caused by a number of effects, particularly how the word list items are structured. A major result of our research so far, both of non-verbal, culture-free tests such as block or digit sequence tests, as well as the verbal lists studied here, has been to explain recall difficulty in terms of informational entropy (see section 2.2). It should be easier to recall a more ordered sequence of less entropy.

Our previous studies of IR have included *frequency* (i.e., how frequently each word occurs in its language) as an explanatory variable, although it is found to contribute little to item task difficulty compared with the major contributions from the sequence length, i.e., the number of symbols (words) in each list (Melin et al., 2021a; Pendrill et al., 2021). The minor contribution from word frequency might however be due to the fact that the words in the list studied are all very short and common in everyday language, and therefore not expected to lead to any significant variation in recall difficulty.

In contrast to RAVLT with 15 words with a fixed order on repeated trials 1 - 5, the word learning list (WLL) test included in the CERAD test battery has only 10 words and the word order changes with each of the three repeated trials. With only 10 words, SPE are expected to be less pronounced (Murdock, 1962) but repeated trials may include learning effects similar to RAVLT (Goldberg et al., 2015; Zhan et al., 2018).

The European NeuroMET2 18HLT09 project has brought together clinicians, academics, metrologists and industry to address measurement challenges in current neurodegenerative diseases. Our part in NeuroMET includes how to properly handle cognitive data and in this paper we will present how task difficulty and SPE change with repeated trials in word recalling tests, as predicted with our entropy-based theory.

2. Methods

2.1 Participants and data collection

The NeuroMET cohort has been recruited and tested bi-annually from 2016 to 2022 at Charité hospital in Berlin. Measurements administered include neuropsychological assessments with a battery of legacy cognitive tests, clinical laboratory data for protein biomarkers and ultra-high field magnetic resonance imaging and spectroscopy (Quaglia et al., 2021).

For this work, data have been included from baseline and follow-up visits from the WLL CERAD cognitive tests (German) from 214 individual assessments of healthy controls (HC, n=73), persons with subjective cognitive decline (SCD, n=44) as well as patients with mild cognitive impairment (MCI, n=43) and suspected dementia due Alzheimer's Disease (AD, n=54).

In trial 1 of WLL CERAD, the test person is asked to freely recall as many as possible of the 10 common but unrelated words read by the test leader. In the second trial, the same 10 words are repeated but in a different order and the person is again asked to freely recall as many as possible. This is then repeated in a third trial, again with a different word order.

The study was approved by the Ethics Committee of the Charité - Universitätsmedizin Berlin, Germany, and was conducted in accordance with the declaration of Helsinki.

2.2 Data analyses

The ordinal responses (raw scores) to the WLL CERAD (classification number 1 for pass or classification number 0 for fail) were restituted through a logistic regression of the data to a dichotomous Rasch (1960) model using the WINSTEPS ® 5.2.0. This restitution process yields separate and linear measures for each memory task difficulty, δ, and individual person memory ability, θ, and compensates for ordinality:

$$P_{success} = \frac{e^{(\theta-\delta)}}{1+e^{(\theta-\delta)}}$$

The focus of this study is primarily on measures of memory task difficulties, δ.

Secondly, a state-of-the-art multivariate formulation is made of a construct specification equation (CSE) (Pendrill, 2019) for the quantity Z of the construct (in this case memory task difficulty, δ), expressed as a sum of a number of covariates, $\boldsymbol{X_k}$ (explanatory variables) in the causal associative relation: $Z = \sum_k \beta_k \cdot X_k$.

Explanatory variables $\boldsymbol{X_k}$ were identified in line with our previous work on RAVLT IR (Melin et al., 2021a; Pendrill et al., 2021) based on information theoretical entropy. In this case, the amount of information in these messages (G symbols with N repeats) according to the well-known Shannon (1948) expression of 'surprisal' in the work of Brillouin (1962), is given by:

$$I = M \cdot \left[ln(G!) - \sum_{j=1}^{N} ln(N_j!) \right]$$

where the normalisation constant, $M = \frac{1}{ln(G)}$

This general expression gave us the following definitions for explanatory variables for the different contributions to memory IR task difficulty for each word, j:

$$\delta_{Mr,j} = 2 \cdot M \cdot ln(G_j!);\ G = L/2$$

$$\delta_{Pr,j} = -M \cdot ln(G_j!);\ G = item\ order$$

$$\delta_{Rr,j} = -M \cdot ln(G_j!);\ G = L - 1 - item\ order$$

$$\delta_{freq,j} = -M \cdot lnf_j$$

Finally, formulation of a CSE for overall task difficulty (Pendrill 2019) for each trial included three steps in a principal component regression (PCR):

i. A PCA amongst the set of explanatory variables, $\boldsymbol{X_k}$, using the entropy-based estimates of δ given above
ii. A linear regression of the empirical task difficulty values δ_j against $\boldsymbol{X'} = \boldsymbol{X} \cdot \boldsymbol{P}$ in terms of the principal components, $\boldsymbol{P}$; and
iii. A conversion back from principal components to the explanatory variables, $\boldsymbol{X_k}$

3. Results

3.1 Overall task difficulty

Figure 1 presents how task difficulty for individual items is found empirically to change over the three trials. On the y-axis lower values imply an easier task and vice versa, and the x-axis represents each item in order of appearance in each trial.

Blue dots represent trial 1 with a clear parabolic fit line, indicating easier tasks in the beginning and at the end, i.e., the SPE for Pr and Rr, and qualitatively similar to our earlier RAVLT observations. The variation in task difficulty with order is successively reduced for trials 2 and 3 (orange and grey dots in figure 1). Overall task difficulty also decreases with the three repeated trials.

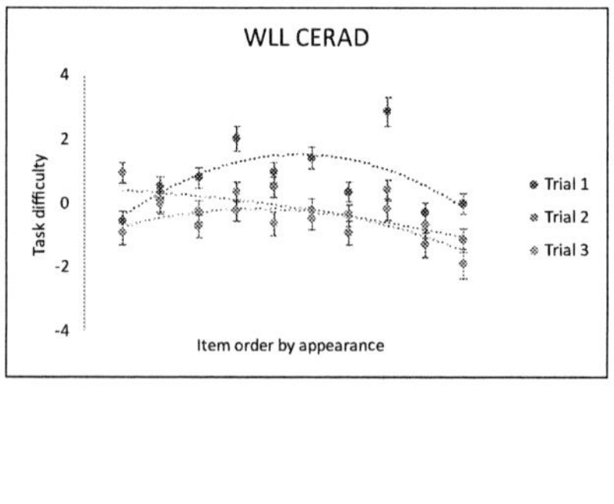

Figure 1. Empirical task difficulty values on the y-axis (lower values implies an easier task), and the x-axis represent each item ordered by appearance in each trial. Error bars show measurement uncertainties with coverage factor k=2.

Smaller contributions from SPE to task difficulty in trials 2 and 3 are also confirmed by the CSEs formulated as described in section 2.2, yielding the following expressions for the three different trials:

$$zR_{WLL1,j} = 6(5) + 0.8(6) \times \delta_{Pr,j} + 1.2(1.2) \times \delta_{Rr,j} - 0.2(1) \times \delta_{freq,j} \quad (1)$$

$$zR_{WLL2,j} = 1(4) + 0.3(8) \times \delta_{Pr,j} + 0.1(6) \times \delta_{Rr,j} - 0.1(1) \times \delta_{freq,j} \quad (2)$$

$$zR_{WLL3,j} = 1(1) + 0.2(3) \times \delta_{Pr,j} - 0.0(3) \times \delta_{Rr,j} - 0.26(4) \times \delta_{freq,j} \quad (3)$$

Figures 2a-c illustrate contributions from each explanatory variable according to eqs. 1-3 across the ten items, clearly showing how primacy disappears in the later trials, while there seems to be a small contribution from recency remaining also in trial 2 and 3.

Because of the rapidly diminishing SPE due to learning effects on repeated trials of relatively short word lists, in contrast to our previous studies on RAVLT IR/trial 1, by WLL trial 3 frequency has become the dominating explanatory variable. One must remember, however, that the variation in empirical task difficulty values is small; in fact, only the second and last items can be separated from the others by amounts significantly larger than the measurement uncertainties.

Furthermore, in figures 2a-c the predicted (zR) can graphically be compared with the empirical task difficulties (same as Figure 1). Pearson correlation coefficients were for trial 1: 0.70, trial 2: 0.65 and trial 3: 0.93, which are of comparable strength to the results for RAVLT (Melin, et al., 2021n) but not as strong as for the block and number recalling tests (Melin et al., 2021b)

In the figures, error bars show measurement uncertainties with coverage factor $k=2$ for each memory task's difficulty, U(δ), which propagate through the PCR (section 2.2). In turn the U(δ) have implications for U(β) and UzR together with uncertainties in the fit itself, which is an issue of sample size, collinearity and measurement disturbance. In the present case when comparing the less cognitive able patients (MCI and AD) with the more cognitive able persons (HC and SCD), the un-even sample sizes may bias the interpretations. However, this can indicate that there are sources of dispersion when making the multivariate regression which are not yet accounted for.

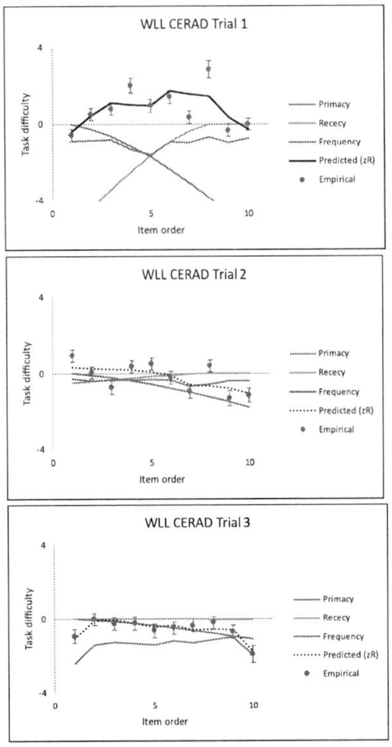

Figures 2a-c. Corresponding plots presenting the contribution from each explanatory variable as well as the empirical and predicted task difficulty values for all three WLL trials. Task difficulty values on the y-axis (lower values implies an easier task), and the x-axis represents each item ordered by appearance in each trial. Error bars show measurement uncertainties k=2.

3.2 Differences between sub-groups

For trial 1, the "intercept" value + 6(5) (first term on the right-hand side (RHS) of each CSE for task difficulty) can be compared with $\delta_{Mr,j} = 2 \cdot M \cdot ln(5!) = +4.2$ logits for the whole cohort. Our model for the learning effects observed for the 5 RAVLT trials (Melin et al., 2022), where the intercept value decreases in inverse proportion to the root of the number of trials performed, would predict that the intercept value would be $\frac{4{,}2}{\sqrt{2}} = 3\ logits$ at trial 2 and $\frac{4{,}2}{\sqrt{3}} = 2.5\ logits$ at trial 3. These predictions are within measurement uncertainties of the observed intercept values given in equations (1), (2) and (3).

When comparing CSEs for the two groups of cohort members, for the second trial the intercepts were found to differ slightly (albeit with large uncertainties):

$$zR_{WLL2\ HC+SCD,j} = 1(1) + 0.0(5) \times \delta_{Pr,j} - 0.1(2) \times \delta_{Rr,j} - 0.4(2) \times \delta_{freq,j} \quad (4)$$

$$zR_{WLL2\ MCI+AD,j} = 2(1) + 0.3(4) \times \delta_{Pr,j} + 0.2(4) \times \delta_{Rr,j} - 0.2(0) \times \delta_{freq,j} \quad (5)$$

In line with what one may expect, this difference in intercept might indicate a faster learning for the more cognitive able cohort members. Further, a difference between the cohort groups was observed in terms of the contributions to task difficulty from primacy and recency; for the more cognitive able cohort members, the contributions from primacy and recency are negligible already at the second trial.

4. Conclusion

Our entropy-based theory earlier developed for RAVLT was successfully replicated for WLL CERAD trial 1 in the present study, although the effects of SPE are not as pronounced with repeated WLL trials. This may be explained by the fact that WLL CERAD comprises only 10 words in contrast to RAVLT as well as a different word ordering per trial.

In the present work we have shown i) how the variation in task difficulty reduces successively for trials 2 and 3, ii) how SPE change with repeated trials as predicted with our entropy-based theory, and iii) how possibilities to separate cohort members according to cognitive health status are limited.

These findings depend mainly on the test design itself: A test with only 10 words, where SPE do not dominate over trials, requires more challenging words to increase the variation in task difficulty, and in turn to challenge the test persons.

In the present case of WLL CERAD, the 10 words are all common but unrelated. Thus, it was no surprise that frequency provided relatively little explanation in the CSE, particularly in the first trial where SPE dominate. However, including less common, i.e., less frequently used, words is expected to make a greater contribution to recall difficulty from frequency. Moreover, other related aspects to consider could be: word length (Surprenant et al., 2011), semantics (Earles & Kersten, 2017; Hyde & Jenkins, 1973), phonetics (Rezvanfard et al., 2011).

The work here is not only novel, but also necessary for more consistent ways of defining and analyzing memory task difficulty, and in turn opens up for more practical and accurate measurement in clinical practice, research and trials.

The observed response in any word learning list test, as well as for other tests of human abilities, typically gets classification numbers. As in the present case, 0 for fail and 1 for pass (section 2.2). Such observed response constitutes raw data, $x_{i,j}$, for test person i and item j, which is characterized by ordinality and is not a measure of the person's memory ability nor the memory task difficulty. We have previously shown that metrological methods to simple syntax studies provide opportunities for more practical and accurate measurement in clinical practice, research and trials (Melin et al., 2021c). In this work, together with ongoing work on word learning list test (Melin et al., 2022; Melin et al., 2021a; Pendrill et al., 2021) we advance a novel metrological approach to cover more consistent ways of defining and analysing memory task difficulty.

9. Acknowledgements

This project 18HLT09 NeuroMET2 has received funding from the EMPIR programme co-financed by the Participating States and from the European Union's Horizon 2020 research and innovation programme.

10. Bibliographical References

Brillouin, L. (1962). *Science and Information Theory* (Second Edition). https://www.amazon.com/Science-Information-Theory-Second-Physics/dp/0486497550

Earles, J. L., & Kersten, A. W. (2017). Why Are Verbs So Hard to Remember? Effects of Semantic Context on Memory for Verbs and Nouns. *Cognitive Science*, *41 Suppl 4*, 780–807. https://doi.org/10.1111/cogs.12374

Goldberg, T. E., Harvey, P. D., Wesnes, K. A., Snyder, P. J., & Schneider, L. S. (2015). Practice effects due to serial cognitive assessment: Implications for preclinical Alzheimer's disease randomized controlled trials. *Alzheimer's & Dementia: Diagnosis, Assessment & Disease Monitoring*, *1*(1), 103–111. https://doi.org/10.1016/j.dadm.2014.11.003

Hawkins, K. A., Dean, D., & Pearlson, G. D. (2004). Alternative Forms of the Rey Auditory Verbal Learning Test: A Review. *Behavioural Neurology*, *15*(3–4), 99–107. https://doi.org/10.1155/2004/940191

Hyde, T. S., & Jenkins, J. J. (1973). Recall for words as a function of semantic, graphic, and syntactic orienting tasks. *Journal of Verbal Learning & Verbal Behavior*, *12*(5), 471–480. https://doi.org/10.1016/S0022-5371(73)80027-1

Melin, J., Regnault, A., Cano, S., & Pendrill, L. (2021a). *Neuropsychological assessments: Word learning tests and diagnostic potential of serial position effects*. The International Metrology Congress, Lyon, France.

Melin, J., Cano, S. J., Flöel, A., Göschel, L., & Pendrill, L. R. (2021b). Construct specification equations: 'Recipes' for certified reference materials in cognitive measurement. *Measurement: Sensors*, *18*, 100290. https://doi.org/10.1016/j.measen.2021.100290

Melin, J., Cano, S., & Pendrill, L. (2021c). The Role of Entropy in Construct Specification Equations (CSE) to Improve the Validity of Memory Tests. *Entropy*, *23*(2), 212. https://doi.org/10.3390/e23020212

Melin, J., Kettunen, P., Wallin, A., & Pendrill, L. (2022). *Entropy-based explanations of serial position and learning effects in ordinal responses to word list tests.*

Murdock, B. B. (1962). The serial position effect of free recall. *Journal of Experimental Psychology*, *64*(5), 482–488. http://dx.doi.org.ezproxy.ub.gu.se/10.1037/h0045106

Pendrill, L. (2019). *Quality Assured Measurement: Unification across Social and Physical Sciences*. Springer International Publishing. https://doi.org/10.1007/978-3-030-28695-8

Pendrill, L, Melin, J., & Cano, S. J. (2021). *Entropy-based explanations of multidimensionality in ordinal responses*. MSMM.

Quaglia, M., Cano, S., Fillmer, A., Flöel, A., Giangrande, C., Göschel, L., Lehmann, S., Melin, J., & Teunissen, C. E. (2021). The NeuroMET project: Metrology and innovation for early diagnosis and accurate stratification of patients with neurodegenerative diseases. *Alzheimer's & Dementia*, *17*(S5), e053655. https://doi.org/10.1002/alz.053655

Rasch, G. (1960). *Studies in mathematical psychology: I. Probabilistic models for some intelligence and attainment tests*. Nielsen & Lydiche.

Rezvanfard, M., Ekhtiari, H., Noroozian, M., Rezvanifar, A., Nilipour, R., & Javan, G. K. (2011). *The Rey Auditory Verbal Learning Test: Alternate Forms Equivalency and Reliability for the Iranian Adult Population (Persian Version)*. 6.

Shannon, C. E. (1948). *A Mathematical Theory of Communication*. *1948*, 55.

Surprenant, A. M., Brown, M. A., Jalbert, A., Neath, I., Bireta, T. J., & Tehan, G. (2011). Backward recall and the word length effect. *The American Journal of Psychology*, *124*(1), 75–86. https://doi.org/10.5406/amerjpsyc.124.1.0075

Weitzner, D. S., & Calamia, M. (2020). Serial position effects on list learning tasks in mild cognitive impairment and Alzheimer's disease. *Neuropsychology*, *34*(4), 467–478. https://doi.org/10.1037/neu0000620

Zhan, L., Guo, D., Chen, G., & Yang, J. (2018). Effects of Repetition Learning on Associative Recognition Over Time: Role of the Hippocampus and Prefrontal Cortex. *Frontiers in Human Neuroscience*, *12*, 277. https://doi.org/10.3389/fnhum.2018.00277

Proceedings of the RaPID-4 @LREC 2022, pages 22–30
Marseille, 25 June 2022

Extraction and Classification of Acoustic Features from Italian Speaking Children with Autism Spectrum Disorders

Federica Beccaria[1], Gloria Gagliardi[1], Dimitrios Kokkinakis[2]
[1] University of Bologna – Department of Classical Philology and Italian Studies
[2] University of Gothenburg – Department of Swedish, Multilingualism, Language and Technology
federica.beccaria@studio.unibo.it, gloria.gagliardi@unibo.it, dimitrios.kokkinakis@svenska.gu.se

Abstract

Autism Spectrum Disorders (ASD) are a group of complex developmental conditions whose effects and severity show high intraindividual variability. However, one of the main symptoms shared along the spectrum is social interaction impairments that can be explored through acoustic analysis of speech production. In this paper, we compare 14 Italian-speaking children with ASD and 14 typically developing peers. Accordingly, we extracted and selected the acoustic features related to prosody, quality of voice, loudness, and spectral distribution using the parameter set eGeMAPS provided by the openSMILE feature extraction toolkit. We implemented four supervised machine learning methods to evaluate the extraction performances. Our findings show that Decision Trees (DTs) and Support Vector Machines (SVMs) are the best-performing methods. The overall DT models reach a 100% recall on all the trials, meaning they correctly recognise autistic features. However, half of its models overfit, while SVMs are more consistent. One of the results of the work is the creation of a speech pipeline to extract Italian speech biomarkers typical of ASD by comparing our results with studies based on other languages. A better understanding of this topic can support clinicians in diagnosing the disorder.

Keywords: Autism Spectrum Disorders, acoustic analysis, machine learning, openSMILE, eGeMAPS

1. Introduction

The American Psychiatry Association defines Autism Spectrum Disorders (ASD) as a group of complex developmental conditions whose effects and severity are different in each person. However, some common symptoms have been found whose presence represents the criteria used during the diagnosis. According to the DSM-5, one of them is the presence of impairments in social communication (Criterion A). Thus, the quality of language is an essential indicator during the diagnosis of ASD, both in comprehension and production. Even if these linguistic characteristics are present in a spectrum that showcases a wide variety, they still have something in common. Social interaction is mainly completed using different language skills.

In the present study, we investigated the speech production of Italian-speaking children with ASD to understand if there are acoustic features that can be shared along the spectrum. Indeed, there are already many English contributions showing abnormalities of autistic speech at the prosodic level. Unfortunately, there are few studies on this promising field in Italian. To conduct this investigation, we performed an acoustic feature extraction and a supervised learning classification between the speech production of Italian-speaking children with ASD and their peers with typical neurodevelopment (TD).

2. Prosody in ASD Speech

The study of prosodic traits in people with autism is relatively new and, compared to other linguistics domains, still little explored (Diehl & Paul, 2013; Kiss et al., 2012; Tanaka et al., 2014; Van Santen et al., 2010). As a result, this research field was called by some experts the "Cinderella of speech" that remains "in the cellar, with few visitors" (Crystal, 2009; p. 257). Nevertheless, the research on the typical acoustic features in people with different neurodevelopmental disorders is promising. Through various methods, usually based on multimodal investigations (i.e., behavioural assessments, acoustic analysis, electrophysiological measures, brain imaging), it has been demonstrated that the speech of autistic people shows some anomalies from the prosodic point of view. Indeed, common variabilities along the spectrum have been recorded in the movements and the pitch types produced (Shriberg et al., 2001). This acoustic pattern is the speakers' attitude and emotional status medium.

Based on these features, two main prosodic behaviours are commonly identified during the speech act: the pragmatic (or linguistic) and the affective functions (Anolli, 2002). The first represents the illocutive force, which is the act itself of talking by the speaker (see Searle & Vanderveken, 1985). Moreover, it distinguishes the type of sentence produced, e.g., interrogative or affirmative. On the other hand, the second function represents the medium - sometimes unintended - of the emotional status felt by the speaker. Thus, people with alterations of these prosodic productions may exhibit impairments in elaborating the vocal chants and sentences showing their emotional status. Moreover, these impairments affect their comprehension of other people, causing difficulties in social interaction and communication (Olivati et al., 2017).

From its first descriptions, the speech of people with autism has been defined as being monotonous, robotic, and pedant (Kanner, 1943). The patients present difficulties both in the production and perception skills. For instance, Kanner (1943; p. 228) wrote about one of the children he studied: "It made no difference whether one spoke to him in a friendly or a harsh way". Thus, the scholar who first defined autism gave an implicit focus on prosodic and affective traits in the speech production and comprehension of people with the disorder. However, the researchers ignored this part of Kanner's study in the decades that followed. Nevertheless, through prosody, we can detect the acoustic patterns that show the speaker's emotional status, one of the most visible symptoms in the atypical communication of people with ASD. Thus, during the last years, the research moved to the study of acoustic correlates while analysing these typical features of the disorder.

3. The Dataset

The participants in the present study come from a pool of Italian-speaking children in a homogeneous geographical area from the region between Florence, Pistoia, and Prato. The corpus consists of audio recordings collected from two cohorts: children with ASD and their peers with typical neurodevelopment (TD). The data are balanced on the number of participants and their demographic characteristics. The children are 14 for each group with the same age (from 6 to 10 years) and sex (11 M, 3 F). Gender disparity is taken from the epidemiology of the disorder recorded by the DSM-5 (APA, 2013), i.e., four males every one female.

The participants in the study were recruited from a previous project on discourse and storytelling in autism (Biancalani, 2019), where the children were asked to tell a story from six pictures stimulating a semi-spontaneous speech during the interviews. The images illustrate a story about a birthday party and are easily interpretable by neurotypical children of different ages. The pictures come from the toy Shubi collection *Storie da raccontare* (in English, 'Story to tell'). The children from the ASD group were recruited from the speech and language therapy service of AUSL Toscana Centro and the Onlus foundation "Opera Santa Rita". The diagnosis was made by a neuropsychiatrist according to DSM-5 criteria. The data collection was carried out by a designed speech therapist in June 2019, after receiving the written consent of the caregivers of the children. The recordings were realised with a video camera placed on a tree-legged support. The setting was designed so that the child would feel comfortable. Therefore, the meeting was conducted in the room where they usually play. The interview started with activities generally done during the treatment session so the child would act in the most spontaneous way.

It was necessary to conduct new data collection for the TD group. The recording was done for qualitative analysis in the previous study, and the audio quality was not good enough to realise an acoustic investigation. In particular, the background noise was so high that it was impossible to identify the child's voice automatically. It was attempted to denoise the recordings with the software Audacity, but this solution would have significantly changed the shape of the waveforms and their quality in general. The participants were chosen from the same geographical area and had the same demographic characteristics as those from the ASD group. Moreover, due to the COVID-19 pandemic, it was impossible to collect the data *in situ,* so the parents of each child did the recording using their phones. Even though we are aware that this might eschew our results, we consider that it will not have that significant impact because the storytelling task remained the same, and the quality of the recordings was high (i.e., there was no background noise).

4. Extraction, Selection, and Classification of Acoustic Features

In the present study, we decided to use the *Munich open-Source Media Interpretation by Large feature-space Extraction* (openSMILE) to extract the acoustic features. In the area of autistic vocalisation detection, this software has been used in previous studies, reaching satisfying results (Asgari & Shafran, 2018; Cho et al., 2019; Kim et al., 2017; Lee et al., 2013; Li et al., 2019; Marchi et al., 2015; Pokorny et al., 2017). After extracting the acoustic features, we selected the most statistically significant between the two groups of our dataset (ASD and TD). Then, we tested the features selection by implementing machine learning algorithms with a binary classification task. The role of training supervised learning methods is to classify them and show if they are significant in the speech production of people with ASD, according to the performance of each model. This model may evolve, through further studies, into a tool that helps the clinician determine whether Italian children have ASD at a young age.

4.1 Methods

We used openSMILE version 2.1, developed for the Interspeech challenge (Schuller et al., 2013). Among the feature sets currently available – i.e., GeMAPS (Geneva Minimalistic Standard Parameter Set), eGeMAPS (Eyben et al., 2015), and ComParE (Schuller et al., 2016) - we applied the second that was specifically ideated by its developers to become a tool used in paralinguistics and clinical speech analysis.

Moreover, we chose this feature set over the other two proposed by openSMILE for several reasons. First, we decided against using ComParE, given that the size of the feature space (n = 6376) vastly outnumbers the sample size of our dataset. Furthermore, this would have caused our machine learning models to overfit, which is highly undesirable. On the other hand, we chose eGeMAPS over GeMAPS, given that the former extracts features based on their relation to various psychological changes in voice production (Eyben et al., 2015), which has proven useful in previous studies (Julião et al., 2020; Lee et al., 2020; Marchi et al., 2015; Memari et al., 2020; Pokorny et al., 2017; Ringeval et al., 2016; Rybner et al., 2022; Schmitt et al., 2016). The acoustic features extracted by eGeMAPS are related to the frequency, energy, amplitude, and distribution on the spectrum. These are presented in Table 1 - 3 with a short explanation extracted from Eyben et al. (2015; pp. 4-5).

Features	Explanation
Pitch	Logarithmic F0 on a semitone frequency scale, starting at 27.5 Hz
Jiitter	Deviations in individual consecutive F0
Formants 1, 2, 3 frequencies and bandwidth	The centre frequency and the bandwidth of the first, second, and third formant

Table 1: Frequency related features

Features	Explanation
Harminics-to-Noise Ratio	Relation of energy in harmonic components to energy in noise-like components
Loudness	Estimate of perceived signal intensity from an auditory spectrum
Shimmer	Difference of the peak amplitudes of consecutive F0 cycles

Table 2: Energy and amplitude related features

Features	Explanation
Alpha Ratio	Ratio of the summed energy from 50–1000 Hz and 1–5 kHz
Formants 1, 2, 3 with relative energies	Ratio of the energy of the spectral harmonic peak at the first, second, third formant's centre frequency to the energy of the spectral peak at F0
Hammarberg Index	Ratio of the strongest energy peak in the 0–2 kHz region to the strongest peak in the 2–5 kHz region
Harmonic difference H1–H2	Ratio of energy of the first F0 harmonic (H1) to the energy of the second F0 harmonic (H2)
Harmonic difference H1–A3	Ratio of energy of the first F0 harmonic (H1) to the energy of the highest harmonic in the third formant range (A3)
MFCC 1-4	Mel-Frequency Cepstral Coefficients 1-4
Spectral flux	Difference of the spectra of two consecutive frames
Spectral Slope 0–500Hz and 500–1500 Hz	Linear regression slope of the logarithmic power spectrum within the two given bands

Table 3: Spectral (balance) related features

Once the acoustic features presented in Tables 1 - 3 were extracted, we selected the most statistically significant ones by implementing a non-parametrical statistical test, namely Mann-Whitney U-test (Mann & Whitney, 1947; Wilcoxon, 1945). Thus, with the Mann-Whitney U-test, we tested whether the features had similar values between the two groups and selected the ones presenting the more significant distance. In the final discussion, we introduced the features selected by comparing them with those obtained by other studies. In doing so, we considered the different methods applied to the data collection and the analysis itself.

Having irrelevant features can decrease the accuracy of machine learning models, especially when dealing with linear models such as support vector machines. On the other hand, the feature selection operated on clinical recorded data can lead to high performances of the classifier, which are not reproducible on new data considering all the speech production. This aspect produces a bias in the results obtained by the classifier when used to create a tool able to distinguish the speech productions of the disease. For instance, while performing the same task on people with Alzheimer Dementia's speech, Luz et al. (2020) report that the performance evaluation metrics drop consistently if applied to the same dataset without performing the feature selection. However, this work aims to test the feature extraction effectiveness and not automatically classify ASD from new speech data. This goal could be reached by future studies conducted on larger datasets.

We pre-processed the data obtained through feature selection to prepare it for the supervised learning methods. Then we normalised the data and implemented the K-fold Stratified cross-validation to train the models (k = 3). Thus, we split the training set into k parts, denominated folds. Next, we train a model that uses that fold as a validation set and the rest as its training set for each fold. This helps avoid overfitting the noise in the data. We split 80% for the train and 20% for the test sets. Given the small number of samples on our corpus (ASD = 14, TD = 14, total features = 16), the data processed on the sets were 22 by the train and six by the test sets.

The machine learning methods implemented are all supervised: Decision Trees (DTs), K-Nearest Neighbours (KNNs), Random Forests (RFs), and Support Vector Machines (SVMs). First, we evaluate the performances of each model trained using different metrics: accuracy, recall, precision, F1-score, and Area under the Curve (AUC). Then, we chose the best ten models obtained by running each supervised method and comparing them with the others. Finally, we selected the best performing model of each method.

All the computational steps are done by implementing different algorithms in Python (Chollet, 2021; Downey et al., 2012; Van Rossum & Drake, 2011) with the aid of the Jupyter Notebook (Kluyver et al., 2016). Moreover, all the machine learning methods performed are implemented using the Scikit-learn module for the Python programming language (Pedregosa et al., 2011). The code used is publicly available on GitHub: https://github.com/federica-bcc/speech-autism.

4.2 Results

We extracted 88 parameters concerning the frequency, energy, and spectral distribution. Table 4 reports the parameters selected with their respective functionals in parenthesis (μ = mean, σ = standard deviation), the values obtained from both the groups with the number of outliers in parenthesis if found. The last column indicates the significance levels through the p-value (p).

The best models of each supervised method reach high accuracy, with the highest being Decision Tree, Random Forest, and Support Vector Machine (accuracy = 83%), while the lowest KNN (accuracy = 67%). The AUC metric's highest values are reached by DT and SVM (AUC = 88%), while the KNN and the RF have lower performances (AUC = 75%). Tables 5 and 6 report the results obtained by the best model of each classifier on these metrics and the others (recall, precision, and F1-score), both on the train and the test sets, respectively.

On the other hand, Table 7 reports the mean of the evaluation metrics obtained by all the models for each method giving a clearer view of their overall behaviour on the classification task.

4.3 Discussion

In the present study, we analysed the speech production of Italian speaking children with ASD. Our corpus comprises 28 audio recording files divided into two groups: 14 children with ASD and 14 controls. First, we implemented the acoustic feature extraction using eGeMAPS provided by the openSMILE toolkit. Next, we extracted 88 parameters for each audio file and selected the most statistically significant between the two groups. Finally, we implemented four supervised learning algorithms to test the validity of the feature selection.

In the following sections, we discuss the features obtained with the feature selection (Section 4.3.1) and the results from the classification task (Section 4.4.2).

Feature	ASD	TD	p-value
Pitch falling slope (σ)	168.81 ± 61.29 (0)	137.27 ± 130.12 (2)	0.0409*
F2 Frequency (σ)	0.17 ± 0.013 (3)	0.15 ± 0.017 (0)	0.0030**
F2 bandwidth (σ)	0.33 ± 0.038 (0)	0.38 ± 0.075 (1)	0.0326*
Jitter (μ)	0.036 ± 0.008	0.024 ± 0.011	0.0094**
Jitter (σ)	1.69 ± 0.21 (2)	1.88 ± 0.26 (1)	0.0094**
Shimmer (μ)	1.23 ± 0.067	1.04+ 0.14	0.0016**
Shimmer (σ)	0.46 ± 0.02 (1)	0.66 ± 0.16 (0)	0.0010***
Harmonics-to-Noise Ratio (μ)	5.04 ± 1.14	7.88 ± 2.10	0.0012**
Harmonics-to-Noise Ratio (σ)	1.03 ± 0.29	0.64 ± 0.28	0.0016**
Loudness (μ)	1.16 ± 0.44	0.82 ± 0.30	0.0508
Loudness rising slope (σ)	7.87 ± 2.25	0.04 ± 0.02	0.0409*
Loudness (Percentile 20.0)	0.59 ± 0.21	0.32 ± 0.18	0.0035**
Spectral Flux (μ)	0.72 ± 0.38	0.42 ± 0.24	0.0366*
Spectral Flux voiced segments (μ)	0.86 ± 0.43	0.51± 0.26	0.0409*
Slope unvoiced segments, 0-500 Hz (μ)	0.056 ± 0.02	0.04 ± 0.02	0.0456*
Slope unvoiced segments, 500-1500 Hz (μ)	-0.0096 ± 0.0022 (0)	-0.0027 ± 0.0071 (1)	0.0026**

Table 4: Values of the acoustic features with statistical significance between the ASD and TD groups.
Results are expressed as *means ± standard deviations (n. outliers)*. Asterisks indicate when the group-related difference is significant under the Mann-Whitney U-test: * $p < 0.05$; ** $p < 0.01$, *** $p < 0.001$.

Methods	Acc.	Rec.	Prec.	F1-sc.	AUC
DT	82	92	100	96	96
KNN	77	83	77	80	77
RF	77	67	89	67	78
SVM	73	83	71	77	72

Table 5: Values of the evaluation metrics obtained on the train set by the best models

Methods	Acc.	Rec.	Prec.	F1-sc.	AUC
DT	83	100	96	80	88
KNN	67	100	50	67	75
RF	83	50	100	67	75
SVM	83	100	67	80	88

Table 6: Values of the evaluation metrics obtained on the test set by the best models

Methods	Acc.	Rec.	Prec.	F1-sc.	AUC
DT	68.2 (16.40)	100 (0)	54.5 (13.50)	69.5 (11.46)	76.3 (12.92)
KNN	58.5 (12.02)	75 (26.35)	42 (10.05)	52.1 (11.83)	59.8 (12.66)
RF	70.1 (10.33)	65 (24.15)	64 (25.03)	59.2 (8.48)	68.5 (6.85)
SVM	79.8 (6.75)	95 (15.81)	63.6 (7.17)	77.4 (5.48)	84.9 (5.44)

Table 7: Means and (sd) of the evaluation metrics obtained on the test set by running the models ten times

4.3.1 Typical Acoustic Features of ASD Speech

To discuss the features selected, we divided them into thematic groups according to their linguistic qualities: frequency-related parameters (pitch and second formant), voice quality (shimmer, jitter, and Harmonics-to-Noise Ratio), loudness, and spectrum-related parameters (spectral flux and slope).

Frequency-related parameters. The pitch is one of the main features of prosodic analysis. In general, there are opposite findings in the literature regarding the mean values of the pitch. The present study found higher values in this functional, but the difference between the two groups is not statistically significant. However, the increasing pitch could suggest chasing away the idea that the speech of people with ASD is robotic, monotonous and without melodic variation, as reported in the past literature (Kissine & Geelhand, 2019; Nayak et al., 2019; Olivati et al., 2017).

We found interesting results on the standard deviation of the pitch falling slope. Moreover, even if not statistically significant, the same pattern is observed in the rising slope. These results confirm the high variation in the general prosody production, specifically on the intonation contours. Sharda et al. (2010) related these pitch excursions to their range and showed similarities to the one observed during "motherese" speech postulating a delayed developmental trajectory of speech. Nevertheless, even if interesting, Bonneh et al. (2011) disproved these results and showed that this trend does not always hold.

Another explanation can be found in some interesting results on impairments controlling the cortical pitch. The most relevant finding on these assumptions is related to auditory processing in autism (Boddaert et al., 2004; Rosenhall et al., 1999). The research in this field has increased in the past few years, mainly thanks to neuro-imaging techniques applied to experiments through a multimodal optic study.

Moreover, the extreme variation in the pitch values shows the difficulties of people with autism to perceive and, consequently, produce prosody in the same way as their peers (Olivati et al., 2017). This can lead to many difficulties in social interaction and communication because of the lack of others' speech intention comprehension than the production itself (Bonneh et al., 2011). Moreover, on the correlation between production and perception, many studies conducted on the comprehension of the emotions communicated by the interlocutor show that children with ASD have less capacity than their peers. The same trend is reflected in their speech, especially in using different intonations to transmit each emotion (Chiew et al., 2017; Hubbard et al., 2017; Schelinski & Kriegstein., 2019).

Finally, another problem described in the literature is the influence of external factors on the recording and the inhomogeneity in extracting the correlations. First, the feature related to the formants, including the fundamental frequency, is sensitive to the speaker's age, gender, and height (Bone et al., 2014). Second, as reported in McCann and Peppe (2003), it would be expected that these descriptors for prosodic abnormalities should appear in many studies. However, the findings do not show coherent discussions because the evaluation measures are not well defined.

For these reasons, in future studies, it will be interesting to investigate both the correlation of voice features to the personal characteristics of the speakers (age, gender, and height) and compare all the results with other studies that used the same metrics.

Voice quality. The voice quality is measured as the difficulty in controlling the vocal fold vibrations, transforming the production into hoarseness, breathiness, and creaky voice. These irregularities can be quantified through the analysis of some features that "reflect mathematical properties of the sound wave" (Robin et al., 2020; p. 102), such as the jitter for the pitch, the shimmer for the intensity and the Harmonics-to-Noise Ratio (HNR) for the description of the periodic and aperiodic acoustic propagation (Tsanas et al., 2011). The present study found interesting results on all these parameters, confirming the observations drawn by other investigations.

Jitter and shimmer are related: the first measures periodicity in the speech signal, while the second the difference from a cycle to the next one. As done in other studies, these values were calculated using the local method by evaluating the pitch period and magnitude once per each span of the period (Boersma, 2001; Bone et al., 2012). However, they are also related to another aspect: they are valuable parameters to measure in a speech pathology analysis because the voice with language impairment is likely to have higher values than a healthy one (Styler, 2021).

In the present study, two populations are compared with the assumption that one of them (ASD) shows impairments in vocal production. The results we obtained from the jitter and the shimmer confirm this hypothesis. Indeed, the means are higher in the speech of ASD, with statistically significant differences described by the p-values obtained by the Mann-Whitney U-test (0.0094 for jitter and 0.0016 for shimmer). However, the results are the opposite for the standard deviations. The findings suggest that these acoustic features vary consistently less in children with autism but have higher values on average.

This trend has also been observed in previous studies. For instance, in Kissine & Geelhand (2019), the authors noted a highly statistically significant difference between these two parameters, with a higher rate in the production of ASD (jitter $p < 0.001$; shimmer $p = 0.001$). Moreover, their sample was composed by adults (mean age: about 28 years old) while, in the present study, the participants were children. Hence, future studies might explore if this trend is typical of autism throughout life, meaning a turning point in the early diagnosis of the disease. Indeed, the analysis of these correlations, combined with the pitch, intensity, and pause count, supports the hypothesis of assessing the speech modulation in ASD through studying the measure of dynamic-intonation variability (Bone et al., 2015).

Moreover, the jitter and the shimmer show the noise present in the speech, and their values can be sensitive to its presence in the recording. For this reason, it is essential to analyse also the HNR that usually detects the friction in the vocal tract, attributed to hoarse, breathy, or laryngeal pathologies when it decreases significantly (Styler, 2021).

In Bone et al. (2014), the mean of the HNR is shown to be strictly related to the jitter: when this latter increases, the other decreases. In the present study, we found this trend with significant results both on the means (jitter: p = 0.0094**, HNR: p = 0.0012**) and on the standard deviations (jitter: p = 0.0094**, HNR: p = 0.0016**) that follows the opposite growth for both the mean and the standard deviation.

The negative correlation between jitter and HNR is observed in many studies concerning the analysis of breathless, hoarseness and roughness voices, where they are also correlated to an increase in the cepstral values (Halberstam, 2004; Hillenbrand et al., 1994). McAllister et al. (1998) correlated in their studies the jitter to the breathy, hoarse, nasal speech and the shimmer to the breathiness, but no correlation with the cepstral values was found in this type of speech. In the same way, the present study did not find statistically significant results on these latter features. Bone et al. (2014) reported the same trend that we obtained. Therefore, we agree with the authors that it is necessary to conduct more analysis regarding voice quality to confirm this trend and to be able to use it during the diagnosis (Bone et al., 2014: 1173).

The loudness. The loudness is defined as the energy intensity produced by a sound wave. We found a statistically significant difference on the 20th percentile (p = 0.0035), in the standard deviation (p = 0.0409), and in the general mean (p = 0.0508). Even if these functionals measure different distribution aspects, they all present the same trend, showing higher values for the ASD group. These results are confirmed in Bone et al. (2012), where the role of intensity in the perception of abnormal volume is underlined with the increasing rate of atypicality. Moreover, these findings suggest that ASD intonation might not be as monotonous as described in other studies since a higher variation influences the perceived expressivity in the intensity contours. Thus, loudness could measure the dynamic intonation of autistic speech production (Bone et al., 2015), especially in tasks where affective prosody is investigated (Hubbard et al., 2017).

However, many researchers report the problem of having opposite results on intensity in the literature of reference.

For instance, in Mohanta et al. (2020; Mohanta & Mittal, 2022), the authors reported higher values in ASD (Quigley et al., 2016; Filipe et al., 2014) but also lower (Scharfstein et al., 2011). Furthermore, in addition to a trend of papers that present lower intensity in autistic speech (Chevallier et al., 2011; Ochi et al., 2019), there is also a consistent number of papers that did not find statistically significant results at all (Diehl & Paul, 2012; 2013; Filipe et al., 2014; Grossman et al., 2010). Moreover, in many studies, the authors decided not to study the intensity levels to avoid the risk of obtaining unclear results (Bisson et al., 2014; Dahlgren et al., 2018).

This difference in the results could be caused by the most reported problems: the recording environment and the microphone's position. The first cause reflects a common problem while doing a clinical speech collection and analysis since it is crucial to do so in a comfortable space for the patient. For the microphone, it would be necessary that all the participants wear it simultaneously from their mouths to ensure that all the variations are due to the actual speech production.

For these reasons, we decided not to consider the results obtained as relevant for the present. However, further studies could solve these impediments by rethinking the data collection process based on these observations.

Spectral-related parameters. In the present study, we found two spectral-related parameters with statistically significant results: the means of the spectral flux and the one from the slope of all the segments (voiced and unvoiced). Regarding the spectral flux, we found a statistically significant difference between both groups under all features extracted: voiced and unvoiced segments and the general mean that depends on them. Unfortunately, we did not find many literature studies for these features in the same context. Therefore, we hypothesised that these results show a trend typical of autistic speech. For example, Haider et al. (2019) report that jitter, shimmer, and spectral flux are valuable features to measure speech instability.

Furthermore, using a speech sample from patients with dementia, the authors demonstrated that these features make the difference in higher accuracy levels between different classifiers. The same observation was done by Bonnet et al. (2011) regarding the spectral characteristics and the pitch values. However, we did not find any other relevant studies to confirm the importance of spectral features to detect ASD, but we found in Pokorny et al. (2017) the same trends as the present study. They also used eGeMAPS to extract the acoustic features and found results shared with ours. Indeed, the ten most significant features between ASD and TD groups are slope in the 0-500 Hz range of unvoiced segments and mean of the length of these and voiced segments.

Furthermore, Volkmar (2017) posits the difficulty in registering the voice volumes visible on the spectrum because of the trend in autistic speech of having a small number of voice volumes that are usually louder than the typical speech. This trend may reflect the impairments in indicating areas of emphasis and higher values in some parameters, such as the spectral slope and flux.

Further studies can clarify these results with more focused research on the spectral-related parameters and show whether the differences between the unvoiced and voiced segments are significant in the early detection of the disorder.

4.3.2 Classification of Speech Samples through Machine Learning Algorithms

The previous sections explained the methods and the results obtained by applying supervised machine learning methods to the feature selection applied to the dataset. The final aim of these implementations is to test whether these acoustic features are typical in the speech production of Italian-speaking children with ASD. Good results in the performances of the classifiers would confirm this assumption. Moreover, testing the effectiveness of the extraction represents a general evaluation of the feature set used (eGeMAPS) since it was proposed as a standard for clinical purposes in acoustic analysis (Eyben et al., 2015).

The best DT, RF, and SVM models reach a high accuracy value (83%), meaning that the feature selection implemented obtained good results on the classifiers. Moreover, the DT, KNN, and SVM reach an optimal value of recall (100%) that indicates the recognition as true of all the acoustic features in the ASD speech.

However, by comparing the metrics obtained by the four best models implemented, we can exclude KNN because it has a poor performance overall, presenting overfitting between the train and the test sets.

Concerning RF, it had a decent performance without overfitting, and it is the model that reaches the highest level of precision (100%). Furthermore, it has the same values on accuracy as DT and SVM. However, these consistently outclassed RF for the other metrics, especially for the recall (50%).

Between the DTs and the SVMs models, if we only look at Table 3, the first can be selected as the best classifier on this dataset. Moreover, it is the only one reaching a recall of 100% on the test set of all the models trained (Table 4). However, if we compare the results of all the models obtained by the k-folds average on the test set, it likely overfits more than RF and SVM. Half of the ten best models of all the ones trained for DT are good in the classification task, but the others tend to decrease their performances drastically from the train to the test sets.

On the other hand, SVM reached high performances on almost all the evaluation metrics of the models trained. (Accuracy = 83% in eight models, Recall = 100%, Precision = 67% in nine models, F1-score = 80% in eight models, AUC = 88% in seven models out of ten).

In the literature, we found the same trend in the implementation of supervised classifiers on the features extracted by eGeMAPS (Asgari & Shafran, 2018; Lee et al., 2020; Li et al., 2019; Pokorny et al., 2017; Rybner et al., 2022; Schmitt et al., 2016). Shahin et al. (2019) used the same SVM model and described it as the most performant compared to GeMAPS, the previous features set. The linear kernel on SVM was also used in Li et al. (2019), and the authors aimed to reach high performances since this supervised method is the best to use when dealing with small datasets.

5. Conclusion

The present work analysed the speech production of Italian speaking children with Autism Spectrum Disorders (ASD) compared with their peers with typical neurodevelopment (TD). Unfortunately, there are no other similar studies on Italian compared with other languages to the best of our knowledge.

The main aim of this study was to determine whether the features reflected in both the qualitative and quantitative literature for English and other languages are also relevant for autistic production in Italian. Therefore, we performed an acoustic analysis on a specific dataset and implemented different types of supervised machine learning methods.

Our findings show that in the speech of Italian children with ASD, some typical acoustic features can be extracted and analysed as previously done in other languages. Furthermore, this task can be done using the extended Geneva Minimalistic Acoustic Parameter Set (eGeMAPS) by considering the small sizes of the dataset used. However, further studies need to consider a larger collection of data and compare the performance of different feature subsets. In this way, it would be possible to create a standard set of typical acoustic features for children with ASD. The next step will be the ideation of a tool from a classifier able to distinguish the typical productions of the disorder from the not typical ones.

Further studies can analyse pitch and intensity features by paying attention to the recording process to satisfy all the requirements. However, due to the necessity of maintaining some environmental comforts for the patients in a clinical condition, we assume it is important to rethink the recording process to satisfy these requirements and collect audio data. Moreover, as pointed out by De La Fuente et al. (2020), the studies should use the same feature set to conduct the feature extraction to have the possibility to better compare the results between different languages.

To conclude, most of the problems found in this work concern the quality of recordings and the dataset size. However, the results obtained on the features extraction and classification are promising for developing a tool that can help the clinician diagnose the disorders at a young age.

6. Acknowledgements

The authors are deeply grateful to Sara Biancalani who collected the clinical data. The precious help of Annalisa Raffone and Ricardo Muñoz Sánchez is also acknowledged.

7. Bibliographical References

American Psychiatric Association (2013). *Diagnostic and Statistical Manual of Mental Disorders, fifth ed.* (DSM-5). Washington (D.C.) / London: American Psychiatric Publishing.

Anolli, L. (2002). *Le emozioni.* Milano: Unicopoli.

Asgari, M., & Shafran, I. (2018). Improvements to harmonic model for extracting better speech features in clinical applications. *Computer Speech & Language*, 47, 298-313.

Biancalani, S. (2019). *Aspetti soprasegmentali e non verbali nel Disturbo dello Spettro Autistico: uno studio pilota.* Thesis dissertation, University of Florence.

Bisson, J. I., Cosgrove, S., Lewis, C., & Roberts, N. P. (2015). Post-traumatic stress disorder. *Bmj*, 351, h6161.

Boddaert, N., Chabane, N., Belin, P., Bourgeois, M., Royer, V., Barthelemy, C., Mouren-Simeoni, M. C., Philippe, A., Bunelle, F., Samson, Y., & Zilbovicius, M. (2004). Perception of complex sounds in autism: abnormal auditory cortical processing in children. *American Journal of Psychiatry*, 161(11), 2117-2120.

Boersma, P. (2001). Praat, a system for doing phonetics by computer. *Glot International*, 5(9-10), 341-345.

Bone, D., Black, M. P., Lee, C. C., Williams, M. E., Levitt, P., Lee, S., & Narayanan, S. (2012). Spontaneous-speech acoustic-prosodic features of children with autism and the interacting psychologist. *Proceedings of Interspeech 2012*, 1043-1046.

Bone, D. Lee, C. C., Black, M. P., Williams, M. E., Lee, S., Levitt, P., & Narayanan, S. (2014). The psychologist as an interlocutor in autism spectrum disorder assessment: Insights from a study of spontaneous prosody. *Journal of Speech, Language, and Hearing Research*, 57(4), 162-1177.

Bone, D., Black, M. P., Ramakrishna, A., Grossman, R. B., & Narayanan, S. S. (2015). Acoustic-prosodic correlates of 'awkward' prosody in story retellings from adolescents with autism. *Interspeech*, 616-1620.

Bonneh, Y. S., Levanon, Y., Dean-Pardo, O., Lossos, L., & Adini, Y. (2011). Abnormal speech spectrum and increased pitch variability in young autistic children. *Frontiers in human neuroscience*, 4(237), 1-7.

Chevallier, C., Noveck, I., Happé, F., & Wilson, D. (2011). What's in a voice? Prosody as a test case for the Theory of Mind account of autism. *Neuropsychologia*, 49(3), 507-517.

Chiew, J., Kjelgaard, M., Chiew, J., & Kjelgaard, M. (2017). The perception of affective prosody in children with autism spectrum disorders and typical peers. *Clinical Archives of Communication Disorders*, 2(2), 128-141.

Cho, S., Liberman, M., Ryant, N., Cola, M., Schultz, R. T., & Parish-Morris, J. (2019). Automatic Detection of Autism Spectrum Disorder in Children Using Acoustic and Text Features from Brief Natural Conversations. *Proceedings of Interspeech 2019,* 2513-2517.

Chollet, F. (2021). *Deep learning with Python.* Shelter Island (NY): Manning Publications Co.

Crystal, D. (2009). Persevering with prosody. *International Journal of Speech-Language Pathology,* 11(4), 257.

Dahlgren, S., Sandberg, A., D., Strömbergsson, S. Wenhov, L. Råstam, M., & Nettelbladt, U. (2018). Prosodic traits in speech produced by children with autism spectrum disorders–Perceptual and acoustic measurements. *Autism & Developmental Language Impairments*, 3, 1-10.

De La Fuente Garcia, S., Ritchie, C. W., & Luz, S. (2020). Artificial Intelligence, Speech, and Language Processing Approaches to Monitoring Alzheimer's Disease: A Systematic Review. *Journal of Alzheimer's disease. JAD*, 78(4), 1547-1574.

Diehl, J. J., & Paul, R. (2012). Acoustic differences in the imitation of prosodic patterns in children with autism spectrum disorders. *Research on Autism Spectrum Disorder*, 6(1), 123-134.

Diehl, J. J., & Paul, R. (2013). Acoustic and perceptual measurements of prosody production on the profiling elements of prosodic systems in children by children with autism spectrum disorders. *Applied Psycholinguistics*, 34(1), 135-161.

Downey, A. (2012). *Think python. 2.0.* Needham (MA): Green Tea Press.

Eyben, F., Scherer, K. R., Schuller, B. W., Sundberg, J., André, E., Busso, C., Devillers, L., Epps, J., Laukka, P., Narayanan, S., & Truong, K. P. (2015). The Geneva minimalistic acoustic parameter set (GeMAPS) for voice research and affective computing. *IEEE transactions on affective computing*, 7(2), 190-202.

Filipe, M. G., Frota, S. Castro, S. L., & Vicente, S. G. (2014). Atypical Prosody in Asperger Syndrome: Perceptual and Acoustic Measurements. *Journal of Autism and Developmental Disorders*, 44, 1972-1981.

Grossman, R. B., Bemis, R. H., Skwerer, D. P., & Tager-Flusberg, H. (2010). Lexical and affective prosody in children with high-functioning autism. *Journal of Speech, Language, and Hearing Research*, 53(3), 778-793.

Haider, F., De La Fuente, S., & Luz, S. (2019). An assessment of paralinguistic acoustic features for detection of Alzheimer's dementia in spontaneous speech. *Journal of Selected Topics in Signal Processing*, 14(2), 272-281.

Halberstam, B. (2004). Acoustic and perceptual parameters relating to connected speech are more reliable measures of hoarseness than parameters relating to sustained vowels. *ORL; Journal for oto-rhino-laryngology and its related specialties*, 66(2), 70-73.

Hillenbrand, J., Cleveland, R. A., & Erickson, R. L. (1994). Acoustic correlates of breathy vocal quality. *Journal of Speech, Language, and Hearing Research*, 37(4), 769-778.

Hubbard, D. J., Faso, D. J., Assmann, P. F., & Sasson, N. J. (2017). Production and perception of emotional prosody by adults with autism spectrum disorder. *Autism Research*, 10(12), 1991-2001.

Julião, M., Abad, A., & Moniz, H. (2020). Comparison of Heterogeneous Feature Sets for Intonation Verification. Proceedings of *International Conference on Computational Processing of the Portuguese Language*, 13-22.

Kanner, L. (1943). Autistic disturbances of affective contact. *Nervous Child*, 2(3), 217-250.

Kim, J. C., Azzi, P., Jeon, M., Howard, A. M., & Park, C. H. (2017). Audio-based emotion estimation for interactive robotic therapy for children with autism spectrum disorder. *The 14th International Conference on Ubiquitous Robots and Ambient Intelligence (URAI)*, 39-44.

Kiss, G., Santen, J. P. V., Prud'Hommeaux, E., & Black, L. M. (2012). Quantitative analysis of pitch in speech of children with neurodevelopmental disorders. *13th Annual Conference of the International Speech Communication Association*, vol.2, 1342-1345.

Kissine, M., & Geelhand, P. (2019). Brief report: Acoustic evidence for increased articulatory stability in the speech of adults with autism spectrum disorder. *Journal of autism & developmental disorders*, 49(6), 2572-2580.

Kluyver, T., Ragan-Kelley, B., Pérez, F., Granger, B.E., Bussonnier, M., Frederic, J., Kelley, K., Hamrick, J.B., Grout, J., Corlay, S., & Ivanov, P. (2016). Jupyter Notebooks - A publishing format for reproducible computational workflows. In Loizides, F., Schmidt, B. (Eds.), *Positioning and Power in Academic Publishing: Players, Agents, and Agendas. Proceedings of the 20th International Conference on Electronic Publishing*, Amsterdam: IOS, 87-90.

Lee, H. Y., Hu, T. Y., Jing, H., Chang, Y. F., Tsao, Y., Kao, Y. C., & Pao, T. L. (2013). Ensemble of machine learning and acoustic segment model techniques for speech emotion and autism spectrum disorders recognition. *Proceedings of Interspeech 2013*, 215-219.

Lee, J. H., Lee, G. W., Bong, G., Yoo, H. J., & Kim, H. K. (2020). Deep-learning-based detection of infants with autism spectrum disorder using auto-encoder feature representation. *Sensors*, 20(23), 6762.

Li, M., Tang, D., Zeng, J., Zhou, T., Zhu, H., Chen, B., & Zou, X. (2019). An automated assessment framework for atypical prosody and stereotyped idiosyncratic phrases related to autism spectrum disorder. *Computer Speech & Language*, 56, 80-94.

Luz S., Haider F., de la Fuente S., Fromm D., & MacWhinney, B. (2020). Alzheimer's Dementia Recognition through Spontaneous Speech: The ADReSS Challenge. *Proceedings of Interspeech 2020*, 2172–2176.

Mann, H. B., & Whitney, D. R. (1947). On a test of whether one of two random variables is stochastically larger than the other. *Annals of mathematical statistics*, 18(1), 50-60.

Marchi, E., Schuller, B., Baron-Cohen, S., Golan, O., Bölte, S., Arora, P., & Häb-Umbach, R. (2015). Typicality and emotion in the voice of children with autism spectrum condition: Evidence across three languages. *Proceedings of Interspeech 2015*, 115-119.

Mcallister, A., Sundberg, J., & Hibi, S. R. (1998). Acoustic measurements and perceptual evaluation of hoarseness in children's voices. *Logopedics Phoniatrics Vocology*, 23(1), 27-38.

McCann, J., & Peppe, S. (2003). Prosody in autism spectrum disorders: A critical review. *Journal of Language & Communication Disorders*, 38(4), 325-350.

Memari, N., Abdollahi, S., Khodabakhsh, S., Rezaei, S., & Moghbel, M. (2020). Speech analysis with deep learning to determine speech therapy for learning difficulties. *International Conference on Intelligent and Fuzzy Systems*, Springer, 1164-1171.

Mohanta, A., Mukherjee, P., & Mirtal, V.K. (2020). Acoustic Features Characterization of Autism Speech for Automated Detection and Classification. *National Conference on Communications (NCC)*, 1-6.

Mohanta, A., & Mittal, V. K. (2022). Analysis and classification of speech sounds of children with autism spectrum disorder using acoustic features. *Computer Speech & Language*, 72, 101287.

Nayak, V., Deshmukh, R., & Waghmare, S. (2019). Pitch pattern analysis in speech of children with autism spectrum disorder. *Journal of Innovative Technology Exploring Engineering*, 9(1), 4209-4212.

Ochi, K., Ono, N., Owada, K., Kojima, M., Kuroda, M, Sagayama, S., & Yamasue, H. (2019). Quantification of speech and synchrony in the conversation of adults with autism spectrum disorder. *PLOS ONE*, 14(12).

Olivati, A. G., Assumpção, F. B., & Misquiatti, A. R. N. (2017). Acoustic analysis of speech intonation pattern of individuals with Autism Spectrum Disorders. *CoDAS*, 29(2).

Pedregosa, F., Varoquaux, G., Gramfort, A., Michel, V., Thirion, B., Grisel, O., Blondel, M., Pretenhofer, P., Weiss, R., Dubourg, V., Vanderplas, J., Passos, A., Cournapeau, D., Brucher, M., & Duchesnay, M. P. E. (2011). Scikit-learn: Machine Learning in Python. *Journal of Machine Learning Research*, 12, 2825-2830.

Pokorny, F., Schuller, B., Marschik, P., Brueckner, R., Nyström, P., Cummins, N., Bölte, S., Einspieler, C., & Falck-Ytter, T. (2017). Earlier Identification of Children with Autism Spectrum Disorder: An Automatic Vocalisation-Based Approach. *Proceedings of Interspeech 2017*, 309-313.

Quigley, J., McNally, S., & Lawson, S. (2016). Prosodic patterns in interaction of low-risk and at-risk-of-autism spectrum disorders infants and their mothers at 12 and 18 months. *Language Learning and Development*, 12(3), 295-310.

Rybner, A., Jessen, E. T., Damsgraad Mortensen, M., Larsen, S. N., Grossman, R., Bilenberg, N., Cantio, C., Jepsen, J. R. M., Weed, E., Simonsen, A., & Fusaroli, R. (2021). Vocal markers of Autism Spectrum Disorder: Assessing the generalizability of machine learning models. *Autism Research,* 1-13.

Ringeval, F., Marchi, E., Grossard, C., Xavier, J., Chetouani, M., Cohen, D., & Schuller, B. (2016). Automatic Analysis of Typical and Atypical Encoding of Spontaneous Emotion. *Proceedings of Interspeech 2016,* 1210-1214.

Robin, J., Harrison, J. E., Kaufman, L. D., Rudzicz, F., Simpson, W., & Yancheva, M. (2020). Evaluation of speech-based digital biomarkers: review and recommendations. *Digital Biomarkers*, 4(3), 99-108.

Rosenhall, U., Nordin, V., Sandström, M., Ahlsén, G., & Gillberg, C. (1999). Autism and hearing loss. *Journal of autism and developmental disorders*, 29(5), 349-357.

Sharda, M., Subhadra, T. P., Sahay, S., Nagaraja, C., Singh, L., Mishra, R., Sen, A., Singhal, N., Erickson, D., & Singh, N. C. (2010). Sounds of melody. Pitch patterns of speech in autism. *Neuroscience letters*, 478(1), 42-45.

Searle, J. R. S., & Vanderveken, D. (1985). *Foundations of illocutionary logic.* Cambridge: Cambridge University Press.

Shahin, M., Ahmed, B., Smith, D. V., Duenser, A., & Epps, J. (2019). Automatic Screening of Children with Speech Sound Disorders Using Paralinguistic Features. *2019 IEEE 29th International Workshop on Machine Learning for Signal Processing (MLSP)*, 1-5.

Scharfstein, L. A., Beidel, D. C., Sims, V. K., & Finnell, L. R. (2011). Social skills deficits and vocal characteristics of children with social phobia or Asperger's disorder: A comparative study. *Journal of abnormal child psychology*, 39(6), 865–875.

Schelinski, S., & von Kriegstein, K. (2019). The relation between vocal pitch and vocal emotion recognition abilities in people with autism spectrum disorder and typical development. *Journal of Autism and Developmental Disorders*, 49(1), 68-82.

Schmitt, M., Marchi, E., Ringeval, F., & Schuller, B. (2016). Towards cross-lingual automatic diagnosis of autism spectrum condition in children's voices. *Speech Communication. ITG Symposium*, 12, 1-5.

Schuller, B., Steidl, S., Batliner, A., Vinciarelli, A., Scherer, K., Ringeval, F., Chetouani, M., Weninger, F., Eyben, F., Marchi, E., Mortillaro, M., Salamin, H., Polychroniou, A., Valente, F., & Kim, S. (2013). The Interspeech 2013 computational paralinguistics challenge: Social signals, conflict, emotion, autism. *Proceedings of Interspeech 2013,* 148-152.

Schuller, B., Steidl, S., Batliner, A., Hirschberg, J., Burgoon, J. K., Baird, A., Elkins, A., Zhang, Y., Coutinho, E., & Evanini, K. (2016). The Interspeech 2016 computational paralinguistics challenge: Deception, sincerity & native language. *Proceedings of, Interspeech 2016,* 2001-2005.

Sharda, M., Subhadra, T. P., Sahay, S., Nagaraja, C., Singh, L., Mishra, R., Amit, S., Singhal, N., Erickson, D., & Singh, N. C. (2010). Sounds of melody. Pitch patterns of speech in autism. *Neuroscience letters*, 478(1), 42-45.

Shriberg, L. D., Paul, R., McSweeny, J. L., Klin, A., Cohen, D. J., & Volkmar, F. R. (2001). Speech and Prosody Characteristics of Adolescents and Adults with High-Functioning Autism and Asperger Syndrome. *Journal of Speech, Language, and Hearing Research*, 44(5), 1097-1115.

Styler, W. (2021). *Using Praat* for *Linguistic Research.* Version*: 1.8.3.* Last Update*:* March 12, 2021.

Tanaka, H., Sakti, S., Neubig, G., Toda, T., & Nakamura, S. (2014). Linguistic and acoustic features for automatic identification of autism spectrum disorders in children's narrative. *Proceedings of the workshop on computational linguistics and clinical psychology: From linguistic signal to clinical reality*, 88-96.

Tsanas, A., Little, M. A., McSharry, P. E., & Ramig, L. O. (2011). Nonlinear speech analysis algorithms mapped to a standard metric achieve clinically useful quantification of average Parkinson's disease symptom severity. *Journal of the Royal Society Interface*, 8(59), 842-855.

Van Rossum, G., & Drake, F. L. (2011). *The Python Language Reference Manual.* United Kingdom: Network Theory Limited.

Van Santen, J. P., Prud'Hommeaux, E. T., Black, L. M., & Mitchell, M. (2010). Computational prosodic markers for autism. *Autism*, 14(3), 215-236.

Volkmar, F. R., & Wiesner, L. A. (2017). *Essential Clinical Guide to Understanding and Treating Autism.* United Kingdom: Wiley.

Wilcoxon, F. (1945). Some uses of statistics in plant pathology. *Biometrics Bulletin*, 1(4), 41-45.

Proceedings of the RaPID-4 @LREC 2022, pages 31–40
Marseille, 25 June 2022

Classification of German Jungian Extraversion and Introversion Texts with Assessment of Changes during the COVID-19 Pandemic

Dirk Johannßen[1,2], Chris Biemann[1], David Scheffer[2]
[1]MIN Faculty, Dept. of Informatics, Universität Hamburg, [2]Dept. of Economics, Nordakademie
[1]22527 Hamburg, Germany [2]25337 Elmshorn, Germany
{biemann, johannssen}@informatik.uni-hamburg.de, {david.scheffer, dirk.johannssen}@nordakademie.de
http://lt.informatik.uni-hamburg.de/

Abstract

The corona pandemic and countermeasures such as social distancing and lockdowns have confronted individuals with new challenges for their mental health and well-being. It can be assumed that the Jungian psychology types of extraverts and introverts react differently to these challenges. We propose a Bi-LSTM model with an attention mechanism for classifying introversion and extraversion from German tweets, which is trained on hand-labeled data created by 335 participants. With this work, we provide this novel dataset for free use and validation. The proposed model achieves solid performance with $F_1 = .72$. Furthermore, we created a feature engineered logistic model tree (LMT) trained on hand-labeled tweets, to which the data is also made available with this work. With this second model, German tweets before and during the pandemic have been investigated. Extraverts display more positive emotions, whilst introverts show more insight and higher rates of anxiety. Even though such a model can not replace proper psychological diagnostics, it can help shed light on linguistic markers and to help understand introversion and extraversion better for a variety of applications and investigations.

Keywords: NLP, COVID-19, Implicit Motives, Introversion, Extraversion

1. Introduction

The first cases of individuals reportedly being infected with the SARS-CoV-2 or COVID-19 virus appeared in December of 2019. Ever since, a global pandemic of this highly infectious disease has emerged, which has been met with countermeasures. Those countermeasures include social distancing and temporary lockdowns (Balasa, 2020). Governments stand in the dichotomy of restricting social and public interactions as a measure of safety and risking the mental health of the people affected, as reports of declining mental well-being emerge (Hämmig, 2019).

Even though professional mental consultation and support do exist, it is difficult to identify and contact heavily impacted individuals (Lester and Howe, 2008). The direct approach would not be feasible, as it would tie up the capacities of mental health workers. Broad information campaigns might cause high costs and still not reach individuals in need. Lastly, affected people might not even be aware of their mental health risks and thus not reach out to available mental health consultations. Depression detection systems or even sentiment analyses of e.g. social media posts could potentially support mental health workers (Coppersmith et al., 2018). But those systems often rely on sufficient self-reports or on topics of mental health or loneliness being directly discussed, which require the individuals to already self-reflect and openly discuss their well-being, resp. the decline thereof (Zirikly et al., 2019).

Furthermore, the well-established safety net of e.g. educational facilities, whose staff could identify troubled individuals, can be unavailable due to the lockdown restrictions. Thus, it might be worthwhile to explore alternative and ideally automated approaches. Carl Gustav Jung researched psychological types (also known as psychological archetypes, (Jung, 1921)), and proposed two perceiving types – sensation and intuition – and two judging types – thinking and feeling. Furthermore, those types are moderated or influenced by the main attitude – extraversion and introversion.

Mental health detection often focuses on introverts due to their self-inflicted distancing and more frequent occurrence of signs of depression compared with extraverts. Recent empirical research on the effects of the pandemic confirms those findings (Wei, 2020). Other findings, however, contradict those results and report empirical findings of extraverts' suffering to be comparably worse (Wijngaards et al., 2020).

As with many psychometrics, manual assessment of psychology types can be costly (Johannßen et al., 2019). Furthermore, burdened individuals might not be reachable by broadly conducted surveys amongst a population. Thus, automation of those types with a focus on introverts and extraverts might reveal the additional potential for identifying individuals in need of support. Therefore, with this work, we aim to classify the Jungian psychological types of *extraversion* and *introversion* from German text and to apply such a model to utterances in 2019 compared with 2020 to investigate whether there are noteworthy well-being differences.

In this work, we will first discuss related work to automated psychometrics, depression detection, and some psychometrics in Section 2. Thereafter, the basics of the Jungian psychological types will be laid out in Section 3. The implicit personality test (IPT) utilized in this work is described in Section 4, followed by the description of the dataset for training neural models and for identifying anxious individuals in Section 5. Section 6 discusses the methodology and approach. The results will be presented in Section 7 and will be discussed in Section 9. We conclude our findings in Section 10 and discuss future outlooks.

2. Related Work

The automated assessment of personality or personality traits is a rather recent application domain. Whilst earlier approaches relied more heavily on rule-based systems, themselves mostly divided into wordlist-based versus corpus-induced methods (Johannßen and Biemann, 2018), machine learning has become more widely utilized in recent years (Mehta et al., 2019). Accordingly, the MBTI and the five-factor model of personality (also called *Big Five*, (Goldberg, 1993)) have been (Angleitner, 1991) and are amongst the most widely utilized personality tests, both of which rely on the Jungian psychological typologies (see Section 3).

Jungian types have successfully been classified from natural language texts by employing a BERT model by Keh et al. (2019). For training their model, the authors scraped data from a self-reporting web forum. The resulting model was utilized for generating personality-induced natural language texts.

The effects of the COVID-19 pandemic have been researched extensively during its outbreak at the end of 2019. Johannßen & Biemann (2020) analyzed social unrest indicators on the application of the pandemic and found that an increase of an implicit motive *power* paired with a self-regulatory passive coping with fears were correlated with signs of crises.

Empirical research on the impacts of the COVID-19 pandemic on introverts and extraverts is somewhat contradictory. Whilst some recent works found extraverts to be more in danger of mental health degradation (Wijngaards et al., 2020; Gubler et al., 2020), other works come to the opposite conclusion (Wei, 2020).

3. Jungian psychological typologies

In "Psychological Types", Jung (1921) distinguished two main types, the Persona, and the Shadow. Whilst the Persona of a person is being shown to the environment and is individualistic, the Shadow remains disguised and is part of a collective unconsciousness. With this view, Jung differed from his tutor Freud to the extent that Freud assumed for the psyche to only be individual. Jung, on the other hand, assumed for humanity to share a collective unconsciousness, which manifests in the form of collectively shared psychological types, that determine our intrinsic desires.

Accordingly, there are two main types, namely the extraverts (e), and the introverts (i). A person either belongs to the former or the latter. Those two types moderate (i.e. influence) all other types, namely sensation (s) vs. intuition (n), thinking (t) vs. feeling (f), and judging (j) vs. perceiving (p).

Based on Jung's psychological types, many psychological tests, and psychometrics emerged thereafter, partly applying the theory directly or extending it. The modality and methodology of measuring types are versatile. Some employ direct questionnaires (e.g. the original Myers-Briggs Type-Indicator (MBTI), (Myers et al., 2000)), some employ visual assertions (e.g. the visual questionnaire or ViQ, (Scheffer and Manke, 2018)) and others analyze natural language (e.g the IPT, which will be described in Section 4).

Even though many of those testing procedures were not psychologically asserted in terms of reliability, stability and validity (e.g. the Big Five or MBTI), those psychological tests that are based on Jung's psychological types have nevertheless frequently been utilized for typing individuals, and were correlated with behavioral observations (Rammstedt et al., 2018).

4. Implicit personality test (IPT)

It is difficult to measure the psyche or personality directly (Fried and Flake, 2018). The research field of psychology has developed and researched different approaches for measuring manifestations of the underlying mental processes, all of which have advantages and shortcomings. E.g. psychoanalysis tries to assume cognitive mechanisms and past events in dialogues, whilst behaviorism strictly limits statements on empirical and reproducible observations (Mahoney, 1984). Both approaches require controlled environments, extensive manual labor, and time. Testing procedures try to determine personality traits with limited time and budget and thus oftentimes balance reliability (i.e. are results reproducible?), validity (i.e. do results correspond to other observations and measures?), and limited testing resources (Schultheiss and Brunstein, 2010, p. 76f).

Some personality testing procedures utilize questionnaires with high reliability. However, standardized surveys and direct questionnaires at times suffer from socio-expectation bias, i.e. participants rather worry about, what testing personnel might think about them, when answering a question in a certain way, rather than answering freely. This bias can occur if the intentions of questions can be guessed or are assumed (Bogner and Landrock, 2016).

Implicit or projective testing procedures overcome this shortcoming by providing participants with ambiguous and situational imagery and asking them to answer questions e.g. who the main character is and what that individual experiences and feels. Those projective methods reveal intrinsic desires. Since there is no socially accepted or wrong answer, the socio-expectation bias is said to be less severe. However, projective methods have been criticized for their reliability (Schultheiss and Brunstein, 2010, p. 119ff).

The IPT is such an implicit test and confronts participants with imagery such as displayed in Figure 1. Participants chose the main person and answer questions about what is happening and how that person feels. Some of those answers, manually labeled with either i (introvert) or e (extravert) are displayed in Listing 1. The human annotators are psychologists and receive extensive training, which initially is wordlist centered but shifts to narrations over time[1]. The IPT is based on the MBTI and has mainly been utilized for business-oriented aptitude diagnostics.

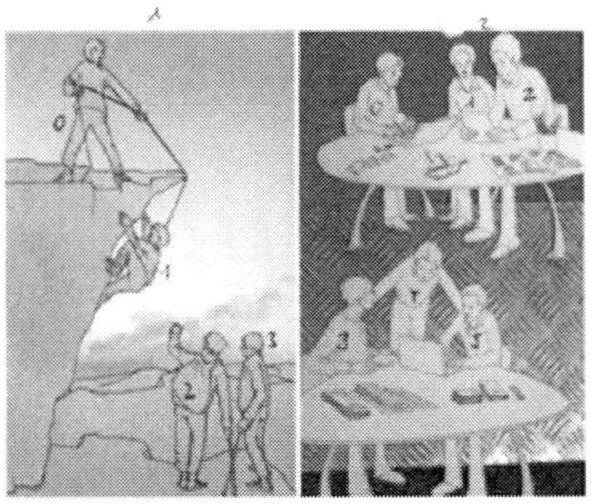

Figure 1: During the IPT, participants are presented with projective imagery, to which they answer questions such as who the main person might be and what that person is experiencing. Such projective or implicit tests are designed to reveal intrinsic desires (Schultheiss and Brunstein, 2010).

```
I    Sie sieht ihre Schüler. das die
     Schüler nach hause gehen. genervt
E    Erklärt jemandem etwas. Es
     richtig zu machen. Er kann es
———— Translated from German ————
I    she sees her students. That the
     students go home. Annoyed
E    Explains something to someone.
     To do it right. He can do it
```

Listing 1: Short examples of answers given during the IPT and corresponding manual labels

5. Data

Since manually asserting natural language texts on introversion or extraversion is costly and would not be scalable, we will first train a neural model (see Section 6) on the data described in this section. We collected German natural language textual data before and from the COVID-19 pandemic and apply said model to this data set. Furthermore, we train in-domain Twitter models.

Model training data

The German natural language textual data utilized for creating the model was collected by a company specialized in aptitude diagnostical testing[2] and is being made public for free use and validation[3]. 2,680 textual answers to provided projection imagery were given by 335 individuals. The population was drawn from the workforce with ages ranging from 18 to 65. Further demographic information was omitted under German data protection laws. The data has been split by separating participants into training (~90%, n=2,360), development, and held-out testing data sets (~5%, n=160 each). Since all 8 answers per participant remained in a data set without being shuffled and separated, we aim to increase the generalization of the model (i.e. rather training to learn the target label and not perform speaker identification). The distribution of answers labeled as extraversion is displayed in Table 1. The two labels are distributed unevenly with the vast majority being extraversion (67.4% of all labels with comparable distributions overall data sets). Answers consist of an average of 42 words and thus can be considered short texts. Each answer has been manually labeled with the four typology pairs. Compared to data sources like Twitter, the training data is rather clean without a lot of noise such as spelling mistakes, spam, or unusual characters. The Kohen's Cappa measure for annotator agreement on the task of extraversion and introversion IPT scores $K = .47$ – only *moderate agreement* (McHugh, 2012).

# extra	8	7	6	5	4	3	2	1	0
%	9.7	22.0	21.4	17.3	13.5	8.5	5.9	1.5	.3

Table 1: Distribution of answers labeled as extraversion in the training material. The upper row displays the counts of answers labeled as extraversion per participant (8 answers in total), the lower row displays the corresponding percentages. 67.4% of all instances were labeled with extraversion and 32.6% with introversion.

Experimental data

One goal of this work is to research transferability across different data domains, namely from the IPT to tweets. Before utilizing any model for validation purposes on tweets, we first need to measure transferability. For this validation data, we sampled 1,100 tweets from a corpus described hereafter, and had them manually labeled by experts on extraversion and introversion. The agreement scores $K = .68$ – which is a *strong agreement* (McHugh, 2012). The data is also made available[4].

Validation data

The experimental data was drawn from Twitter[5], a

[1] For a closely related testing procedure, please refer to Kuhl & Scheffer (1999)

[2] WafM Wirtschaftsakademie GmbH https://www.wafm.de/.

[3] https://www.inf.uni-hamburg.de/en/inst/ab/lt/resources/data/ipt-introextra-2022.html.

[4] https://www.inf.uni-hamburg.de/en/inst/ab/lt/resources/data/ipt-introextra-2022.html.

[5] Twitter https://www.twitter.com

micro-messaging service. The service offers an API for downloading 1% of the worldwide traffic of the social network (Gerlitz and Rieder, 2013). Since the goal of this research is to find new ways of identifying individuals in need during the COVID-19 pandemic, we crawled the Twitter API for the period from March to May 2019 and from March to May 2020. Linguistically, the samples are comparably similar (e.g. equal average lengths, equal part-of-speech (POS) tags, sentence lengths, etc).
The crawled instances were filtered by a German flag to only include posts from German individuals. Furthermore, we filtered non-German samples via language detection (Google translate python library[6].). Besides the texts themselves, the field *date time* was included, which functions both as an identifier hence the inclusion of milliseconds, and as an inclusion criterion for the experimental setup. In total, 10,000 instances were sampled, 5,000 per time period (2019, 2020). An answer from 2019 contains 19.77 words on average and 19.76 from 2020, which makes this a short-text classification task. Bias effects have to be assumed when comparing two different time periods. We aimed to reduce this bias by spreading the selection period over three months, hence selective topics like sports, weather, or cultural events should not overshadow the overreaching effects the pandemic might have.

6. Methodology

In this methodology section, we propose a two-stage approach to asserting domain transferability, describe two employed model architectures, and present the experimental setup.

Two-stage approach
Since there is a considerable difference in labeled data quality and availability between the training data from the IPT and the experimental validation data from Twitter, and since it can be assumed that domain transferability does not produce convincing results, we propose two consecutive experimental stages: i) first, we will train two models from previous experiments (Johannßen et al., 2019; Johannßen and Biemann, 2020) on the IPT data set and validate them on the Twitter dataset, and ii) secondly, we will train those models directly on the Twitter validation set. We critically evaluate transferability and validation applicability, as it is often aspired when performing NLP on psychological textual data (Stajner and Yenikent, 2021; Plank and Hovy, 2015a).

Bi-LSTM attention Model
Previous work on German natural language textual data with a focus on psychological measures have resulted in a viable model, which has reached state-of-the-art results on a shared task dataset and is being utilized for this work as well (Johannßen et al., 2019; Johannßen and Biemann, 2020).

The first model is displayed in Figure 2 and consists of a bi-directional long short-term memory (LSTM, (Hochreiter and Schmidhuber, 1997)) neural network, combined with an attention mechanism.

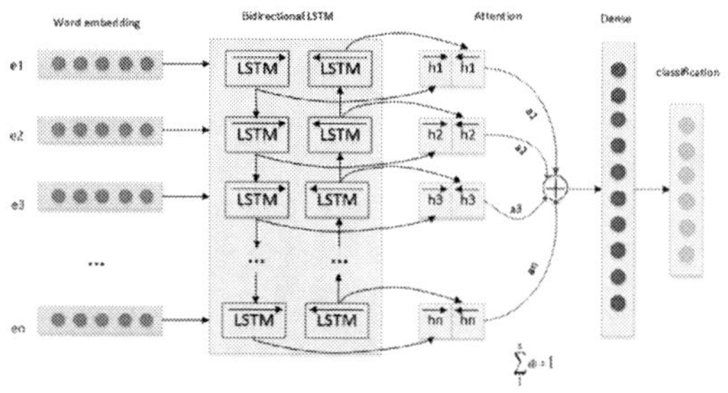

Figure 2: The employed model is a bi-directional long short-term memory neural network, combined with an attention mechanism (image by (Zhou and Wu, 2018)). This type of architecture allows for the model to observe the input from both sides, left and right. The attention supports algorithmic decisions made and at times allows for an analysis of more algorithmic important parts of an input or instance.

In addition to weight connections between each layer to its successor, LSTMs (a special type of Recurrent Neural Network (RNN)) also possess connections between units of the same layer. Furthermore, LSTMs possess a so-called forget gate, which can control which part of an unlimited memory to keep for decisions and which to *forget*. A bi-directional network combines both directions – forward and backward – of input and concatenates the impacts of a token in dependence of the previous and following context of this token. Lastly, the attention mechanism (Bahdanau et al., 2014) models the algorithmic importance of a network by multiplying hidden states with an alignment score to create a context vector, which then gets concatenated with a previous output.
The model is constructed with 5 layers (1 input, 3 hidden, 1 output) and contains 256 units in each hidden layer. Input tokens are represented by 300-dimensional fasttext embeddings, pre-trained on *Common Crawl*[7] and *Wikipedia*[8] (Grave et al., 2018). As optimizer we chose Adam (Kingma and Ba, 2017) and the loss was calculated via cross-entropy. Training parameters were set to a step-width of 1e-6, a dropout rate of .5, and mini-batch training of size 32 in 50 epochs.

Logistic Model Tree (LMT) Model
Since previous approaches (Johannßen et al., 2019) have shown strong results from trained logistic model trees on small datasets (LMT, Landwehr et al. (2005)), we trained an LMT, which is a decision tree with logistic regressions at its leaves, as a second model to be considered. We performed feature engineering but opted

[6]https://pypi.org/project/googletrans/

[7]Common Crawl, https://commoncrawl.org/.
[8]Wikipedia, https://www.wikipedia.org/.

for two different sets of hand-crafted features: one set of features for modeling the IPT and one set of features for modeling the same task on tweets directly.

IPT LMT: As described in our previous work (Johannßen et al., 2019), for firstly engineering the IPT features, the texts mostly were tokenized and processed per token. Engineered features were the type-token-ratio, the ratio of spelling mistakes, and frequencies between 3 and 10 appearances. Further features are LIWC and language model perplexities. The psychometric dictionary and software *language inquiry and word count* (LIWC) was developed by Pennebaker et al. (1999) and later transferred to German by Wolf et al. (2008). LIWC is a simple wordlist-based but well-established tool amongst psychologists and has been utilized for both, the private sector and research. When analyzing a text, LIWC increments categories (i.e. positive emotions, cognitive processes, or anxiety) based on matching dictionary terms per category, which have previously been psychologically validated (Wolf et al., 2008). E.g. the category *family* contains words such as sister, father, mother, mom, etc. The counts per category then get normalized over the length of the input. The results are percentages of words belonging to each category. The German LIWC allows for 96 categories to be assigned to each token, ranging from rather syntactic features such as personal pronouns to rather psychometric values such as familiarity, negativity, or fear. Part-of-speech (POS) tags were assigned to each token and thereafter counted and normalized to form a token ratio. We trained a POS tagger via the natural language toolkit (NLTK) on the TIGER corpus, assembled by Brants at al. (2004) and utilizing the STTS tagset, containing 54 individual POS tags.

We trained a bigram language model for each class and incorporated Good-Turing smoothing for calculating the perplexity. During training, we tuned parameters (e.g. which smoothing to use) via development set and tested the model with the held-out test set. The perplexity of a model q is: $2^{-\frac{1}{N}\sum_{i=1}^{N}\log_2 q(x_i)}$, with p being an unknown probability distribution, $x_1, x_2, \ldots x_N$ being the sequence (i.e. the sentence) drawn from p and q being the probability model.

Twitter model: Secondly, we engineered features for the same task on the labeled Twitter data directly. For the class extraversion, the most influential tasks reflected upon stimulus *from the outside*, such as many add symbols (@) and hashtags (#), plural forms, and plural pronouns. Furthermore, multiple exclamation marks (often used by German speakers to emphasize and *shout*), instances written in all caps, and emojis indicate extraversion in tweets. As for introversion, mostly the opposite features indicate the class: only few emojis, exclamation marks, hashtags, or add symbols. Singular forms and singular pronouns indicate introversion, as well as lowercased tokens (unusual in German, since common and proper nouns are spelled with an initial uppercase).

Pre-processing

Since additional features did not enhance the model's performance metrics in preliminary experiments, we decided against adding any (e.g. POS tags, spelling mistakes, or linguistic inquiry and word count (LIWC, (Pennebaker et al., 2007; Wolf et al., 2008)) category counts). We follow the pre-processing steps by Johannßen & Biemann (2020) by removing stop-words, numbers, emojis, or Twitter-typical special characters, as well as auto-correcting spelling mistakes. 1.000 remaining pre-processed tweets were drawn.

Experimental setup

As described in Section 1, there are contradictory empirical findings on whether introverts or extraverts are more mentally challenged during the pandemic. To investigate this contradiction, we collected data from 2019 and 2020, as described in Section 5. The proposed models (see Section 6) will be trained on the task of classifying extraverts and introverts by their use of natural textual language and will thereafter be utilized for classifying labels to the tweets from 2019 and 2020. Finally, we will divide extraverts and introverts of both years and investigate their linguistic tone and mood. This investigation will be performed by the use of LIWC. From those LIWC category word percentages, we will investigate, whether the tone of extraverts and introverts have significantly changed and in which way.

7. Results

Model benchmarks

Firstly, we performed benchmarks to confirm our model choices. The Benchmarks displayed in Table 2 have shown that the proposed Bi-LSTM model with attention mechanism achieves the best results on this classification task, even outperforming a BERT base model. It can be assumed that BERT base fails to capture the task due to little training data and diverging content meanings compared with everyday use of language (Ezen-Can, 2020).

Model	Accuracy	Precision	Recall	F1 Score
BERT base	.70	.49	.70	.58
CNN	.72	.70	.72	64
LMT + features	.66	.65	.66	.65
RNN	.66	.64	.66	.65
Self attention	.68	.71	.68	.69
LSTM	**.73**	.70	**.73**	.69
Bi-LSTM attn.	.71	**.73**	.71	**.72**

Table 2: Benchmark performances of different model architectures. The proposed Bi-LSTM model with attention mechanism achieves the highest F1 score. Whilst oftentimes BERT outperforms other architectures, the employed BERT base might fail to capture the signals due to diverging content meanings compared with everyday language use (Ezen-Can, 2020).

IPT model performances and Twitter validation

The confusion matrix of the IPT Bi-LSTM is displayed

in Table 4. The current state-of-the-art (SOTA) approach for classifying English introversion and extraversion by Plank & Hovy (2015b) scores $F_1 = .72$. Even though those scores are not comparable due to the differing languages and datasets, the proposed model nonetheless achieves comparable results with $F_1 = .72$ on the task with German textual data. The performance of the IPT LMT model is slightly worse than the performance of the Bi-LSTM attention model with $F_1 = .69$ with perplexity (and thus introversion/extraversion bigram language models) being the discriminating feature on its root node.

Model	Bi-LSTM att.	LMT
Precision	.736	.693
Recall	.7125	.685
F-Measure	.7203	.689

Table 3: Bi-LSTM attention model and LMT model performance measures of precision, recall, and the F-measure for the task of classifying the Jungian psychology types of extraversion and introversion. The model was trained on the IPT.

Actual \ Predicted	Extra	Intro	Σ
Extra	83	29	112
Intro	17	31	48
Σ	100	60	160

Table 4: The confusion matrix of the Bi-LSTM attention model on the IPT classification task test set.

Despite the proposed Bi-LSTM model scoring well on the held-out test IPT dataset, it does not validate well on the experimental Twitter dataset. When utilizing this model on a held-out test set ($n = 160$) of the 1,000 hand-labeled tweets and measuring its performance, the model scores $F_1 = .5$, indicating uninformed decisions based on chance. The same can be observed for the proposed IPT LMT model, which scores an even worse $F_1 = .3$, rendering it unapplicable for cross-domain tweet classification.

In-domain Twitter model and validation

The proposed Bi-LSTM model with attention mechanism fails to capture the aspects of introversion and extraversion from the small Twitter dataset. The model scores a mere $F_1 = .4$ on the Twitter held-out test set and thus is not applicable for being utilized for any further predictions.

In contrast to the Bi-LSTM model, the feature engineered and in-domain trained LMT twitter model achieves good results on the held-out Twitter test set with $F_1 = .69$. The LMT model's confusion matrix is displayed in Table 5, showing that the model performs sufficiently well on both classes and especially introversion, which seems to be harder to model in general (Stajner and Yenikent, 2021). Influential features include the POS tags KOUI, PPOSAT, VAPP, and pronouns, as well as LIWC categories Other, Past, School, and Physical. Lastly, frequencies of exclamation marks, hashtags, emojis, and add tags.

From those results, we can conclude that the out-of-domain transferability between IPT models and tweets does not validate. The Bi-LSTM model performs well on the IPT but fails when being trained directly on the Twitter dataset. The LMT IPT model performs slightly worse. When training a feature-engineered LMT directly on tweets, it performs sufficiently. Hereafter, we will only discuss the IPT Bi-LSTM and Twitter LMT. Additionally, we will utilize the Twitter LMT for further validation studies on the Covid-19 validation dataset described in Section 5.

Actual \ Predicted	Extra	Intro	Σ
Extra	37	21	58
Intro	13	37	50
Σ	50	58	108

Table 5: The confusion matrix of the LMT model on the Twitter data test set.

Error Analysis

The employed attention mechanism at least partially allows for the investigation of the algorithmic importance of single input tokens for the IPT Bi-LSTM classification task at hand. As Kain & Wallace (2019) point out, the distribution of attention weight mass does not necessarily correspond to the underlying theories of the task at hand. However, in earlier work, we have explored the attention weights of the proposed model in more depth and found them to be in line with implicit test theory (Johannßen and Biemann, 2019). With the limitations and the possibility of some explainability in mind, we present the attention weight mass during the training phase in Table 6. Those tokens with higher mass indeed appear to correspond with the psychological theory of introversion and extraversion. In those examples, calmness is rather associated with introversion and togetherness rather than extraversion.

verwenden use	erschaffen create	ruhe calm	arbeit work	vertieft being absorbed	intro
gemeinsam together	ideen ideas	nachbar neighbour	vertrauen trust	gedicht poem	extra

Table 6: Visualization of the attention weight mass per German token with corresponding translations during the training phase. Pre-processing steps were applied, e.g. stop-words removal (thus the choppy utterances). The tokens that received the highest mass do correspond with the psychological theory of extroversion vs. introversion (in this example calmness for introverts vs. togetherness for extraverts).

The errors made by the IPT Bi-LSTM attention model are displayed in Table 7. Very short and uncontextualized answers were more often mistaken by the model and classified incorrectly. Furthermore, instances that require broader world knowledge (e.g. holding a rope being equivalent to team mountaineering) were misclassified.

Label	Text	Pred.
E	King kills; kills; drill in his hand	I
E	Hears his volleagues; to understand everything	I
I	Persons climbing; secures rope; in focus; reaction	E
I	sees landscape; holds rope; feels responsible	E

Table 7: Errors made by the Bi-LSTM attention model. Apparently, short answers and those that require broader world knowledge were difficult to model. The labels read E for Extraversion and I for Introversion.

The LMT Twitter model made similar mistakes as the IPT Bi-LSTM model, which indicates, that despite the data sources being different (IPT vs. tweets), there are overreaching linguistic challenges when attempting to model the task of classifying Jungian introversion and extraversion. Once again, short and noisy instances are prone to being misclassified, as well as those instances, which require world knowledge. This is in line with the findings from Stajner et al. (2021) on why the MBTI (including introversion and extraversion) is difficult to model.

8. Twitter LMT Model & LIWC categories

The most precise method of identifying individuals in need of support would either be self-reports or medical diagnoses made by trained physicians. Both information are sparse and those individuals with the most severe threat of mental suffering oftentimes do not self-report their struggling or visit facilities. With limited information, we aim to determine whether classifications of introversion and extraversion differentiate the observed tweets not only into those two psychological types, but also into groups that are challenged by the pandemic at different levels.

As described in Section 6, we utilize the psychological dictionary tool LIWC. Table 8 displays those results. Six LIWC categories were investigated that correspond to mental health and the social background (Pennebaker et al., 2007). Those are *inhibition positive feeling*, *insight*, *anxiety*, *sad*, *sex* and *eat*.

Table 8 is divided into three table paragraphs. The first displays tweets classified as introversion from 2019 compared with 2020. The second table paragraph displays tweets classified as extraversion, and the third table paragraph compares the whole instance data set without this introversion/extraversion differentiation in order to provide a comparison point (whether those changes are specific for either of the two psychological types or are present in the entire data set).

Even though we investigated the changes from 2019 compared with 2020 a confounding analysis showed differences in LIWC categories between extraversion and introversion in multiple categories, including those in Table 8, indicating an unrecognized explanatory variable.

		Inhibition	Positive feeling	Insight	Anxiety	Sad	Sex	Eat
Introversion	'19	.27	.20	1.35	.12	.34	.33	.13
	'20	.31	.21	1.71	.20	.28	.25	.09
	Δ	.04	.24	.36	.08	-.06	-.09	-.04
	%	12.4	3.7	22.1	40.3	-21.8	-35.0	-56.7
Extraversion	'19	.29	.21	1.54	.13	.31	.24	.13
	'20	.27	.27	1.57	.12	.37	.35	.17
	Δ	-.02	.06	-.03	-.01	-.07	.10	.04
	%	-7.1	24.2	3.0	-9.8	18.9	30.1	26.7
Control	'19	.28	.21	1.42	.12	.33	.30	.13
	'20	.29	.23	1.65	.16	.32	.29	.12
	Δ	.01	.04	.23	.04	.01	-.01	.01
	%	5.2	13.3	14.9	26.2	-2.7	-3.3	-8.6

Table 8: The first table paragraph displays psychological LIWC categories per instance with noticeable fluctuations from 2019 compared with 2020, which were classified as introversion. The displayed LIWC values represent the percentages of words of an instance (i.e. an answer) belonging to a category. In each case, the first row displays the LIWC category counts in 2019, the second in 2020, the third displays the absolute differences (Δ), and the fourth row displays the relative percentage difference. The second table paragraph displays the corresponding LIWC categories for extraversion predictions. A control investigation is displayed in the third and last table paragraph, where all instances from 2019 are compared with 2020 as a point of comparison of the change magnitudes.

Table 8 shows some fundamental differences between the groups of tweets classified as introverted and extraverted. Accordingly, *inhibition* declined for rose by 12%, whilst having increased by 7% for extraverts. While *positive feelings* barely changed for introverts, they increased by 24% for extraverted. Insight was greatly increased for introverts (+ 22%). The big difference occurs for anxiety, which sharply increased by 40% for individuals classified as introverts, whilst having declined roughly 10% for extraverted instances.

Noteworthy, *sad* did increase for extraverts (+19%), whilst having decreased for introverts (-22%). The category includes utterances such as crying, grief, or sadness. Instance examinations showed that instances high in *sadness* mostly read 'i miss you' or missing someone or something.

The social factors of *sex* and *eat* (being physical closeness and topics such as restaurants, dining, etc.) further differentiate those two groups by having decreased for introverts (-35% and -57%), whilst being increased in its frequency for instances classified as extraversion (+30% and +27%).

Needless to say, neither the attention weights, the binary classifications, nor the LIWC psychological categories can assert the individual's state of mind for certain. Nonetheless, they can serve as indicators. Following, we will discuss those findings, put them into relation to the pandemic, and will discuss the current research on this topic from Section 2 with regard to those findings.

9. Discussion

As shown in Section 7, the proposed IPT Bi-LSTM model reaches comparably strong performances on the binary classification task between introversion and extraversion. The attention weights during training as displayed in Table 6 appear to be aligned with the theory of Jungian psychology types. For tweets, an in-domain LMT was trained.

The results in Table 8 add novel findings to the current discussion. Whilst introverts expressed fewer optimistic utterances, those worries did not increase for extraverts. Rather than that, negative emotions rose sharply for introverts, which can be interpreted as clear signs of worry. Anxiety generally increased but slightly more for introverts. Noteworthy, sadness increased for extraverts. But as single instance observations reveal, instances high in *sadness* mostly miss persons or e.g. restaurants. This direction of energy towards the outside suits extraversion and would explain this rather negative emotion being increased for extraverts. The last two observed LIWC categories with remarkable changes from 2019 compared with 2020 are of social relevance (*sex* and *eat*). Firstly, utterances associated with physical closeness are less frequent for introverts, whilst being by far more frequent for extraverts. Utterances associated with dining, eating, or visiting restaurants decreased for introverts, whilst being increased for extraverts. This, again, suits the understanding of Jungian extraversion (see Section 3).

Extraversion has been interpreted as sensitivity to positive affect and optimism, introversion, on the other hand, as lacking sensitivity to positive affect and pessimism (Watson and Clark, 1997; Watson and Tellegen, 1985). Positive affect (i.e. extraversion) is crucial in times of crisis to see the broader picture, cope with depressive thoughts and ruminations, and stay action-oriented. Introverts, which lack this disposition to experience positive affect tend to be "state-oriented" and even depressed, especially in times of crisis (Kuhl and Kazén, 1999). This could explain the higher frequencies of negative emotions in the tweets.

All of those characteristics are unfavorable during lockdowns or other inclined types of isolations and social distancing. Those findings are supported by current empirical research, such as conducted by Wei (2020), who also found introverts to be rather inclined to suffer during the pandemic.

10. Conclusion & Outlook

The Corona or COVID-19 pandemic can be described as an event of a century. Many governments have resorted to measurements of social distancing or lockdowns. Even though those measurements save lives and help to fight this menacing disease, it also burdens individuals. The aim of this work to build an NLP binary classifier of the Jungian psychology types of introverts and extraverts and investigate whether they react differently to those methods has been reached with comparably strong results. Even though the model showed strong results on the held-out test set, the Bi-LSTM model was not applicable for out-of-domain data from Twitter. Therefore, we crafted a second model on hand-labeled tweets. All data was made public.

Experiments on Twitter data from 2019 compared with 2020 differentiated by introverts and extraverts revealed that the mental suffering of introverts during the pandemic is comparably more severe, adding novel findings to the current and contradictory debate. Introverts show a higher frequency of utterances associated with isolation, showed less optimism, spoke less about social interactions, and showed more frequent anxiety utterances. Meanwhile, extraverts showed less frequent utterances of isolation and more frequent friendships. With our approach, we offer an approach to identify individuals, that show elevated signs of worry. With those findings, those individuals could be supported by mental health services. Furthermore, it underlines the necessity as a society to look out for those individuals, that have become especially retracted or express themselves with isolating language.

A future outlook, some indicators such as the confounding analysis, some already infrequent LIWC counting measures, and the rather weak introversion classification capabilities of the model should be taken into account for further critical analyzations. The findings in this paper should be viewed critically and examined with complementary experiments. Furthermore, we aim to deepen those findings and provide systems for automated personality detections, which then could help society to better overall mental health.

11. Ethical Consideration

Even though this research is intended to foster psychological diagnostic research and mental health, such work poses the problem of an ethical dilemma between risks and promises (Johannßen et al., 2020). NLPsych systems can be misused (dual use (Williams-Jones et al., 2014)), misunderstood (Luhmann system theory (Görke and Scholl, 2006)), and will contain severe biases, which are hard to detect due to data protection laws (Diehl et al., 2015).

The proposed classification approach can neither replace clinical examinations nor should it be used for anything else than the performed validation study: mass observations with in-domain data for research purposes and without the intention of diagnosing individuals. This, however, is not what this work intends to provide. Rather, we aimed to support psychologists with additional and evaluation objectivity tools and shed validating light on the effects of the pandemic. We believe this work to add insights into human well-being during the COVID-19 pandemic and hope to foster research for increased mental health, which is a result of a wide range of research findings.

12. References

Angleitner, A. (1991). Personality psychology: trends and developments. *European journal of personality*, 5(3).

Bahdanau, D., Cho, K., and Bengio, Y. (2014). Neural Machine Translation by Jointly Learning to Align and Translate. *arXiv:1409.0473 [cs, stat]*, 1409.

Balasa, A. (2020). COVID – 19 on Lockdown, Social Distancing and Flattening the Curve – A Review. *European Journal of Business and Management Research*, 5.

Bogner, K. and Landrock, U. (2016). *Response Biases in Standardised Surveys (Version 2.0)*. GESIS - Leibniz-Institut für Sozialwissenschaften.

Brants, S., Dipper, S., Hansen, S., Lezius, W., and Smith, G. (2004). The TIGER treebank. *Journal of Language and Computation*, 2:597–620.

Coppersmith, G., Leary, R., Crutchley, P., and Fine, A. (2018). Natural Language Processing of Social Media as Screening for Suicide Risk. *Biomedical Informatics Insights*, 10.

Diehl, C., Hunkler, C., and Kristen, C. (2015). *Ethnische Ungleichheiten im Bildungsverlauf: Mechanismen, Befunde, Debatten*. Springer VS.

Ezen-Can, A. (2020). A Comparison of LSTM and BERT for Small Corpus. *CoRR*, abs/2009.05451. arXiv: 2009.05451.

Fried, E. I. and Flake, J. K. (2018). Measurement Matters. *APS Observer*, 31(3).

Gerlitz, C. and Rieder, B. (2013). Mining One Percent of Twitter: Collections, Baselines, Sampling. *M/C Journal*, 16(2)(620).

Goldberg, L. R. (1993). The structure of phenotypic personality traits. *The American Psychologist*, 48(1):26–34.

Grave, E., Bojanowski, P., Gupta, P., Joulin, A., and Mikolov, T. (2018). Learning Word Vectors for 157 Languages. In *Proceedings of the International Conference on Language Resources and Evaluation (LREC 2018)*, pages 3483–3487, Miyazaki, Japan.

Gubler, D. A., Makowski, L. M., Troche, S. J., and Schlegel, K. (2020). Loneliness and Well-Being During the Covid-19 Pandemic: Associations with Personality and Emotion Regulation. *Journal of Happiness Studies*, 22(5):2323–2342.

Görke, A. and Scholl, A. (2006). Niklas Luhmann'S theory of social systems and journalism research. *Journalism Studies*, 7:644–655.

Hochreiter, S. and Schmidhuber, J. (1997). Long Short-term Memory. *Neural computation*, 9:1735–1780.

Hämmig, O. (2019). Health risks associated with social isolation in general and in young, middle and old age. *PLoS ONE*, 14(7).

Jain, S. and Wallace, B. C. (2019). Attention is not Explanation. In *Proceedings of the 2019 Conference of the North American Chapter of the Association for Computational Linguistics: Human Language Technologies, Volume 1 (Long and Short Papers)*, pages 3543–3556, Minneapolis, MN, USA.

Johannßen, D. and Biemann, C. (2020). Social media unrest prediction during the COVID-19 pandemic: Neural implicit motive pattern recognition as psychometric signs of severe crises. In *Proceedings of the Third Workshop on Computational Modeling of People's Opinions, Personality, and Emotion's in Social Media*, pages 74–86, Barcelona, Spain (Online), December. Association for Computational Linguistics.

Johannßen, D., Biemann, C., and Scheffer, D. (2019). Reviving a psychometric measure: Classification and prediction of the operant motive test. In *Proceedings of the Sixth Workshop on Computational Linguistics and Clinical Psychology*, pages 121–125, Minneapolis, Minnesota, June. Association for Computational Linguistics.

Johannßen, D. and Biemann, C. (2018). Between the Lines: Machine Learning for Prediction of Psychological Traits - A Survey. In *Proceedings of the International Cross-Domain Conference*, pages 192–211, Hamburg, Germany.

Johannßen, D. and Biemann, C. (2019). Neural classification with attention assessment of the implicit-association test OMT and prediction of subsequent academic success. In *Proceedings of the 15th Conference on Natural Language Processing, KONVENS 2019, Erlangen, Germany, October 9-11, 2019*.

Johannßen, D. and Biemann, C. (2020). Social Media Unrest Prediction during the COVID-19 Pandemic: Neural Implicit Motive Pattern Recognition as Psychometric Signs of Severe Crises. In *Proceedings of the Third Workshop on Computational Modeling of People's Opinions, Personality, and Emotion's in Social Media*, pages 74–86, Barcelona, Spain (Online).

Johannßen, D., Biemann, C., and Scheffer, D. (2019). Reviving a psychometric measure: Classification of the Operant Motive Test. In *Proceedings of the Sixth Annual Workshop on Computational Linguistics and Clinical Psychology (CLPsych)*, pages 121–125, Minneapolis, MN, USA.

Johannßen, D., Biemann, C., and Scheffer, D. (2020). Ethical considerations of the GermEval20 Task 1. IQ assessment with natural language processing: Forbidden research or gain of knowledge? In *Proceedings of the GermEval 2020 Task 1 Workshop in conjunction with the 5th SwissText & 16th KONVENS Joint Conference 2020*, pages 30–44, Zurich, Switzerland (online).

Jung, C. G. (1921). *Psychologische Typen*. Zürich, Rascher.

Keh, S. S. and Cheng, I.-T. (2019). Myers-Briggs Personality Classification and Personality-Specific Language Generation Using Pre-trained Language Models. *ArXiv*, abs/1907.06333.

Kingma, D. P. and Ba, J. (2017). Adam: A Method for Stochastic Optimization. *arXiv:1412.6980 [cs]*.

Kuhl, J. and Kazén, M. (1999). Volitional facilitation

of difficult intentions: Joint activation of intention memory and positive affect removes Stroop interference. *Journal of Experimental Psychology: General*, 128(3):382–399.

Kuhl, J. and Scheffer, D. (1999). *Der operante Multi-Motiv-Test (OMT): Manual [The operant multimotive-test (OMT): Manual]*. Impart, Osnabrück, Germany: University of Osnabrück.

Landwehr, N., Andrew Hall, M., and Frank, E. (2005). Logistic Model Trees. *Machine Learning*, 59(1):161–205.

Lester, H. and Howe, A. (2008). Depression in primary care: three key challenges. *Postgraduate Medical Journal*, 84(996):545–548.

Mahoney, M. J. (1984). Psychoanalysis and Behaviorism. In *Psychoanalytic Therapy and Behavior Therapy: Is Integration Possible?*, pages 303–325. Springer US, Boston, MA.

McHugh, M. (2012). Interrater reliability: The kappa statistic. *Biochemia medica: časopis Hrvatskoga društva medicinskih biokemičara / HDMB*, 22:276–82.

Mehta, Y., Majumder, N., Gelbukh, A., and Cambria, E. (2019). Recent trends in deep learning based personality detection. *Artificial Intelligence Review*, 53(4):2313–2339.

Myers, I. B., Kirby, L. K., and Myers, K. D. (2000). *Introduction to Type: A Guide to Understanding Your Results on the Myers-Briggs Type Indicator*. Oxford Psychologists Press.

Pennebaker, J., Francis, M. E., and John Booth, R. (1999). Linguistic inquiry and word count (LIWC). *Software manual*.

Pennebaker, J., Chung, C., Ireland, M., Gonzales, A., and Booth, R. (2007). The Development and Psychometric Properties of LIWC2007. *Software manual. http://liwc.wpengine.com*.

Plank, B. and Hovy, D. (2015a). Personality traits on Twitter—or—How to get 1,500 personality tests in a week. In *Proceedings of the 6th Workshop on Computational Approaches to Subjectivity, Sentiment and Social Media Analysis*, pages 92–98, Lisboa, Portugal, September. Association for Computational Linguistics.

Plank, B. and Hovy, D. (2015b). Personality Traits on Twitter—or—How to Get 1,500 Personality Tests in a Week. In *Proceedings of the 6th Workshop on Computational Approaches to Subjectivity, Sentiment and Social Media Analysis*, pages 92–98, Lisboa, Portugal.

Rammstedt, B., Lechner, C. M., and Danner, D. (2018). Relationships between Personality and Cognitive Ability: A Facet-Level Analysis. *Journal of Intelligence*, 6(2):28.

Scheffer, D. and Manke, B. (2018). The significance of implicit personality systems and implicit testing: Perspectives from PSI theory. In *Why people do the things they do: Building on Julius Kuhl's contributions to the psychology of motivation and volition*, pages 281–300. Hogrefe Publishing, Boston, MA, US.

Schultheiss, O. and Brunstein, J. (2010). *Implicit Motives*. Oxford University Press, 1 edition.

Stajner, S. and Yenikent, S. (2021). Why Is MBTI Personality Detection from Texts a Difficult Task? In *Proceedings of the 16th Conference of the European Chapter of the Association for Computational Linguistics: Main Volume*, pages 3580–3589, Online.

Watson, D. and Clark, L. A. (1997). Chapter 29 - Extraversion and Its Positive Emotional Core. In *Handbook of Personality Psychology*, pages 767–793. Academic Press, San Diego, CA, USA.

Watson, D. and Tellegen, A. (1985). Toward a consensual structure of mood. *Psychological Bulletin*, 98(2):219–235.

Wei, M. (2020). Social Distancing and Lockdown – An Introvert's Paradise? An Empirical Investigation on the Association Between Introversion and the Psychological Impact of COVID19-Related Circumstantial Changes. *Frontiers in Psychology*, 11.

Wijngaards, I., Sisouw de Zilwa, S. C. M., and Burger, M. J. (2020). Extraversion Moderates the Relationship Between the Stringency of COVID-19 Protective Measures and Depressive Symptoms. *Frontiers in Psychology*, 11.

Williams-Jones, B., Olivier, C., and Smith, E. (2014). Governing 'Dual-Use' Research in Canada: A Policy Review. *Science and Public Policy*, 41:76–93.

Wolf, M., Horn, A. B., Mehl, M. R., Haug, S., Pennebaker, J. W., and Kordy, H. (2008). Computergestützte quantitative Textanalyse: Äquivalenz und Robustheit der deutschen Version des Linguistic Inquiry and Word Count. *Diagnostica*, 54(2):85–98.

Zhou, Q. and Wu, H. (2018). NLP at IEST 2018: BiLSTM-Attention and LSTM-Attention via Soft Voting in Emotion Classification. In *Proceedings of the 9th Workshop on Computational Approaches to Subjectivity, Sentiment and Social Media Analysis*, pages 189–194, Brussels, Belgium.

Zirikly, A., Resnik, P., Uzuner, Ö., and Hollingshead, K. (2019). CLPsych 2019 Shared Task: Predicting the Degree of Suicide Risk in Reddit Posts. In *Proceedings of the Sixth Workshop on Computational Linguistics and Clinical Psychology*, pages 24–33, Minneapolis, MN, USA.

Proceedings of the RaPID-4 @LREC 2022, pages 41–55
Marseille, 25 June 2022

The Post-Stroke Speech Transcription (PSST) Challenge

Robert C. Gale,[†] **Mikala Fleegle,**[‡] **Gerasimos Fergadiotis,**[‡] **Steven Bedrick**[†]
[†]Oregon Health and Science University, Portland, Oregon, USA
[‡]Portland State University, Portland, Oregon, USA
galer@ohsu.edu, soroka@pdx.edu, gf3@pdx.edu, bedricks@ohsu.edu

Abstract

We present the outcome of the Post-Stroke Speech Transcription (PSST) challenge. For the challenge, we prepared a new data resource of responses to two confrontation naming tests found in AphasiaBank, extracting audio and adding new phonemic transcripts for each response. The challenge consisted of two tasks. Task A asked challengers to build an automatic speech recognizer (ASR) for phonemic transcription of the PSST samples, evaluated in terms of phoneme error rate (PER) as well as a finer-grained metric derived from phonological feature theory, feature error rate (FER). The best model had a 9.9% FER / 20.0% PER, improving on our baseline by a relative 18% and 24%, respectively. Task B approximated a downstream assessment task, asking challengers to identify whether each recording contained a correctly pronounced target word. Challengers were unable to improve on the baseline algorithm; however, using this algorithm with the improved transcripts from Task A resulted in 92.8% accuracy / 0.921 F1, a relative improvement of 2.8% and 3.3%, respectively.

Keywords: anomia, aphasia, speech language pathology assessment, automatic speech recognition

1 Introduction

Anomia, or word-finding difficulty, is the primary feature of aphasia (Goodglass and Wingfield, 1997; Raymer and Rothi, 2001), an acquired neurogenic language disorder that affects 2.5-4 million people in the US (Simmons-Mackie, 2018). The primary cause of aphasia is stroke, and 21%–40% of acute stroke patients are diagnosed with anomia by the time they are discharged. Anomia is believed to be indicative of disruption in accessing a semantic description of the target concept, and/or retrieving a fully phonologically specified representation (Dell, 1986; Dell et al., 1997).

Specifically, paraphasias, which are unintended word production errors, typically result from reduced or insufficiently persistent activation of target representations relative to competing non-target representations and/or noise in the system (Dell et al., 1999; Dell et al., 1997). In some cases, people with aphasia produce real word errors. For example, reduced activation of lexical-semantic representations may result in semantic errors (e.g., "dog" for the target "cat") or unrelated errors, sharing no obvious semantic or phonological features with the target word ("chair" for "cat"). Activation of inappropriate phoneme representations may sometimes result in real word errors (e.g., "dog" for the target "log"). However, breakdowns in phonological processing may also lead to non-word productions known as neologisms that may or may not be phonologically related to the target (e.g., "tat" for the target "cat" and "blat" for the target "dog", respectively).

Given the prevalence of anomia in the aphasic population and its tendency to persist even when other symptoms of aphasia remit (Goodglass and Wingfield, 1997), professionals typically assess anomia using confrontation naming tests (Cho-Reyes and Thompson, 2012; Roach et al., 1996; Kaplan et al., 2001), during which a patient is presented with pictures of simple objects and they are asked to name them. The overall accuracy on such tests is an important clinical metric that has been found to be a good indicator of overall aphasia severity (Schuell et al., 1964; Walker and Schwartz, 2012) and is predictive of the ability to convey information during discourse production (Fergadiotis et al., 2019). Furthermore, improvement in naming accuracy has been linked to improvement in overall communicative skills (Carragher et al., 2012; Herbert et al., 2008).

Further, in research settings, professionals develop individualized profiles based on the different types of errors elicited through confrontation naming tests (e.g., phonological, semantic, non-word errors, etc.) and then use these profiles to characterize patients' cognitive-linguistic deficits. Such individualized error profiles have informed theoretical accounts of the cognitive machinery underlying word production (Dell, 1986; Dell et al., 1997; Dell and O'Seaghdha, 1992); lesion-symptom mapping (Schwartz et al., 2009; Schwartz et al., 2012; Walker et al., 2011); personalization of treatments (Best et al., 2013); treatment efficacy studies (Brookshire et al., 2014; Kendall et al., 2003; Kendall et al., 2006; Kendall et al., 2008); the understanding of cross-linguistic treatment generalization (Edmonds and Kiran, 2006); and cortical reorganization investigations after a stroke (Fridriksson et al., 2012)

Error profiles also have the potential to be highly informative in clinical settings for developing individualized intervention plans (Abel et al., 2007). However, currently, developing a patient's profile is prohibitively time- and labor-intensive because it requires phonemic transcriptions for determining response accuracy and the nature of the errors. For naming tests with dozens or hundreds of items, this is rarely feasible in fast-paced clinical settings. As such, there is much interest in the clinical community in automating this process.

To this end, we introduce the Post-Stroke Speech Transcription Challenge (PSST). The Challenge is a shared task consisting of two sub-tasks, one for phonemic transcription (Task A), one for binary classification (Task B). The goals of the PSST Challenge are threefold: first, to produce an accessible dataset relating to these clinical tasks for use by the machine learning community; second, to establish benchmarks for these tasks; and third, to lay the groundwork for a community of practice for machine learning researchers interested in aphasia and other similar disorders.

2 Background

2.1 Orthographic vs. Phonemic ASR

An automatic speech recognizer (ASR) typically implies an orthographic system (e.g. one that produces words written in the English alphabet). Phonemic ASR, by contrast, uses symbols like ARPABet or the International Phonetic Alphabet (IPA) to indicate how the utterance was pronounced. Unlike their orthographic counterparts, phonemic ASRs might transcribe the same word several different ways, capturing linguistic variability (e.g. dialect, coarticulation) or identifying errors (e.g. mispronunciations, paraphasias).

The previous generation of orthographic ASRs used a layered architecture, with an intermediate layer mapping phoneme sequences to words using a pronunciation dictionary (Mohri et al., 2001). However, the last decade saw a push toward so-called "end-to-end" systems to directly predict orthographic sequences, enabled by deep neural networks, unassisted and unbound by phoneme-to-word constraints (Graves and Jaitly, 2014). This period coincided with the introduction of Librispeech (Panayotov et al., 2015), a corpus extracted from the collection of public domain audiobooks LibriVox. With 1,000 hours of training data available as a free download, LibriSpeech not only became a standard resource in research toolkits, it also came to serve as a primary benchmark for orthographic ASR. In a flurry of activity, the word error rate (WER) for LibriSpeech's `test-clean` dropped from 5.5% (established with its introduction) to under 1.5% just five years later (Zhang et al., 2020). By comparison, the go-to benchmark for phonemic ASR, TIMIT (Garofolo et al., 1993), was less competitive, though phoneme error rates (PER) still halved: an early end-to-end system had a PER of 17.7% (Graves et al., 2013) compared to 8.3% more recently (Baevski et al., 2020).

2.2 ASR for Aphasic Speech

End-to-end ASRs rely heavily on statistical methods, learning acoustic and linguistic patterns from large speech corpora. By definition, aphasic speech breaks from typical linguistic patterns, with highly variable error patterns exacerbating the difficulty of the ASR task. Previous work with AphasiaBank reflects these difficulties. Le and Provost (2016) reported 47%–76% PER when grouped by severity of aphasia.[1] Perez et al. (2020) improved on this with a PER of 33%–61%. Le et al. (2018) reported results in terms of WER: 37.4% overall, ranging 34%–63% per severity group.

Small datasets are another hindrance to aphasic ASR, though recent innovations enabled ASRs to be trained on far less data. Similar to recent work in natural language processing (Mikolov et al., 2013; Radford and Narasimhan, 2018; Devlin et al., 2019), the self-supervised methods behind wav2vec 2.0 (Baevski et al., 2020) use large amounts of *unlabeled* speech data, pretraining a model to predict its own abstract feature representations using a contrastive loss function (van den Oord et al., 2018). These pretrained models are intended to be fitted with new output layers and fine-tuned for specific tasks like ASR, and are readily available for download. Using this technique, Baevski et al. (2020) showed how a viable ASR could be trained with as little as 10 minutes labeled data, highlighting its utility for low-resource languages. Applying this to aphasic ASR, Torre et al. (2021) achieved a 22.3–55.5% WER on English AphasiaBank, depending on severity. Remarkably, the authors also trained an ASR using only 1 hour of Spanish AphasiaBank, with a 42.8 WER and a character error rate (CER) of 24.8%.

2.3 Automating Aphasia Assessment Tasks

As discussed earlier (§1), the development of a robust ASR system for aphasic speech has the potential to transform clinical practice for the assessment of aphasia. Currently, our group has been developing novel methods to automatically classify clinically relevant types of paraphasias in confrontation picture naming tests (Fergadiotis et al., 2016; Cowan et al., 2021; Casilio et al., 2019; McKinney-Bock and Bedrick, 2019). Our algorithms determine the lexical status of erroneous productions using a word frequency model, use grapheme-to-phoneme analysis to assess phonological similarity between productions and target words, and employ a neural network to measure semantic similarity. Then, information across these three dimensions is combined automatically to classify paraphasias in clinically relevant categories. However, automated analyses of this sort still require that language samples be manually transcribed which represents a major barrier to their translation into practice. Without the ability to automatically produce accurate phonemic transcripts an ASR system, human experts must perform this laborious and error-prone task. For a naming test with dozens or hundreds of items, this is rarely feasible in a clinical setting. As a first step in evaluating the potential of an ASR system for aphasic speech to be used in such a pipeline, Task B in this challenge is focused on

[1] Although they report PER, AphasiaBank's transcripts are (mostly) orthographic. Supplementary materialscontained transcripts tokenized as words (not phonemes) and a pronunciation dictionary, suggesting their ASR targeted a fixed vocabulary instead of free-form phoneme prediction.

a simpler task: assess the ability of the ASR system to generate phonemic transcriptions not for error classification but rather to determine response accuracy.

3 Preparing the PSST Corpus

Funding for the dataset preparation and baseline model development activities, and for the shared task itself, originated from the National Institutes of Health's Office of Data Science Strategy, under the "Administrative Supplements to Support Collaborations to Improve the AI/ML-Readiness of NIH-Supported Data" program (NOT-OD-21-094). The goal of this funding mechanism was to support efforts to promote and facilitate the use of existing biomedical datasets by the AI/ML community.

The PSST Corpus is comprised of short speech segments from English AphasiaBank (MacWhinney et al., 2011), specifically responses to the Boston Naming Test Short Form (BNT-SF) (Mack et al., 1992) and Verb Naming Test (VNT) (Thompson, 2012) portions of the protocol. Participants included 107 individuals with aphasia who completed both BNT-SF and VNT as retrieved from English AphasiaBank on September 1, 2021. We defined aphasia as an Aphasia Quotient (AQ) of <93.8 on the Western Aphasia Battery - Revised (Kertesz, 2007) or <11 on the BNT-SF. Participants were right-handed, predominantly English-speaking, with a history of a single, left-hemispheric stroke, adequate hearing and vision, and no significant comorbid neurological or psychiatric illness. Individuals with concomitant motor speech disorders were also included. The extracted segments averaged 3.9 seconds in length, include 3291 utterances from 107 speakers, and total approximately 3.5 hours of audio.

Ground truth phonemic transcriptions for the BNT-SF and VNT were derived from two previous studies and adapted for the purposes of this ASR project. Naming attempts were originally identified and phonemically transcribed by trained research assistants and disagreements resolved by a licensed speech-language pathologist. Transcriptions were entered and time-aligned to audiovisual recordings using ELAN (Max Planck Institute for Psycholinguistics, 2022). Using the time alignments, we automatically extracted audio from the full AphasiaBank videos, applying filters for loudness and clarity (see Appendix B.2). A trained research assistant and licensed speech-language pathologist updated transcriptions to reflect the present study's conventions, then the transcripts were normalized and mapped to ARPAbet for ASR purposes (see Appendix B.3). Correctness labels were assigned to all responses by a licensed speech-language pathologist, followed by an audit and resolution process by consensus. We defined correctness as the presence of the target word anywhere within the segmented response. Pronunciation variations of the target word that could be explained by an individual's dialectal pattern and/or typical patterns of coarticulation were scored as correct.

	Train	Validation	Test
Hours	2.59 (73%)	0.36 (10%)	0.59 (17%)
Segments	2173 (70%)	325 (10%)	624 (20%)
Speakers	74 (69%)	11 (10%)	22 (21%)

Table 1: Quantities of data for each split of the PSST dataset in terms of hours of audio, number of segments, and number of speakers.

Data splits targeted train, valid, and test proportions of 70%, 10%, and 20% respectively, with quantities measured as hours of audio. As shown in Table 1, the final proportions were approximately 73%, 10%, and 17%. Each speaker was included in no more than one of the splits. To stratify the splits by overall severity of aphasia, we categorized each participant as mild ($75 < AQ$), moderate ($50 < AQ \leq 75$), severe ($25 < AQ \leq 50$), or very severe ($AQ \leq 25$) per the criteria from the WAB (Kertesz, 2007). To find the optimal split, 1000 candidate configurations were computed, then we chose the configuration with the lowest average KL divergence for duration of audio across the three splits (with a value of about 0.007). Table 1 shows the hours of audio, number of segments, and number of speakers in each split.

4 Task A: ASR for Aphasic Speech

Task A asked participants to automatically transcribe the phonemes in each segment of recorded audio. We provided ARPAbet transcripts for the train and validation splits described in §3. We provided code to compute FER and PER for these splits, and we made available our baseline model's source code and pretrained weights. Shortly before the deadline, we released the audio from the test split with the transcripts withheld. Challengers submitted the transcripts their models produced for the test set, and we used the same scripts to compute final metrics. We received entries from two challengers (Yuan et al., 2022; Moël et al., 2022), who submitted transcripts for 7 models apiece.

4.1 Evaluation

Task A was evaluated in terms of PER and FER. To calculate PER, we computed the Levenshtein distance (phoneme errors, i.e. the minimum insertions, deletions, and replacements) between target and ASR transcripts. PER is defined as this distance divided by the total length (in phonemes) of the target transcripts.

Like PER, the FER was computed as the errors (in terms of feature distance) divided by the expected length (number of phonemes $\times$ 24 features). Our implementation of feature distance is very similar to one found in panphon (Mortensen et al., 2016), specifically the `feature_edit_distance()` algorithm. As discussed in Appendix A, phonological features specified as present/absent ([+feature] / [−feature]) o͡ʊ p ʊ ʃ ɪ ŋ j ɚ

o͡ʊ m ʊ ʃ ɪ ŋ ʌ

Utterance

FER	PER
15.4%	37.5%

Action	Cost	From	To	Features
EQ	0 / 24	o͡ʊ	o͡ʊ	
SUB	3.5 / 24	p	m	-sonorant → +sonorant -delayedrelease → 0delayedrelease -nasal → +nasal -voice → +voice
EQ	0 / 24	ʊ	ʊ	
EQ	0 / 24	ʃ	ʃ	
EQ	0 / 24	ɪ	ɪ	
EQ	0 / 24	ŋ	ŋ	
SUB	5 / 24	j	ʌ	-syllabic → +syllabic +high → -high +front → -front -back → +back +tense → -tense
DEL	21 / 24	ɚ		+syllabic -consonantal +sonorant +continuant 0delayedrelease +approximant -tap -nasal +voice -spreadglottis -labial -round -labiodental +coronal -anterior +distributed -strident -lateral -dorsal 0high 0low 0front 0back 0tense

Figure 1: An error analysis generated by the `pssteval-viewer` tool we provided with the challenge materials. The tool shows the PSST transcript (top) aligned to an ASR's output, the FER and PER for the utterance, and then the feature analysis used to compute the FER. This example is utterance id `ACWT01a-VNT20-shove` as transcribed by Moëll/O'Regan et al.'s MO4 model.

or unspecified ([0feature]). If two phonemes differed and the feature was specified in both, that feature error had a cost of 1; if the feature was unspecified in one phoneme, it cost ½. Insertions and deletions were treated as if each feature of missing phoneme was unspecified. The values for each feature align with Hayes (2009), with the exception of diphthongs. While English diphthongs are usually represented by two letters, they behave more like a single sound (Ladefoged and Johnson, 2015); further, each diphthong has only one ARPAbet token. Neither Hayes (2009) nor `panphon` defines features for diphthongs, so we synthesized these definitions, prompting some special rules for feature error calculation. See Appendix A for more details, including the full table of features.

4.2 Models

Baseline Model (*PSST–A*) For the PSST baseline ASR model (*PSST–A*), we began with a pretrained wav2vec2.0 acoustic model downloaded from fairseq (Ott et al., 2019), specifically the BASE model described in Baevski et al. (2020). This model contains 95m parameters pretrained on 960 hours from the LibriSpeech dataset (Panayotov et al., 2015). We fitted the model with an output layer corresponding to the phoneme inventory of the PSST transcripts, then fine-tuned the model targeting a connectionist temporal classification (CTC) loss. Details on the fine-tuning process can be found in Appendix C.

Yuan et al. (Y1–Y7) The approach taken by Yuan et al. focused on data augmentation, exploring outside data sets prepared in a variety of ways. For the challenge, they submitted 7 configurations for our summary, which we will call Y1 through Y7. Each model used a wav2vec2.0 approach comparable to *PSST–A*, but began with the LARGE variant, which uses 315 million parameters, and is trained on 60,000 hours of unlabeled audio from Librivox (from which LibriSpeech is extracted). Y5 was trained only with PSST data, serving as a baseline for their augmentation experiments.

Y2 augmented PSST with 3.9 hours of TIMIT. Adhering to convention, the 61 labels in TIMIT were collapsed to 39 phonemes (Lopes and Perdigao, 2011a; Lee and Hon, 1989), resulting in labels similar to those provided for the PSST challenge, except /ɾ/ was merged with /d/, and /ʒ/ was merged with /ʃ/.

Y4, Y6, and Y7 augmented PSST with LibriSpeech data in various quantities. To prepare LibriSpeech for use with phonemic ASR, Yuan et al. automatically generated pseudo-labels from the orthography using a grapheme-to-phoneme (G2P) model, which had a phoneme inventory nearly aligned with the PSST corpus, although like the TIMIT experiment, the flap symbol /ɾ/ was unused.

Y1 and Y3 augmented PSST with 47 hours of Aphasiabank, taking care to exclude the speakers assigned to the PSST test set. To prepare the (mostly) orthographic corpus for phonemic ASR, Yuan et al. used a technique of iterative self-labeling. First, they produced a set of phonemic labels using a model trained on only PSST data. Then they trained a new model, augmenting PSST with the AphasiaBank samples that exceeded an experimentally determined confidence threshold. Confidence scores were computed in two ways: (a) unweighted, using a standard CTC loss; and (b) weighted, adjusting confidence with probabilities found during the pseudo-labeling step. This process was repeated until the model no longer improved. Y1 was unweighted with a 0.9 threshold, trimming 47.0 hours of AphasiaBank to the best 33.3. Y3 was weighted, with a 0.7 threshold, yielding 44.0 hours of AphasiaBank.

Moëll/O'Regan et al. (MO1-MO7) Moëll/O'Regan et al. (2022) also explored data augmentation strategies for their submissions to the ASR challenge. We refer to their 7 configurations as MO1 through MO7. The authors used two off-the-shelf wav2vec2.0 architectures: BASE, which has 95m parameters, which was pretrained on 960 hours of unlabeled audio; and the LS-960 variant of LARGE, with 315m parameters, which was pretrained on the same 960 hours as BASE. Of those we received, only MO3 and MO7 used BASE, while the rest used LARGE. For MO6, they established an unaugmented baseline with the LARGE architecture.

Much of Moëll/O'Regan et al. focused on expanding PSST and the other datasets with audio perturbation techniques. In MO2 and MO5, they synthesized new PSST data by adjusting the pitch of the audio (while preserving time). In MO4, they synthesized new PSST data by time-stretching the audio (while preserving pitch). For MO6, they augmented PSST by adding Gaussian noise to the signals.

In MO1, MO3, and MO5, Moëll/O'Regan et al. augmented PSST with TIMIT data. They chose to omit utterances that conflicted with the PSST corpus' phoneme inventory, resulting in only 1.1 hours of augmentation data drawn from TIMIT's train and test splits. Noting an acoustic mismatch between the dry, studio-quality recordings of TIMIT and the untreated academic environments of the PSST recordings, the authors experimented with artificial reverb on the TIMIT data: using room impulse response (RIR) convolution, they simulated random rooms by applying filters found in online collections.

4.3 Results

Results for the Task A models are shown in Table 2. *PSST–A* showed an FER of 12.1% and a PER of 26.4%. Only two models failed to outperform these metrics: Y6 and Y7, the models using 100 and 960 hours of LibriSpeech. MO1 through MO7 improved on *PSST–A*. Their best-performing model in terms of FER was MO1, which augmented both PSST and TIMIT data using RIR augmentation. MO2 (pitch-shift augmentation) yielded their best PER at 25.1%. The worst-performing models from Moëll/O'Regan et al. were MO6 and MO7 (LARGE, with vs. without noise augmentation) with an FER of 12% each, and a respective PER of 25.9% and 26.1%. Y1 through Y5 were the five best-performing models. The stand-out best was the unweighted pseudo-labeling configuration of the AphasiaBank experiment at 9.9% FER and 20.0% PER. Y2, augmented with TIMIT, was the next best, at 10.3% FER / 21.1% PER. Y3, the weighted AphasiaBank configuration, followed closely behind at 10.4% FER / 21.5% PER. Y5 (no augmentation) had an FER of 11.3% and a PER of 22.3%, and Y4 (3.9 hours of LibriSpeech) improved on this only slightly.

4.4 Discussion

Both challengers were primarily focused on augmentation of the PSST dataset, a sensible approach considering the small size of the corpus. Each emphasized a different augmentation strategy: Yuan et al. explored the effects of domain shift and data quantities, while Moëll/O'Regan et al. synthesized additional data with audio perturbation techniques. For Yuan et al., their best model showed a relative improvement of 9% FER / 10% PER against its unaugmented counterpart Y5. The best model from Moëll/O'Regan et al. showed a relative improvement of 5% FER / 3% PER against its unaugmented counterpart M07.

Another difference between the two challengers' submissions was their respective choices of pretrained model. The models from Yuan et al. were all pretrained on 60,000 hours of unlabeled audio, while every model from Moëll/O'Regan et al. pretrained on 960 hours of unlabeled audio. Comparing each challenger's unaugmented LARGE models (Y5 and MO6), the 60,000-hour model improved on the 960-hour model by a relative 9% FER / 14% PER. By comparison, model size had minimal effect: MO6 improved on *PSST–A* by <1% FER / 3% PER, having 315 million and 95 million parameters, respectively.

Moëll/O'Regan et al. experimented with several different techniques, laying the foundation for future investigations. One interesting question the authors raise is whether their pitch-shift techniques, which preserve time, could be retaining acoustic markers of phonological features more so than their other techniques. The effects of room acoustics could also be explored in more depth: for example, what if RIR filter selection were more intentional, factoring in room size, shape, and construction material? Finally, Moëll/O'Regan et al. were somewhat conservative with the balance of synthetic data to unmodified PSST. With pitch perturbation, 3-fold augmentation is known to be effective and the recommended practice with last-generation ASR toolkits (Ko et al., 2015). Also, several perturbation techniques could be combined for numerous subtle variations of synthetic data.

The Yuan et al. work also prompts fascinating questions. The paper's narrative centers on the effects of various quantities of in- and out-of-domain data. This effect is clearest between the LibriSpeech-augmented models: Y4 (using only 3.9 hours of LibriSpeech) was fourth-best, whereas Y6 (100 hours) and Y7 (960 hours) were the overall worst. The authors hypothesize this is a consequence of domain mismatch. Indeed, LibriSpeech is audibly different from the PSST corpus

Model	Arch	Data (hours of audio) Pretrain	PSST	TIMIT	AphasiaBank	Other	ASR FER	PER
Y1	LARGE	60,000	2.8		33.3^U		**9.9%**	**20.0%**
Y2	LARGE	60,000	2.8	3.9			10.3%	21.1%
Y3	LARGE	60,000	2.8		44.0^W		10.4%	21.5%
Y4	LARGE	60,000	2.8			3.9^L	10.6%	22.2%
Y5	LARGE	60,000	2.8				10.9%	22.3%
MO1	LARGE	960	2.8	1.1^r			11.3%	25.5%
MO2	LARGE	960	5.6^p				11.4%	25.1%
MO3	BASE	960	2.8	1.1^r			11.7%	26.3%
MO4	LARGE	960	5.6^t				11.7%	25.4%
MO5	LARGE	960	5.6^p	1.1^r			11.9%	26.0%
MO6	LARGE	960	2.8				12.0%	25.9%
MO7	BASE	960	5.6^n				12.0%	26.1%
PSST–A	BASE	960	2.8				12.1%	26.4%
Y6	LARGE	60,000	2.8			100^L	12.5%	26.0%
Y7	LARGE	60,000	2.8			960^L	16.7%	38.0%

^{L} Librispeech, pseudo-labeled with G2P
^{U} iteratively pseudo-labeled (unweighted)
^{W} iteratively pseudo-labeled (weighted)
^{p} with pitch-shifted variants
^{t} with time-shifted variants
^{n} with Gaussian noise augmentation
^{r} RIR reverb applied

Table 2: ASR results for Test set. Results are show in terms of feature error rate (FER), phoneme error rate (PER). Values in gray did not improve on *PSST–A*.

in many ways: speaker demographics, recording conditions, and factors concerning the clinical context of PSST. In contrast to these "bottom-up" characteristics, the authors also describe a "top-down" effect, pointing out how a model like wav2vec2.0 tends to develop an implicit language model (LM) As more out-of-domain data is added, this implicit LM is biased toward out-of-domain transcripts. They support this hypothesis with a principal component analysis, illustrating how the model's contextualized representations visibly shift as more out-of-domain data is added to the training data, more so than the in-domain data from AphasiaBank.

These findings are compelling, though we'd like to emphasize how a segment of speech can be transcribed phonemically in many different ways and still be correct, depending on its context. By ASR standards, TIMIT was transcribed using narrow conventions—extremely narrow in the case of stop consonants (e.g. /b/), which are subdivided as closures (e.g. `BCL`) and releases (e.g. `B`) occurring in isolation or as a sequence (e.g. `BCL B`). In ASR systems, these closures are conventionally relabeled as as silence. (Lopes and Perdigao, 2011a) As a result, the word "maybe" is alternately realized with the stop (when `M EY BCL B IY` becomes /me͡ɪ bi/) or without (when `M EY BCL IY` becomes /me͡ɪ i/). In PSST conventions, however, both of these pronunciations are /me͡ɪbi/. Considering how open-ended transcription can be, we note how Yuan et al. used different techniques to generate pseudo-labels: G2P for Librispeech versus iterative pseudo-labeling for AphasiaBank. The G2P model was trained on a word-to-pronunciation dictionary, and the transcripts are a function of orthography, uninfluenced by the recordings. On the other hand, the AphasiaBank labels were generated by a model trained on the PSST labels themselves, and the transcripts are a function of the audio recordings. Unlike their AphasiaBank model, their G2P model has never been exposed to contextually important phenomena like the mispronunciations, neologisms, inter- and intra-word variation, etc. found in the PSST transcripts. So while the LibriSpeech data is out-of-domain, perhaps its pseudo-labels are better characterized out-of-*range*, with the important distinction that the latter could have a remedy. We could learn more if the LibriSpeech experiments were repeated using the iterative pseudo-labeling methods.

5 Task B: Correctness

In Task B, we asked participants to perform a simple example of a downstream task, namely, determining whether a recording contained a target word pronounced correctly. Since the BNT-SF and VNT are confrontation naming tests, they are intended to elicit specific nouns and verbs (respectively) in response. For the challenge, we used the same audio samples as Task A, with true/false labels provided by our annotators (see §3). We also provided a set of acceptable phoneme sequences for each stimulus, including all variations in conjugation, dialect, etc. that we found during data preparation. This allowed us to focus on the question of how to identify and preserve sufficient acoustic-phonetic information from a speech signal to improve on a downstream classification task. Like Task A, we provided scripts for the classification metrics for the train and valid splits, and we provided the source code for the baseline model.

We received a submission from one challenger (Tran, 2022) for Task B. Our baseline model relies on ASR transcripts from Task A, so we also experimented with the Task A transcripts submitted by challengers.

5.1 Evaluation

Task B was evaluated in terms of F1-score, precision, recall, and accuracy. To compute each metric, we tallied the true positives (TP), true negatives (TN), false positives (FP), and false negatives (FN). Precision was computed as $\frac{TP}{TP+FP}$, recall as $\frac{TP}{TP+FN}$, and accuracy as $\frac{TP+TN}{TP+TN+FP+FN}$. F1 is the harmonic mean of precision and recall, or $\frac{2TP}{2TP+FP+FN}$.

5.2 Models

Baseline Model (*PSST–B*) The baseline model for Task B relied on a simple string matching algorithm. We began with the transcripts produced by *PSST–A*, removing any silence and noise labels. If a transcript contained any of the pre-determined "correct" phoneme sequences, uninterrupted and in its entirety, the sample was marked true; otherwise, it was marked false.

Challenge Submission: Tran (2022) The approach in Tran (2022) explored acoustic feature engineering as a supplement to the methods used in the baseline model. Motivated by previous work identifying acoustic markers of mild cognitive impairment (MCI) (Roark et al., 2011), Tran conducted a broad search for relevant acoustic features using speech analysis toolkits. These features were aggregated using statistical functions such as mean, minimum, and maximum. Similarly, aggregates of ASR confidence measurements were also explored in the feature set. Features were selected using a T-test, focusing on those deemed statistically significant: mean/standard deviation of loudness, mean/standard deviation of spectral flux, and mean/max of the ASR confidence measures. The features were concatenated with the *PSST–B* predictions into fixed-length vectors, then used to train support vector machine (SVM) and logistic regression classifiers. Hyperparameters were optimized with grid search, and both linear and non-linear SVM kernels were explored.

The Effects of ASR on Task B Although neither Yuan et al. (2022) nor Moël et al. (2022) applied their work to Task B, we used their transcripts to observe how each ASR model affected the Correctness task. For this experiment, we followed the same methods as *PSST–B*, swapping out the transcripts for those produced by challengers' models. We also computed metrics using the gold standard transcripts to identify this model's ceiling with hypothetically "perfect" ASR.

5.3 Results

The baseline model had an accuracy of 0.903, precision of 0.929, recall of 0.858, and F1 of 0.892. The techniques used in Tran (2022) yielded the same labels as the baseline model, so all metrics were the same.

In the experiment using transcripts from Task A, we found mixed results, which we report in Table 3. The ceiling for "perfect" ASR showed a 0.984 F1, 0.968 precision, 1.000 recall, and 0.985 accuracy. The baseline transcripts had a 0.892 F1, 0.929 precision, 0.858 recall, and 0.903 accuracy. Y2 achieved the top F1 of 0.921, and the top accuracy of 0.985. All of Y1–Y5 improved on the four metrics with one exception: Y5 was below the baseline precision, while obtaining the best recall of 0.914, and the second-best F1 (0.920) and accuracy (0.926). Although Y1 achieved the stand-out best FER and PER in Task A, its transcripts were less effective for identifying correctness, having an F1 of 0.917 and an accuracy of 0.925. Similarly, the gains MO1 through MO7 showed in Task A did not translate to the classification task. Of these, MO7 had the best F1 at 0.888 and accuracy at 0.900. MO4 improved on the baseline in terms of recall (0.865), but at the expense of precision (0.910). MO6, MO3, and MO5 improved on precision (0.934, 0.931, and 0.930, respectively) at the expense of recall (0.842, 0.842, and 0.832, respectively). Y6 and Y7 also improved a bit on precision (0.934 and 0.942, respectively) while taking a heavy hit to recall (0.696 and 0.432, respectively).

5.4 Discussion

As Tran points out, the baseline established by *PSST–B* was quite strong. Surprisingly, while 26% of the phonemes produced by *PSST–A* were incorrect, less than 10% of those transcripts were labeled incorrect by *PSST–A*. When planning the challenge, we chose to avoid more difficult (and more clinically informative) tasks, like those that require subtler judgements phonological similarity judgements. In retrospect, we may have designed Task B to be *too* easy, leaving little room to improve on the baseline.

Tran's experiments showed negative results, producing labels identical to *PSST–B*. This suggests that the acoustic features didn't provide more information than the *PSST–B* algorithm could glean from the transcripts. The author also notes that without including the *PSST–B* predictions as a feature, the performance of the acoustic models was only slightly better than chance. Further, Tran discusses the challenge of retaining valuable information while aggregating time sequences to fixed-length vectors. To this, we note some problem formulation differences between Task B and work like Roark et al. (2011) and Fraser et al. (2014). First, their acoustic markers were found in narrative speech tasks, consisting of several successive sentences, containing more prosodic information than a confrontation naming test. Second, the Task B correctness labels describe an event (a paraphasia) as opposed to a condition like aphasia or MCI; thus, the clinical dementia rating used in the cited work is more analogous to the AQ index included with the PSST data.

Transcripts	F1	Precision	Recall	Accuracy	FER	PER
PSST-Gold	0.984	0.968	1.000	0.985	0%	0%
Y2	**0.921**	0.941	0.901	**0.928**	10.3%	21.1%
Y5	0.920	0.926	**0.914**	0.926	10.9%	22.3%
Y1	0.917	0.941	0.894	0.925	**9.9%**	**20.0%**
Y3	0.903	**0.949**	0.861	0.914	10.4%	21.5%
Y4	0.899	0.930	0.871	0.910	10.6%	22.2%
PSST-Baseline	0.892	0.929	0.858	0.903	12.1%	26.4%
MO7	0.888	0.928	0.851	0.900	12.0%	26.1%
MO4	0.887	0.910	0.865	0.897	11.7%	25.4%
MO6	0.885	0.934	0.842	0.899	12.0%	25.9%
MO1	0.884	0.912	0.858	0.896	11.3%	25.5%
MO3	0.884	0.931	0.842	0.897	11.7%	26.3%
MO2	0.883	0.921	0.848	0.896	11.4%	25.1%
MO5	0.878	0.930	0.832	0.893	11.9%	26.0%
Y6	0.798	0.934	0.696	0.836	12.5%	26.0%
Y7	0.593	0.942	0.432	0.724	16.6%	38.0%

Table 3: Correctness results using the *PSST–B* model, using Test transcripts generated by Task A models Y1-Y7 and MO1-MO7. F1, precision, recall, and accuracy scores are shown, alongside the FER and PER shown in Task A. The first row, *PSST-Gold*, used the gold standard transcripts. Values in gray did not improve on *PSST–A*.

In the experiment using transcripts from Task A, we see how improvements to FER and PER do not necessarily ripple out to the downstream task. FER and PER consider the full transcript, so improvements outside the response boundaries have no effect on correctness. Even if improvements occurred within the response boundary, so long as any errors remain, the *PSST–B* algorithm will mark it as false. A correctness algorithm that considered likelihoods for each token in the sequence might better show a relationship to incremental ASR improvements.

The perfect recall and imperfect precision of *PSST-Gold* indicate that with ideal transcripts, 10 false positives account for all the errors. In these samples, the correct sequence of phonemes were present, but the response was incorrect for other reasons. For example, the string /me͡ɪlbɑks/ ("mailbox") contains /me͡ɪl/, it is incorrect because it is a different word, and a noun rather than a verb. Similarly, /klæfɪŋ/ contains the /læfɪŋ/ ("laughing"), but the production is a non-word. This can be seen as a limitation of the algorithm with no sensitivity to word and syllable boundaries. Unlike *PSST-Gold*, the remaining transcripts had worse recall than precision, suggesting they tended to miss correctly pronounced words (false negatives) more so than they smoothed out mispronunciations (false positives).

We reviewed *PSST–B* errors that were common across the transcripts. In one instance, we provided the transcript /pʊʃɪŋ/ ("pushing") and labeled the response as correct, whereas none of the ASR transcripts agreed. In fact, 7 of 12 transcripts had /m/ as the initial consonant, and upon listening to the sample post-hoc, we tend to agree with the ASR. Another particular challenge pertains to matters of motor planning and articulation. One example included a prolongation of the initial /m/ in the word "mixing", i.e. /mː- mɪksɪŋ/. During the prolongation, the participant was also lowering the jaw with lips closed, introducing more oral resonance than typical for /m/, and demonstrating involuntary pitch fluctuations. This seemed to confuse all the ASR systems, though predictably: 6 were transcribed as /**p**ɪksɪŋ/ and 5 as /**bp**ɪksɪŋ/ In their raw form, our transcripts annotated phenomena like phonological fragments and prolongations, but these annotations were removed during pre-processing. Furthermore, none of our annotations addressed deviations in pitch or resonance.

6 Conclusion

As we hoped, the PSST participants improved on our baseline approach. The ASR metrics FER and PER were improved by a relative 18% and 24%, respectively. Those improvements alone improved the F1 of the Correctness task by a relative 3.3%. These ideas warrant further experimentation, and we expect progress will continue as a result of expanding the PSST data and refining this work.

To this end, as a next step we will investigate which linguistic and clinical characteristics pose the greatest challenge across the ASR systems. Further, we will assess how FER/PER relate to the performance of downstream tasks; and, explore how different approaches to FER computation could improve its utility. At the same, we intent to continue expanding the PSST dataset using AphasiaBank data while also refining our evaluation methods. Given the opportunity to hold another PSST challenge, we see ample opportunity to raise the bar with the downstream tasks: introducing tasks like phonological and morphological similarity assessment, or leaning in to the complexities associated with accents and dialect.

7 Acknowledgements

This research was supported by the National Institute on Deafness and Other Communication Disorders of the National Institutes of Health under award numbers R01DC015999 and R01DC015999-04S1.

We thank past and present Portland State University students Mia Cywinski, Emily Tudorache, and Khanh Nguyen for their contribution to the preparation and annotation of the transcribed dataset, as well as current and past members of the Oregon Health & Science University research team Alexandra Salem, Linying Li, Dr. Brooke Cowan, and Dr. Katy McKinney-Bock. We thank the challenge participants for taking on these important tasks. We thank Brian MacWhinney for above-and-beyond assistance with hosting our challenge data. Finally, we are grateful for AphasiaBank participants, whose voices make this research possible.

Abel, S., Willmes, K., and Huber, W. (2007). Model-oriented naming therapy: Testing predictions of a connectionist model. *Aphasiology*, 21(5):411–447, April.

Baevski, A., Zhou, H., rahman Mohamed, A., and Auli, M. (2020). wav2vec 2.0: A framework for self-supervised learning of speech representations. *ArXiv*, abs/2006.11477.

Best, W., Greenwood, A., Grassly, J., Herbert, R., Hickin, J., and Howard, D. (2013). Aphasia rehabilitation: Does generalisation from anomia therapy occur and is it predictable? A case series study. *Cortex*, 49(9):2345–2357, October.

Brookshire, C. E., Conway, T., Pompon, R. H., Oelke, M., and Kendall, D. L. (2014). Effects of intensive phonomotor treatment on reading in eight individuals with aphasia and phonological alexia. *American Journal of Speech-Language Pathology*, 23(2):S300–S311, May.

Carragher, M., Conroy, P., Sage, K., and Wilkinson, R. (2012). Can impairment-focused therapy change the everyday conversations of people with aphasia? A review of the literature and future directions. *Aphasiology*, 26(7):895–916, April.

Casilio, M., Fergadiotis, G., Bedrick, S., and McKinney-Bock, K. (2019). Can machines classify paraphasias? Evidence from Dell's model.

Cho-Reyes, S. and Thompson, C. K. (2012). Verb and sentence production and comprehension in aphasia: Northwestern Assessment of Verbs and Sentences (NAVS). *Aphasiology*, 26(10):1250–1277, October.

Chomsky, N. and Halle, M. (1968). *The Sound Pattern of English*. Harper & Row, New York, NY.

Cowan, B., McKinney-Bock, K., Casilio, M., Fergadiotis, G., and Bedrick, S. (2021). An evaluation framework for machine learning models of paraphasia classification.

Dell, G. S. and O'Seaghdha, P. G. (1992). Stages of lexical access in language production. *Cognition*, 42(1–3):287–314.

Dell, G. S., Schwartz, M. F., Martin, N., Saffran, E. M., and Gagnon, D. A. (1997). Lexical access in aphasic and nonaphasic speakers. *Psychological Review*, 104(4):801–838, October.

Dell, G. S., Chang, F., and Griffin, Z. M. (1999). Connectionist models of language production: Lexical access and grammatical encoding. *Cognitive Science*, 23(4):517–542, October.

Dell, G. S. (1986). A spreading-activation theory of retrieval in sentence production. *Psychological Review*, 93(3):283–321.

Devlin, J., Chang, M.-W., Lee, K., and Toutanova, K. (2019). BERT: Pre-training of deep bidirectional transformers for language understanding. In *Proceedings of the 2019 Conference of the North American Chapter of the Association for Computational Linguistics: Human Language Technologies, Volume 1 (Long and Short Papers)*, pages 4171–4186, Minneapolis, Minnesota, June. Association for Computational Linguistics.

Edmonds, L. A. and Kiran, S. (2006). Effect of semantic naming treatment on crosslinguistic generalization in bilingual aphasia. *Journal of Speech Language and Hearing Research*, 49(4):729, August.

Fergadiotis, G., Gorman, K., and Bedrick, S. (2016). Algorithmic classification of five characteristic types of paraphasias. *American Journal of Speech-Language Pathology*, 25(4S):S776–S787, December.

Fergadiotis, G., Kapantzoglou, M., Kintz, S., and Wright, H. H. (2019). Modeling confrontation naming and discourse informativeness using structural equation modeling. *Aphasiology*, 33(5):544–560.

Fraser, K. C., Meltzer, J. A., Graham, N., Leonard, C., and Rochon, E. (2014). Automated classification of primary progressive aphasia subtypes from narrative speech transcripts. *Cortex*, 55:43–60.

Fridriksson, J., Richardson, J. D., Fillmore, P., and Cai, B. (2012). Left hemisphere plasticity and aphasia recovery. *NeuroImage*, 60(2):854–863, April.

Goodglass, H. and Wingfield, A. (1997). *Anomia: Neuroanatomical and cognitive correlates*. Academic Press, San Diego, CA.

Graves, A. and Jaitly, N. (2014). Towards end-to-end speech recognition with recurrent neural networks. In Eric P. Xing et al., editors, *Proceedings of the 31st International Conference on Machine Learning*, volume 32(2) of *Proceedings of Machine Learning Research*, pages 1764–1772, Bejing, China, 22–24 Jun. PMLR.

Graves, A., Mohamed, A.-r., and Hinton, G. (2013). Speech recognition with deep recurrent neural networks. In *2013 IEEE International Conference on Acoustics, Speech and Signal Processing*, pages 6645–6649.

Halpern, B. M., Feng, S., Son, R. v., Brekel, M. v. d., and Scharenborg, O. (2022). Low-resource automatic speech recognition and error analyses of oral cancer speech. *Speech Communication*, 141:14–27.

Hayes, B. (2009). *Introductory Phonology*. Wiley-Blackwell, Malde, MA.

Herbert, R., Hickin, J., Howard, D., Osborne, F., and Best, W. (2008). Do picture-naming tests provide a valid assessment of lexical retrieval in conversation in aphasia? *Aphasiology*, 22(2):184–203, January.

Kaplan, E., Goodlgass, H., and Weintraub, S. (2001). *Boston Naming Test*. Lippincott Williams & Wilkins, Philadelphia, PA, 2nd edition.

Kendall, D., Conway, T., Rosenbek, J., and Gonzalez-Rothi, L. (2003). Case study: Phonological rehabilitation of acquired phonologic alexia. *Aphasiology*, 17(11):1073–1095, January.

Kendall, D. L., Rodriguez, A. D., Rosenbek, J. C., Conway, T., and Gonzalez Rothi, L. J. (2006). Influence of intensive phonomotor rehabilitation on apraxia of speech. *Journal of Rehabilitation Research and Development*, 43(3):409–418, June.

Kendall, D. L., Rosenbek, J. C., Heilman, K. M., Conway, T., Klenberg, K., Gonzalez Rothi, L. J., and Nadeau, S. E. (2008). Phoneme-based rehabilitation of anomia in aphasia. *Brain and Language*, 105(1):1–17, April.

Kertesz, A. (2007). *Western Aphasia Battery – R*. Grune & Stratton, New York.

Ko, T., Peddinti, V., Povey, D., and Khudanpur, S. (2015). Audio augmentation for speech recognition. In *Interspeech 2015*, pages 3586–3589. ISCA, September.

Ladefoged, P. and Johnson, K. (2015). *A Course in Phonetics*. Cengage Learning, Stamford, CT, seventh edition.

Le, D. and Provost, E. M. (2016). Improving automatic recognition of aphasic speech with aphasiabank. In *INTERSPEECH*.

Le, D., Licata, K., and Mower Provost, E. (2018). Automatic quantitative analysis of spontaneous aphasic speech. *Speech Communication*, 100:1–12, June.

Lee, K.-F. and Hon, H.-W. (1989). Speaker-independent phone recognition using hidden markov models. *IEEE Trans. Acoust. Speech Signal Process.*, 37:1641–1648.

Lopes, C. and Perdigao, F. (2011a). Phoneme recognition on the TIMIT database. In *Speech Technologies*. InTech.

Lopes, C. and Perdigao, F. (2011b). Phoneme recognition on the timit database. In Ivo Ipsic, editor, *Speech Technologies*, chapter 14. IntechOpen, Rijeka.

Mack, W. J., Freed, D. M., Williams, B. W., and Henderson, V. W. (1992). Boston Naming Test: Shortened Versions for Use in Alzheimer's Disease. *Journal of Gerontology*, 47(3):P154–P158, May.

Max Planck Institute for Psycholingustics. (2022). *ELAN (Version 6.3) [Computer software]*. The Language Archive, Nijmegen, The Netherlands. URL: https://archive.mpi.nl/tla/elan.

McKinney-Bock, K. and Bedrick, S. (2019). Classification of semantic paraphasias: optimization of a word embedding model. In *3rd Workshop on Evaluating Vector Space Representations for NLP*, pages 52–62, Minneapolis, USA. Association for Computational Linguistics.

Mikolov, T., Sutskever, I., Chen, K., Corrado, G. S., and Dean, J. (2013). Distributed representations of words and phrases and their compositionality. In *NIPS*.

Mohri, M., Pereira, F., and Riley, M. (2001). Weighted finite-state transducers in speech recognition. *Departmental Papers (CIS)*, page 11.

Mortensen, D. R., Littell, P., Bharadwaj, A., Goyal, K., Dyer, C., and Levin, L. S. (2016). Panphon: A resource for mapping IPA segments to articulatory feature vectors. In *Proceedings of COLING 2016, the 26th International Conference on Computational Linguistics: Technical Papers*, pages 3475–3484. ACL. URL: https://github.com/dmort27/panphon.

Moël, B., O'Regan, J., Mehta, S., Kirkland, A., Lameris, H., Gustafsson, J., and Beskow, J. (2022). Speech data augmentation for improving phoneme transcriptions of aphasic speech using wav2vec 2.0 for the PSST Challenge. In Nicoletta Calzolari (Conference Chair), et al., editors, *Proceedings of the Thirteenth International Conference on Language Resources and Evaluation (LREC 2022)*, Marseille, France, June 20-25, 2022. European Language Resource Association (ELRA).

Ott, M., Edunov, S., Baevski, A., Fan, A., Gross, S., Ng, N., Grangier, D., and Auli, M. (2019). fairseq: A fast, extensible toolkit for sequence modeling. URL: https://github.com/facebookresearch/fairseq.

Panayotov, V., Chen, G., Povey, D., and Khudanpur, S. (2015). Librispeech: An ASR corpus based on public domain audio books. *2015 IEEE International Conference on Acoustics, Speech and Signal Processing (ICASSP)*, pages 5206–5210.

Perez, M., Aldeneh, Z., and Provost, E. M. (2020). Aphasic Speech Recognition Using a Mixture of Speech Intelligibility Experts. In *Proc. Interspeech 2020*, pages 4986–4990.

Radford, A. and Narasimhan, K. (2018). Improving language understanding by generative pre-training. https://s3-us-west-2.amazonaws.com/openai-assets/research-covers/language-unsupervised/language_understanding_paper.pdf.

Raymer, A. M. and Rothi, L. J. G. (2001). Impairments of word comprehension and production. In Roberta Chapey, editor, *Language intervention strategies in aphasia and related neurogenic communication disorders*, pages 606–625. Lippincott Williams & Wilkins, 4 edition.

Roach, A., Schwartz, M., Martin, N., Grewal, R., and Brecher, A. (1996). The Philadelphia Naming Test:

scoring and rationale. *Clin. Aphasiol.*, 24:121–133, January.

Roark, B., Mitchell, M., Hosom, J.-P., Hollingshead, K., and Kaye, J. (2011). Spoken language derived measures for detecting mild cognitive impairment. *IEEE Transactions on Audio, Speech, and Language Processing*, 19(7):2081–2090.

Schuell, H., Jenkins, J. J., and Jimenez-Pabon, E. (1964). *Aphasia in adults*. Harper & Row, New York, NY.

Schwartz, M. F., Kimberg, D. Y., Walker, G. M., Faseyitan, O., Brecher, A., Dell, G. S., and Coslett, H. B. (2009). Anterior temporal involvement in semantic word retrieval: Voxel-based lesion-symptom mapping evidence from aphasia. *Brain*, November.

Schwartz, M. F., Faseyitan, O., Kim, J., and Coslett, H. B. (2012). The dorsal stream contribution to phonological retrieval in object naming. *Brain*, 135(12):3799–3814, December.

Simmons-Mackie, N. (2018). *Aphasia in North America*. Aphasia Access, Moorestown, NJ.

Tao, T., Yoon, S.-Y., Fister, A., Sproat, R., and Zhai, C. (2006). Unsupervised named entity transliteration using temporal and phonetic correlation. In *Proceedings of the 2006 Conference on Empirical Methods in Natural Language Processing*, pages 250–257, Sydney, Australia, July. Association for Computational Linguistics.

Thompson, C. K. (2012). Northwestern Assessment of Verbs and Sentences (NAVS). https://www.scholars.northwestern.edu/en /publications/northwestern-assessment-of-verbs-and-sentences-navs.

Torre, I. G., Romero, M., and Álvarez, A. (2021). Improving Aphasic Speech Recognition by Using Novel Semi-Supervised Learning Methods on AphasiaBank for English and Spanish. *Applied Sciences*, 11(19):8872, September.

Tran, T. (2022). Post-Stroke Speech Transcription Challenge (Task B): Correctness detection in anomia diagnosis with imperfect transcripts. In Nicoletta Calzolari (Conference Chair), et al., editors, *Proceedings of the Thirteenth International Conference on Language Resources and Evaluation (LREC 2022)*, Marseille, France, June 20-25, 2022. European Language Resources Association (ELRA).

van den Oord, A., Li, Y., and Vinyals, O. (2018). Representation learning with contrastive predictive coding. *CoRR*, abs/1807.03748.

Walker, G. M. and Schwartz, M. F. (2012). Short-form Philadelphia naming test: Rationale and empirical evaluation. *American Journal of Speech-Language Pathology*, pages S140–S153, May.

Walker, G. M., Schwartz, M. F., Kimberg, D. Y., Faseyitan, O., Brecher, A., Dell, G. S., and Coslett, H. B. (2011). Support for anterior temporal involvement in semantic error production in aphasia: New evidence from VLSM. *Brain and Language*, 117(3):110–122.

Yuan, J., Cai, X., and Church, K. (2022). Data augmentation for the Post-Stroke Speech Transcription (PSST) challenge: Sometimes less is more. In Nicoletta Calzolari (Conference Chair), et al., editors, *Proceedings of the Thirteenth International Conference on Language Resources and Evaluation (LREC 2022)*, Marseille, France, June 20-25, 2022. European Language Resources Association (ELRA).

Zhang, Y., Qin, J., Park, D. S., Han, W., Chiu, C.-C., Pang, R., Le, Q. V., and Wu, Y. (2020). Pushing the limits of semi-supervised learning for automatic speech recognition. *ArXiv*, abs/2010.10504.

8 Language Resource References

Garofolo, John and Lamel, Lori and Fisher, William and Fiscus, Jonathan and Pallett, David and Dahlgren, Nancy and Zue, Victor. (1993). *TIMIT Acoustic-Phonetic Continuous Speech Corpus*. Abacus Data Network.

MacWhinney, B., Fromm, D., Forbes, M., and Holland, A. (2011). AphasiaBank: Methods for studying discourse. *Aphasiology*, 25(11):1286–1307. Supported by NIH-NIDCD R01-DC008524 (2007-2022).

Vassil Panayotov and Guoguo Chen and Daniel Povey and Sanjeev Khudanpur. (2015). *Librispeech: An ASR corpus based on public domain audio books*. OpenSLR (https://www.openslr.org).

Appendices

A More on Phonological Features and Feature Error Rate (FER)

Phoneme error rate (PER) is the go-to evaluation metric for phonemic ASR, derived from the edit distance between the predicted and target phonemes. For PSST, we explore a feature error rate (FER) as finer-grained alternative to PER. Instead of the phonemic edit distance, the error in FER is a phonological feature distance (Mortensen et al., 2016; Tao et al., 2006). In short, each phoneme is represented by a quasi-binary vector indicating the presence and absence of each feature described by the system, and these vectors can be used to compute a measure akin to Euclidean distance. Feature distance is then normalized by the sequence length to determine the error rate, much like PER. In other words, FER is a way of giving "partial credit" to an ASR transcript when it produces phonemes which are similar (but not exact) to the target transcript, defining similarity in terms of distinctive phonological features.

Phonological features distill information about how people distinguish the sounds of their language from one another, while also grouping phonemes into natural classes (Chomsky and Halle, 1968). For example, the English words "bead" and "bid" both contain *high*

ARPAbet	IPA	Example Word	Special diphthong features
EY	/e͡ɪ/	"bay"	[-+high, +-tense]
OW	/o͡ʊ/	"beau"	[-+high, +-tense]
OY	/ɔ͡ɪ/	"boy"	[-+high, -+front, +-back, +-round]
AW	/a͡ʊ/	"bough"	[-+high, +-low, -+back, -+round]
AY	/a͡ɪ/	"buy"	[-+high, +-low, -+front]

Table 4: Diphthongs and their unique features used during computation of feature error rate (FER)

Cost	Feature Changes		
1	[–feature]	↔	[+feature]
0.75	[–feature]	↔	[+–feature]
	[–+feature]	↔	[+feature]
0.5	[–feature]	↔	[0feature]
	[–+feature]	↔	[+–feature]
	[0feature]	↔	[+feature]
0.25	[–feature]	↔	[–+feature]
	[–+feature]	↔	[0feature]
	[0feature]	↔	[+–feature]
	[+–feature]	↔	[+feature]
0	[–feature]	↔	[–feature]
	[–+feature]	↔	[–+feature]
	[0feature]	↔	[0feature]
	[+–feature]	↔	[+–feature]
	[+feature]	↔	[+feature]

Table 5: Costs associated with each feature difference during computation of feature error rate (FER)

front vowels. In the feature system proposed by (Hayes, 2009), high front vowels are a natural class primarily described as [+syllabic, +high, +front]. In fact, the two phonemes share all the same features, save for one distinction: the /i/ in **b**ead is [+tense], while the /ɪ/ in "bid" is said to be lax, or [−tense], distinguished by only that feature. Some phonemes do not specify a certain feature, for example, the tense/lax distinction only applies to vowels, so /b/ and /d/ are both [0tense].

Distinctive features are thus used in phonological analysis to classify phonemes and describe their linguistic behavior (e.g. allophonic variations or historical sound changes), and they are empirically validated for that purpose. Recently, however, phonological features have found novel applications in computational linguistics, enhancing statistical models with information about phonemes' features and feature distances (Mortensen et al., 2016).

For the PSST challenge, we use FER as an evaluation metric for ASR. Previous research has used a variation of the concept as a metric for automatic phoneme recognition (Halpern et al., 2022), but the practice is not well established. Our motivation here is to gain insight into what makes an ASR a better fit for our tasks. During transcription, certain feature-adjacent phonemes can be quite difficult to distinguish (by an ASR or a human). Yet in some contexts, feature-adjacent phonemes like /t/ and /d/ are functionally interchangeable (e.g. a sound change attributable to dialect), whereas more distant phoneme errors would invalidate an analysis.

Compared to PER, FER is much more difficult to compute and understand, and all the more difficult for those with no background in phonology. For this reason, we put together the `pssteval-viewer` tool to illustrate how FER was computed for each utterance, which we shared with PSST challengers in our evaluation toolkit. An example feature analysis generated by the software is shown in Figure 1.

To build our table of feature values, we began with the system specified by Hayes (2009). We excluded two features which do not contrast in our ARPAbet transcript (nor English, generally): [constrictedglottis] and [trill]. Diphthongs presented a conundrum: with no single entry for diphthongs in the feature table, the two components would be treated as two phonemes. In other words, if a diphthong replaced a monophthong (or vice versa), the distance would always include an insertion or a deletion, and the feature error would be greater than a full phoneme. To rectify this, we treated diphthongs as individual phonemes (as they are in ARPAbet), adding new entries in the feature table for /e͡ɪ/, /o͡ʊ/, /ɔ͡ɪ/, /a͡ʊ/, and /a͡ɪ/ (the vowels in "bay", "bow/beau", "boy", "bow/bough", and "buy", respectively), and new feature values to capture their movement. These all emphasize the first of their two component vowels (Ladefoged and Johnson, 2015), so when a feature has the new value [$+^{-}$feature] (present toward absent) we consider it between [+feature] and [0feature], while [$-^{+}$feature] (absent toward present) is between [0feature and [−feature]. The five diphthongs and their novel features are highlighted in Table 4 All combinations of feature changes and their costs are shown in Table 5. introduced two new symbols to capture how a diphthong's features moved between its components.

B More Details on Data Preparation

B.1 More on Data Preparation

Approximately one third of the total number of included responses ($n = 3291$) consisted of BNT-SF first responses ($n = 1074$), defined as single-word first complete attempts according to the scoring guidelines of the

ARPAbet	IPA	consonantal	delayedrelease	continuant	sonorant	approximant	syllabic	tap	nasal	voice	spreadglottis	labial	round	labiodental	coronal	anterior	distributed	strident	lateral	dorsal	high	low	front	back	tense
P	p	+	−	−	−	−	−	−	−	−	−	+	−	−	−	0	0	0	−	−	0	0	0	0	0
B	b	+	−	−	−	−	−	−	−	+	−	+	−	−	−	0	0	0	−	−	0	0	0	0	0
T	t	+	−	−	−	−	−	−	−	−	−	−	−	−	+	+	−	−	−	−	0	0	0	0	0
D	d	+	−	−	−	−	−	−	−	+	−	−	−	−	+	+	−	−	−	−	0	0	0	0	0
K	k	+	−	−	−	−	−	−	−	−	−	−	−	−	−	0	0	0	−	+	+	−	0	0	0
G	g	+	−	−	−	−	−	−	−	+	−	−	−	−	−	0	0	0	−	+	+	−	0	0	0
CH	t͡ʃ	+	+	−	−	−	−	−	−	−	−	−	−	−	+	−	+	+	−	−	0	0	0	0	0
JH	d͡ʒ	+	+	−	−	−	−	−	−	+	−	−	−	−	+	−	+	+	−	−	0	0	0	0	0
F	f	+	+	+	−	−	−	−	−	−	−	+	−	+	−	0	0	0	−	−	0	0	0	0	0
V	v	+	+	+	−	−	−	−	−	+	−	+	−	+	−	0	0	0	−	−	0	0	0	0	0
TH	θ	+	+	+	−	−	−	−	−	−	−	−	−	−	+	+	+	−	−	−	0	0	0	0	0
DH	ð	+	+	+	−	−	−	−	−	+	−	−	−	−	+	+	+	−	−	−	0	0	0	0	0
S	s	+	+	+	−	−	−	−	−	−	−	−	−	−	+	+	−	+	−	−	0	0	0	0	0
Z	z	+	+	+	−	−	−	−	−	+	−	−	−	−	+	+	−	+	−	−	0	0	0	0	0
SH	ʃ	+	+	+	−	−	−	−	−	−	−	−	−	−	+	−	+	+	−	−	0	0	0	0	0
ZH	ʒ	+	+	+	−	−	−	−	−	+	−	−	−	−	+	−	+	+	−	−	0	0	0	0	0
HH	h	−	+	+	−	−	−	−	−	−	+	−	−	−	−	0	0	0	−	−	0	0	0	0	0
M	m	+	0	−	+	−	−	−	+	+	−	+	−	−	−	0	0	0	−	−	0	0	0	0	0
N	n	+	0	−	+	−	−	−	+	+	−	−	−	−	+	+	−	−	−	−	0	0	0	0	0
NG	ŋ	+	0	−	+	−	−	−	+	+	−	−	−	−	−	0	0	0	−	+	+	−	0	0	0
L	l	+	0	+	+	+	−	−	−	+	−	−	−	−	+	+	−	−	+	−	0	0	0	0	0
DX	ɾ	+	0	+	+	+	−	+	−	+	−	−	−	−	+	+	−	−	−	−	0	0	0	0	0
Y	j	−	0	+	+	+	−	−	−	+	−	−	−	−	−	0	0	0	−	+	+	−	+	−	+
W	w	−	0	+	+	+	−	−	−	+	−	+	+	−	−	0	0	0	−	+	+	−	−	+	+
R	r	−	0	+	+	+	−	−	−	+	−	−	−	−	+	−	+	−	−	−	0	0	0	0	0
ER	ɝ, ɚ	−	0	+	+	+	+	−	−	+	−	−	−	−	+	−	+	−	−	−	0	0	0	0	0
IY	i	−	0	+	+	+	+	−	−	+	−	−	−	−	−	0	0	0	−	+	+	−	+	−	+
IH	ɪ	−	0	+	+	+	+	−	−	+	−	−	−	−	−	0	0	0	−	+	+	−	+	−	−
UW	u	−	0	+	+	+	+	−	−	+	−	+	+	−	−	0	0	0	−	+	+	−	−	+	+
UH	ʊ	−	0	+	+	+	+	−	−	+	−	+	+	−	−	0	0	0	−	+	+	−	−	+	−
EH	ɛ	−	0	+	+	+	+	−	−	+	−	−	−	−	−	0	0	0	−	+	−	−	+	−	−
EY	e͡ɪ	−	0	+	+	+	+	−	−	+	−	−	−	−	−	0	0	0	−	+	$-^{+}$	−	+	−	$+^{-}$
AH	ʌ, ə	−	0	+	+	+	+	−	−	+	−	−	−	−	−	0	0	0	−	+	−	−	−	+	−
AO	ɔ	−	0	+	+	+	+	−	−	+	−	+	+	−	−	0	0	0	−	+	−	−	−	+	−
OW	o͡ʊ	−	0	+	+	+	+	−	−	+	−	+	+	−	−	0	0	0	−	+	$-^{+}$	−	−	+	$+^{-}$
OY	ɔ͡ɪ	−	0	+	+	+	+	−	−	+	−	+	$+^{-}$	−	−	0	0	0	−	+	$-^{+}$	−	$-^{+}$	$+^{-}$	−
AE	æ	−	0	+	+	+	+	−	−	+	−	−	−	−	−	0	0	0	−	+	−	+	+	−	0
AW	a͡ʊ	−	0	+	+	+	+	−	−	+	−	−	$-^{+}$	−	−	0	0	0	−	+	$-^{+}$	$+^{-}$	−	$-^{+}$	0
AY	a͡ɪ	−	0	+	+	+	+	−	−	+	−	−	−	−	−	0	0	0	−	+	$-^{+}$	$+^{-}$	$-^{+}$	−	0
AA	ɑ	−	0	+	+	+	+	−	−	+	−	−	−	−	−	0	0	0	−	+	−	+	−	+	0

Table 6: The 40 phonemes in this ASR system in ARPAbet and IPA, and their associated phonological features. Features align with Hayes (2009), with the exception of diphthong handling, which are treated as individual phonemes here (using special symbols $-^{+}$and $+^{-}$to describe their movement).

	Split	Mild		Moderate		Severe		Very Severe	
Hours	Train	0.85	(32.8%)	1.39	(53.4%)	0.33	(12.5%)	0.03	(1.0%)
	Validation	0.11	(31.5%)	0.20	(56.3%)	0.04	(12.1%)	0.00	(0.0%)
	Test	0.17	(28.2%)	0.32	(55.0%)	0.08	(13.9%)	0.02	(2.6%)
Segments	Train	1073	(49.3%)	893	(41.0%)	187	(8.6%)	20	(0.9%)
	Validation	121	(37.2%)	170	(52.3%)	34	(10.4%)	0	(0.0%)
	Test	262	(41.9%)	275	(44.0%)	67	(10.7%)	20	(3.2%)
Speakers	Train	33	(44.5%)	32	(43.2%)	8	(10.8%)	1	(1.3%)
	Validation	4	(36.3%)	6	(54.5%)	1	(9.0%)	0	(0.0%)
	Test	8	(36.3%)	10	(45.4%)	3	(13.6%)	1	(4.5%)

Table 7: Detailed breakdown of the data illustrating the attempt to balance aphasia severity across each split. The balance is show for each of hours of audio, number of segments, and number of speakers.

IPA	Example	ARPAbet
/p/	"**p**at"	P
/b/	"**b**at"	B
/t/	"**t**en"	T
/d/	"**d**en"	D
/k/	"**c**oat"	K
/g/	"**g**oat"	G
/ɾ/	"bu**tt**er" (allophone of /t/, /d/)	DX
/ʔ/	"co**tt**on" (allophone of /t/)	*(removed)*
/t͡ʃ/	"**ch**ur**ch**"	CH
/d͡ʒ/	"**j**u**dg**e"	JH
/f/	"**f**an"	F
/v/	"**v**an"	V
/θ/	"**th**in" (voiceless)	TH
/ð/	"**th**en" (voiced)	DH
/s/	"**s**ee"	S
/z/	"**z**oo"	Z
/ʃ/	"**sh**oe"	SH
/ʒ/	"occa**s**ion"	ZH
/h/	"**h**at"	HH
/n/	"**n**ose"	N
/ŋ/	"si**ng**"	NG
/m/	"**m**an"	M

IPA	Example	ARPAbet
/w/	"**w**in"	W
/j/	"**y**es"	Y
/r/	"**r**ed"	R
/l/	"**l**ate"	L
/ɝ/	"h**ear**d" (stressed)	ER
/ɚ/	"p**er**haps" (unstressed)	ER
/i/	"sh**e**"	IY
/ɪ/	"f**i**t"	IH
/u/	"b**oo**t"	UW
/ʊ/	"w**oo**d"	UH
/e͡ɪ/	"st**a**te"	EY
/ɛ/	"r**e**d"	EH
/o͡ʊ/	"v**o**te"	OW
/ɔ͡ɪ/	"b**oy**"	OY
/ɔ/	"d**aw**n"	AO
/ʌ/	"b**u**t" (stressed)	AH
/ə/	"**a**lone" (unstressed)	AH
/ɑ/	"n**o**t"	AA
/æ/	"c**a**t"	AE
/a͡ɪ/	"k**i**te"	AY
/a͡ʊ/	"c**ow**"	AW

Table 8: A list of International Phonemic Alphabet (IPA) notations used by our laboratory and their ARPAbet mappings for ASR, with examples.

PNT. For about a quarter of BNT-SF responses ($n = 155$), first complete attempts were segmented to also contain surrounding connected speech when phonemic boundaries between words were blurred. BNT-SF responses that overlapped with examiner speech as well as responses labeled as non-naming attempts (e.g., descriptions of the target, whispered responses, etc.) were excluded.

Approximately two thirds of the response data consisted of VNT first responses ($n = 2217$), defined as any response from the moment following picture stimulus presentation and a first examiner prompt to the moment preceding a second examiner prompt and/or the administration of the next picture stimulus. Nonverbal cues from the examiner, such as gestures indicating the target verb, were treated as second prompts if they occurred. Examiner speech that overlapped with a response was excluded, and, if possible, exactly one segment of participant speech was retained per test item.

B.2 Audio Preprocessing

When we extracted audio-only segments from the full TalkBank session videos, we applied pre-processing steps using `ffmpeg`. To remove high-energy, low-frequency noise, we used a high-pass filter, rolling off the audio signal below 100Hz (at a rate of 12 dB per octave). Then, we applied adaptive limiting to the audio in two phases. First, we used a applied a filter designed to achieve broadcast-standard loudness normalization (EBU R128), dynamically adjusting to an integrated loudness of –23dB. Second, to remove large peaks (e.g. when a microphone was bumped) we applied a look-ahead limiter set to prevent the signal from exceeding –6dB. Finally, we downsampled and downmixed to a monaural 16KHz (discarding sounds over 8KHz, typical for ASR) and extracted each segment to individual WAV files.

B.3 Transcription Procedures

Phonemic transcriptions were broad with conventions originally developed by our laboratory for the purposes of use with a computer algorithm. For this project, we aimed to apply previously developed conventions in a way that captured some degree of phonetic detail if and when phonemic boundaries were crossed. To this end, research assistants received training from a licensed speech-language pathologist on some typical coarticulation processes and dialectical patterns observed in the participant sample, namely those that could be represented using broad phonemic notation.

B.4 Transcript Pre-Processing for ASR

For ASR purposes, the IPA transcripts were converted to ARPAbet. The full mapping of IPA to ARPAbet symbols is shown in Table 8. Similar to conventional ASR preparation (Lopes and Perdigao, 2011b), some phonemes were combined or removed: /ə/ and /ʌ/ became `AH`, /ɝ/ and /ɚ/ became `ER`, and glottal stops (/ʔ/) were removed from the transcripts. We used a special symbol `SPN` for instances where transcribers noted unintelligible words or speech noises (e.g. laughing, coughing).

C More on baseline model training

The model was fine-tuned for 12,000 total iterations (401 epochs), linearly ramping up to a learning rate of 5×10^{-5} over the first 4000 iterations. For the first 2000 iterations, we froze all but the newly-initialized weights, priming only the output layer. For the final model, we restored the model to the point when it showed the minimum PER on the validation set, at 5964 iterations (200 epochs). We used a maximum batch size of 6.4 million frames of audio (400 seconds). Figure 2 shows the progression of the model's loss over the course of training.

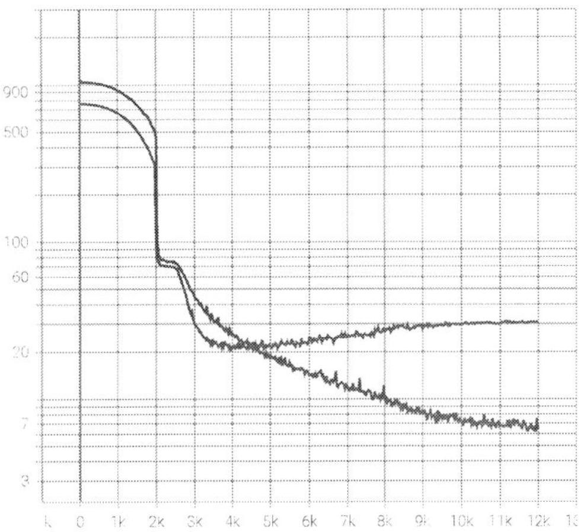

Figure 2: CTC loss over number of updates for the baseline model (at 30 updates per epoch). The red line is loss computed for the train set, and the blue line is loss computed for the test metric.

Proceedings of the RaPID-4 @LREC 2022, pages 56–61
Marseille, 25 June 2022

Post-Stroke Speech Transcription Challenge (Task B): Correctness Detection in Anomia Diagnosis with Imperfect Transcripts

Trang Tran
University of Southern California, Institute for Creative Technologies
Los Angeles, CA, USA
ttran@ict.usc.edu

Abstract

Aphasia is a language disorder that affects millions of adults worldwide annually; it is most commonly caused by strokes or neurodegenerative diseases. Anomia, or word finding difficulty, is a prominent symptom of aphasia, which is often diagnosed through confrontation naming tasks. In the clinical setting, identification of correctness in responses to these naming tasks is useful for diagnosis, but currently is a labor-intensive process. This year's Post-Stroke Speech Transcription Challenge provides an opportunity to explore ways of automating this process. In this work, we focus on Task B of the challenge, i.e. identification of response correctness. We study whether a simple aggregation of using the 1-best automatic speech recognition (ASR) output and acoustic features could help predict response correctness. This was motivated by the hypothesis that acoustic features could provide complementary information to the (imperfect) ASR transcripts. We trained several classifiers using various sets of acoustic features standard in speech processing literature in an attempt to improve over the 1-best ASR baseline. Results indicated that our approach to using the acoustic features did not beat the simple baseline, at least on this challenge dataset. This suggests that ASR robustness still plays a significant role in the correctness detection task, which has yet to benefit from acoustic features.

Keywords: anomia, psst challenge, stroke, aphasia, automatic speech recognition

1. Introduction

Aphasia is a language disorder that affects 2–4 million people annually just in the US alone.[1] Aphasia most commonly occurs after a stroke or head injury, or can be acquired slowly from growing brain tumors or neurological diseases.[2] Patients with aphasia suffer difficulty in communication, which can manifest as various forms of language impairments, including both comprehension and expression.

One of the most prominent symptoms of aphasia is *anomia*, or word finding difficulty. Specifically, aphasia patients with anomia might make word production errors that are semantic (e.g. "dog" for the target "cat"), phonological (e.g. "tat" for the target "cat"), both, or even unrelated (e.g. "chair" for the target "cat"). These errors are typically diagnosed in the clinical setting through confrontation naming tasks, where the patient is presented with hundreds of items to identify/name. The resulting error profiles are then analyzed by professionals to provide overall assessment. Understanding these errors is therefore critical in diagnosis as well development of treatment plans.

However, current approaches for anomia test assessments are labor intensive for clinicians, especially with a large number of patients, each completing a large set of tests. Further, speech recognition for atypical speech, such as that produced by aphasia patients, is especially challenging, since most state-of-the-art automatic speech recognizers (ASR) were trained on clean (and often read) speech in controlled environments.

Recently, self-supervised speech representation approaches (Liu et al., 2020a; Liu et al., 2020b; Baevski et al., 2020), commonly learned from raw audio, have shown promising results on multiple tasks. Their utility has been evaluated on a range of spoken language processing tasks, from word/phoneme recognition to emotion and sentiment analysis (Yang et al., 2021; Shon et al., 2021). The natural question is then whether these systems can be adapted to aphasic speech, especially when the aphasia data is recorded in conditions often much different from the pretrained ASR data. In this work, however, we take a more incremental approach in assessing the possibility of detecting anomia with a simple combination of pretrained ASR output and acoustic features. This approach is inspired by the earlier works showing the utility of prosody (i.e. *how* something is said vs. *what* is said) in aiding spoken language understanding systems, both when applied to hand transcripts and ASR transcripts (Kahn and Ostendorf, 2012; Marin and Ostendorf, 2014; Tran et al., 2019; Tran and Ostendorf, 2021). In particular, we focus on Task B: correctness prediction of naming responses in the Post-Stroke Speech Transcription Challenge (PSST) 2022. We aim to answer the following questions:

- Using a pretrained ASR system, can correctness prediction be improved using acoustic features?
- Are there salient differences in the acoustic patterns of correct vs. incorrect naming responses?

In answering these questions, we hope to understand whether such a simple and low-cost system (i.e. not

[1] https://www.aphasiaaccess.org/white-papers/

[2] https://www.nidcd.nih.gov/health/aphasia

requiring additional aphasia-specific data and annotations) helps predict response correctness, or whether it is worth investing more effort in improving ASR for the domain of aphasic speech and language disorders in general.

2. Related Work

Many researchers have explored the potential of using speech for the diagnosis of language disorders. For example, Roark et al. (2011) showed that both lexical and acoustic signals can help detect mild cognitive impairment (MCI). In particular, noun and verb counts, syntactic complexity (as measured by Yngve score (Yngve, 1960)), pause durations and pause rates seemed to be most useful. For Primary Progressive Aphasia (PPA) detection and subtype classification, Fraser et al. (2013; Fraser et al. (2014) also found that syntactic complexity features were among the most useful. In addition, while acoustic features were not as useful in differentiating PPA from control, they were important in classification of PPA's subtypes.

In an investigation to push towards a fully automated diagnosis pipeline, Zhou et al. (2016) compared using hand-transcribed speech conversations vs. ASR outputs to detect Alzheimer's disease in participants. Not surprisingly, they found that accuracy is higher using perfect transcripts, but also identified key features that have distinguishing power in both gold and ASR transcripts, such as word length and frequency. In addition, the authors observed that accuracies can vary within a narrow band of word error rates (WER), i.e. ASR transcripts with the same low WER can contain drastically different information. For predicting aphasia quotient (AQ), Le et al. (2018) trained a speech recognition system on AphasiaBank (MacWhinney et al., 2011) and achieved a new recognition benchmark for ASR in aphasic speech, in addition to obtaining higher accuracy on AQ prediction.

The research so far has largely been limited by ASR quality, as aphasic speech proves to be a challenge. However, to the best of our knowledge, little has been explored on whether acoustic features are informative in aiding correctness prediction on top of ASR transcripts.

3. Data and Metrics

The dataset we use is provided by the PSST Challenge 2022 organizers (Gale et al., 2022). In particular, the dataset is a subset of AphasiaBank (MacWhinney et al., 2011), a database of multimedia interactions in clinical settings for the study of aphasia. For the PSST challenge, the subset includes responses from the Boston Naming Test – Short Form (BNT) and the Verb Naming Test (VNT). In addition to the audio and metadata from AphasiaBank, Gale et al. (2022) provided human phone-level annotations, as well as the correctness label for the naming responses (i.e. whether the utterance was considered correct by clinicians). The dataset is well-balanced with approximately 50%:50% split of correct vs. incorrect labels (binary classes), both in the training and validation set. The train/validation/test splits were predefined by the challenge organizers. Overall dataset statistics is shown in Table 1.

Split	# Utterances	PER	FER
Train	2298	4.0%	2.4%
Validation	341	22.6%	10.6%
Test	652	n/a	n/a

Table 1: Dataset Statistics for the PSST Challenge

For ASR, we use the pretrained system provided by Gale et al. (2022), and obtained phone transcripts from this off-the-shelf ASR. The phone error rate (PER) and feature error rate (FER) are also reported for each set. PER is a standard metric in ASR research (i.e. % phone recognition errors out of reference phones); FER is a metric provided by the challenge organizers that emphasizes evaluation of errors regarding *distinctive phone features* (i.e. putting more value on transcripts that *sound* correct as opposed to strict comparison with phone representations).

For correctness prediction, we use standard evaluation metrics for binary classification, i.e. F1 score (in addition to reporting precision and recall), as instructed by the organizers (Gale et al., 2022).

4. Methods

4.1. Acoustic Features

Inspired by previous works exploring acoustic features for aphasia classification, we extracted several feature sets reported in literature to be generally useful in speech analysis.

- Librosa (McFee et al., 2015) feature set: we extract the pitch contour for each utterance using librosa's implementation of the pYIN algorithm (Mauch and Dixon, 2014; de Cheveigné and Kawahara, 2002). This gives us the estimated pitch contour, as well as voice activity detection per frame. To summarize the pitch contour and voicing characteristics for the whole utterance, we compute the voice activity rate (active_rate) for each utterance, which we consider the proxy for pause characteristics of the utterance. Pause features have been shown to be useful in acoustic analysis of speech disorders, e.g. as in (Roark et al., 2011; Le et al., 2018). Additionally, we hypothesize that pauses are important indicators of speech fluency, i.e. aphasic speech might be less fluent than healthy speech due communication difficulties reflected by hesitations and self-corrections.

  To potentially alleviate the loss of acoustic information in summarizing features for the whole utterance, we also estimate the polynomial fit coefficients of the pitch contour. We used a 5th order polynomial fit, resulting in a six dimensional feature vector for each utterance, i.e. the coefficients $[a_5, a_4, a_3, a_2, a_1, a_0]$.

- The Geneva Minimalistic Acoustic Parameter Set (GeMAPS) for Voice Research and Affective Computing (Eyben et al., 2010): We extract the low-level descriptors as recommended in (Eyben et al., 2010); this gave us 18 features that cover different pitch, energy, and spectral balance characteristics of the speech utterances. Detailed descriptions for each feature can be found in Eyben et al. (2010). For each feature in this set, we compute the mean and standard deviation of each utterance.

In addition to acoustic features, we explore potentially using ASR scores for the utterances as a proxy of how confident the speech recognizer was. We hypothesize that lower confidences could potentially indicate anomalies in the speech patterns and thus could inform correctness in the naming task. For this, we use the min, max, mean, median, and standard deviation of the softmax normalized logit scores generated by the pretrained ASR system. Specifically, the logit scores were first normalized to sum up to 1 before the sufficient statistics calculations.[3] We did not excluded silent or pad tokens in this work (a possible future tweak), and this was only a simple way to assess the *global* ASR confidence for each utterance.

To select the potentially most useful features for discriminating between correct and incorrect responses, we perform a t-test for each feature between the correct and incorrect samples in the training data. Features that have statistically significant differences ($p < 0.001$, using Bonferroni correction) in correct vs. incorrect samples are the following (henceforth referred to as CoreFeats):

- max_logit: max value of the (normalized) logit scores in each utterance
- mean_logit: mean value of the (normalized) logit scores in each utterance
- mean_Loudness_sma3 (GeMAPS feature): mean value of loudness in each utterance, i.e. mean estimate of perceived signal intensity from an auditory spectrum
- sd_Loudness_sma3 (GeMAPS feature): standard deviation of loudness in each utterance
- mean_spectralFlux_sma3 (GeMAPS feature): mean value of spectral flux in each utterance, i.e. the mean difference of the spectra of two consecutive frames
- sd_spectralFlux_sma3 (GeMAPS feature): standard deviation of spectral flux in each utterance

Interestingly, none of the librosa features were significantly different between correct and incorrect samples. This is surprising since previous work has shown pauses are a useful indicator, but the feature active_rate is not among CoreFeats according to our selection heuristics.

4.2. Classifiers

Our baseline model is a simple string matching procedure as implemented by Gale et al. (2022), i.e. we use the 1-best ASR output and run the program to evaluate whether the transcript is found among acceptable pronunciations. This baseline output also is chosen to be our "base" feature, i.e. a binary feature indicating whether a correct pronunciation is found in the ASR transcripts.

We experimented with all acoustic features listed in Section 4.1. In particular, our classifiers were trained on all the subsets of features listed, as well as those selected through the statistical significance test above, i.e. CoreFeats.

We explored two types of standard classifiers, since the dataset is relatively small: logistic regression (LR) and support vector machine (SVM). Hyperparameter search included the regularization coefficient $C \in [10^{-4}, 10^{-3}, ..., 10^{4}]$ for both LR and SVM, and we additionally experimented with both linear and RBF kernels for the SVM. We use cross validation with 5 folds in the training set to select the hyperparameters. Our models were implemented using the Scikit-learn toolkit (Pedregosa et al., 2011).

5. Results and Discussion

The baseline model (using string match on 1-best ASR output) turned out to be a very strong baseline. All our configurations without using this baseline (i.e. using only acoustic features) yielded very poor results, often comparable to random guessing (F1 ≈ 0.5). Results from experiments with all different combinations of {Librosa, GeMAPS, logit} features as described in Section 4.1 all showed similarly poor performances.

Using only CoreFeats did slightly better than random, but combining CoreFeats with the baseline indicator does not beat simply using the baseline. In fact, the predicted outputs from Baseline and Baseline+CoreFeats were identical.

Table 2 shows the best results with SVM (linear kernel, $C = 0.01$).

On the final test set, our best-performing classifier (Baseline+CoreFeats) obtained F1 score = 0.89 (precision = 0.93, recall = 0.86) and accuracy = 0.90. This result is similar to those on the validation set, likely thanks to similarly balanced data distributions.

[3] Raw "logit scores" are a bit of a misnomer since they are usually not normalized to sum up to 1 for general purposes, e.g. in inference.

Model	Precision	Recall	F1
Baseline	0.92	0.81	0.86
CoreFeats only	0.64	0.59	0.61
Baseline+CoreFeats	0.92	0.81	0.86

Table 2: Results of Classification on the Validation Set

To diagnose our results, we looked specifically at the set of samples where the results from our CoreFeats-only classifier differ from those using Baseline. Our motivation is to see whether particularly difficult samples, i.e. those Baseline got wrong, had any indicators that the acoustic features might have identified.

In both training and validation sets, using only CoreFeats (without baseline) performed better on the VNT set compared to BNT. Specifically, out of 1467 utterances in the training set where CoreFeats obtained correct predictions, 1023 are from VNT while 444 are from BNT. Similarly for the validation set, out of 214 correct predictions by CoreFeats, twice as many are from VNT than BNT (143 vs. 71). This pattern persists even when looking into the subset where CoreFeats managed to predict correctly those Baseline predicted incorrectly. In the validation set, while CoreFeats performed better than Baseline for only 15 utterances, only 2 are from BNT while the rest are from VNT. Anecdotally (from listening to a few samples), we observed that the BNT task involves isolated word naming while VNT elicits potentially longer, more sentence-like speech to include the verb being tested. We hypothesize that this is where acoustic features are likely more useful, as these longer speech samples exhibit more diverse prosodic phenomena easier to model by acoustic features (Tran, 2020).

Figures 1 and 2 show the histograms of subset of samples where the outputs of Baseline and CoreFeats classifiers differ. In the training set, it appears that acoustic features could potentially help identify additional true positives (correct naming responses). However, the majority of instances are correctly classified by Baseline, so it is not obvious that acoustic features could help in a significant way.

The similar analysis on the validation set shows a slightly different trend: here Baseline misses more incorrect responses, i.e. it failed to identify utterances with incorrect pronunciations/reading. Arguably this is the more interesting case where acoustic features should help: for example, while there might be a good string match between the ASR transcript and the true transcript, the acoustic characteristics of the utterance might help flag these as incorrect responses to help reduce misdiagnosis. However, again, the majority of cases are still correctly classified using Baseline.

This difference in behavior between the training and validations sets, coupled with the large difference in PER and FER as shown in Table 1, suggests that the pretrained ASR system might have overfitted on the training set.

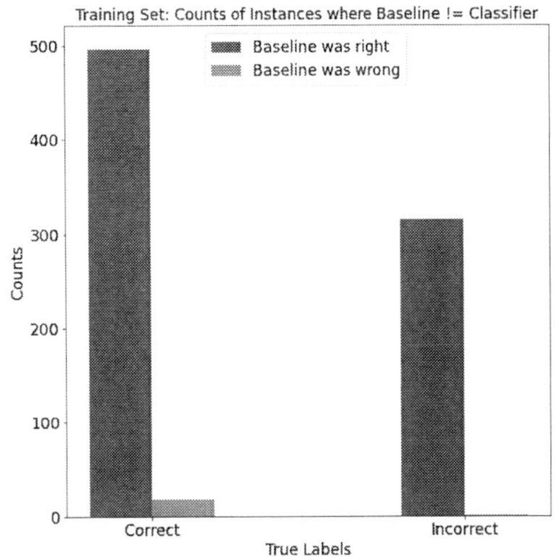

Figure 1: Distribution of samples where Baseline predictions are different from CoreFeats predictions; Training set.

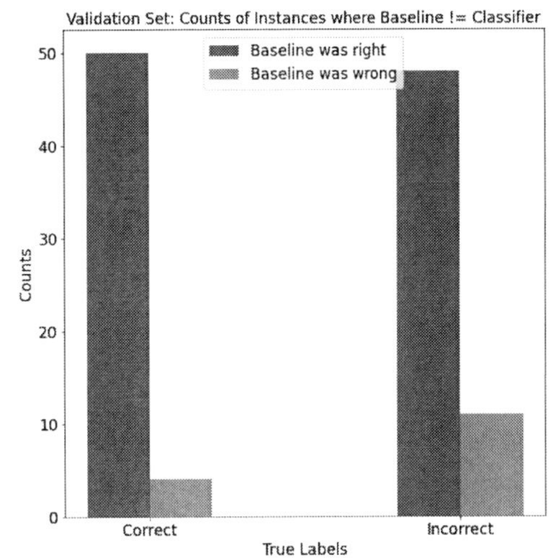

Figure 2: Distribution of samples where Baseline predictions are different from CoreFeats predictions; Validation set.

6. Potential Next Directions

Our first attempt at a simple system to classify correctness of naming responses in anomia diagnosis has yielded negative results so far. Specifically, the challenge seems to be two-fold: (1) acoustic feature selection and (2) over-reliance on robust ASR.

Regarding acoustic feature selection, it is largely unclear how to select the best set of features, despite a large amount of study dedicated to this area. Using acoustic features in this setting is also difficult both from the modeling (how to aggregate frame-level features to the utterance level representation) and the data quality (which features are robust to recording noise, dialects, age, etc.) perspectives. The dataset in this challenge is quite small, and the acoustic feature space is large. Perhaps redoing this feature analysis on a larger aphasia dataset might yield a different result.

Regarding ASR systems, the difference in both classification results and FER/PER between the training and validation sets highlights the difficulty in domain adaptation. One experiment we would have liked to try is to use several off-the-shelf pretrained ASR systems and devise heuristics for ensembling the results. For example, in addition to a Baseline as in this work, we could look at the differences in prediction and confidences of various ASR systems, and use these differences as another proxy the transcription quality.

Overall, from this small study, it appears that the robustness of ASR plays a more important role than acoustic feature exploration.

7. Conclusion

In this work, we focus on Task B: Correctness Evaluation of the PSST Challenge 2022. Our goal was to investigate whether using acoustic features in addition to ASR transcripts would improve correctness prediction. The motivation was that if acoustic features helped, this augmentation approach would only need a relatively good pretrained ASR system without further collecting costly annotations or additional data for fine-tuning ASR. Unfortunately, this was not the case, as our approach to using acoustic features could not improve over a simple baseline (string match between 1-best ASR output and acceptable pronunciations). However, we did find potential indicators of acoustic feature usefulness in tasks eliciting longer speech. Specifically, using acoustic features obtained better results in the verb naming test (VNT) than in the isolated noun naming test (BNT), likely because the former elicits longer, more sentence-like utterances.

Our results suggest that ASR robustness still plays critical role in this task, and that it is worth investing more effort in improving ASR for the domain of aphasic speech and language disorders in general.

8. Acknowledgements

We would like to thank the organizers of the PSST Challenge for initiating this effort and help raise awareness to this important problem in the speech and NLP community. We also thank the organizers for providing the data and baseline codes. We thank the anonymous reviewers for their helpful feedback.

9. Bibliographical References

Baevski, A., Zhou, Y., Mohamed, A., and Auli, M. (2020). wav2vec 2.0: A framework for self-supervised learning of speech representations. In H. Larochelle, et al., editors, *Advances in Neural Information Processing Systems*, volume 33, pages 12449–12460. Curran Associates, Inc.

de Cheveigné, A. and Kawahara, H. (2002). Yin, a fundamental frequency estimator for speech and music. *The Journal of the Acoustical Society of America*, 111 4:1917–30.

Eyben, F., Wöllmer, M., and Schuller, B. (2010). OpenSMILE: The Munich Versatile and Fast Open-Source Audio Feature Extractor. In *Proc. ACM Multimedia*, MM '10, pages 1459–1462, New York, NY, USA. Association for Computing Machinery.

Fraser, K. C., Rudzicz, F., and Rochon, E. (2013). Using text and acoustic features to diagnose progressive aphasia and its subtypes. In FrÃ©dÃ©ric Bimbot, et al., editors, *INTERSPEECH*, pages 2177–2181. ISCA.

Fraser, K. C., Meltzer, J. A., Graham, N. L., Leonard, C., Hirst, G., Black, S. E., and Rochon, E. (2014). Automated classification of primary progressive aphasia subtypes from narrative speech transcripts. *Cortex*, 55:43 – 60. Language, Computers and Cognitive Neuroscience.

Gale, R., Fleegle, M., Bedrick, S., and Fergadiotis, G. (2022). Dataset and tools for the PSST Challenge on Post-Stroke Speech Transcription, March. Project funded by the National Institute on Deafness and Other Communication Disorders grant number R01DC015999-04S1.

Kahn, J. G. and Ostendorf, M. (2012). Joint reranking of parsing and word recognition with automatic segmentation. *Computer Speech & Language*, 26(1):1–51.

Le, D., Licata, K., and Mower Provost, E. (2018). Automatic quantitative analysis of spontaneous aphasic speech. *Speech Communication*, 100:1–12.

Liu, A. T., Li, S.-W., and yi Lee, H. (2020a). TERA: Self-Supervised Learning of Transformer Encoder Representation for Speech.

Liu, A. T., Yang, S.-w., Chi, P.-H., Hsu, P.-c., and Lee, H.-y. (2020b). Mockingjay: Unsupervised Speech Representation Learning with Deep Bidirectional Transformer Encoders. *ICASSP 2020 - 2020 IEEE International Conference on Acoustics, Speech and Signal Processing (ICASSP)*, May.

MacWhinney, B., Fromm, D., Forbes, M., and Holland, A. (2011). AphasiaBank: Methods for Studying Discourse. *Aphasiology*, 25(11):1286–1307.

Marin, A. and Ostendorf, M. (2014). Domain adaptation for parsing in automatic speech recognition. In *Proc. ICASSP*, pages 6379–6383.

Mauch, M. and Dixon, S. (2014). Pyin: A fundamental frequency estimator using probabilistic threshold distributions. In *2014 IEEE International Conference on Acoustics, Speech and Signal Processing (ICASSP)*, pages 659–663.

McFee, B., Raffel, C., Liang, D., Ellis, D. P., McVicar, M., Battenberg, E., and Nieto, O. (2015). "librosa:

Audio and music signal analysis in python". In *Proceedings of the 14th python in science conference*, pages 18–25.

Pedregosa, F., Varoquaux, G., Gramfort, A., Michel, V., Thirion, B., Grisel, O., Blondel, M., Prettenhofer, P., Weiss, R., Dubourg, V., Vanderplas, J., Passos, A., Cournapeau, D., Brucher, M., Perrot, M., and Duchesnay, E. (2011). Scikit-learn: Machine learning in Python. *Journal of Machine Learning Research*, 12:2825–2830.

Roark, B., Mitchell, M., Hosom, J., Hollingshead, K., and Kaye, J. (2011). Spoken language derived measures for detecting mild cognitive impairment. *Audio, Speech, and Language Processing, IEEE Transactions on*, 19(7):2081–2090, Sept.

Shon, S., Pasad, A., Wu, F., Brusco, P., Artzi, Y., Livescu, K., and Han, K. J. (2021). SLUE: new benchmark tasks for spoken language understanding evaluation on natural speech. *CoRR*, abs/2111.10367.

Tran, T. and Ostendorf, M. (2021). Assessing the use of prosody in constituency parsing of imperfect transcripts. In *Proc. Interspeech*, pages 2626–2630.

Tran, T., Yuan, J., Liu, Y., and Ostendorf, M. (2019). On the Role of Style in Parsing Speech with Neural Models. In *Proc. Interspeech*, pages 4190–4194.

Tran, T. (2020). *Neural Models for Integrating Prosody in Spoken Language Understanding*. Ph.D. thesis, University of Washington.

Yang, S.-W., Chi, P.-H., Chuang, Y.-S., Lai, C.-I. J., Lakhotia, K., Lin, Y. Y., Liu, A. T., Shi, J., Chang, X., Lin, G.-T., Huang, T.-H., Tseng, W.-C., Lee, K.-T., Liu, D.-R., Huang, Z., Dong, S., Li, S.-W., Watanabe, S., Mohamed, A., and Lee, H.-Y. (2021). SUPERB: Speech Processing Universal PERformance Benchmark. In *Proc. Interspeech 2021*, pages 1194–1198.

Yngve, V. H. (1960). A model and an hypothesis for language structure. *Proceedings of the American Philosophical Society*, 104:444–466.

Zhou, L., Fraser, K. C., and Rudzicz, F. (2016). Speech recognition in Alzheimer's disease and in its assessment. *Interspeech 2016*, pages 1948–1952.

Proceedings of the RaPID-4 @LREC 2022, pages 62–70
Marseille, 25 June 2022

Speech Data Augmentation for Improving Phoneme Transcriptions of Aphasic Speech using wav2vec 2.0 for the PSST Challenge

Birger Moëll*, Jim O'Regan*, Shivam Mehta, Ambika Kirkland, Harm Lameris, Joakim Gustafsson, Jonas Beskow
Division of Speech Music and Hearing, KTH Royal Institute of Technology
{bmoell, joregan, smehta, kirkland, lameris, jkgu, beskow}@kth.se

Abstract

As part of the PSST challenge, we explore how data augmentations, data sources, and model size affect phoneme transcription accuracy on speech produced by individuals with aphasia. We evaluate model performance in terms of feature error rate (FER) and phoneme error rate (PER). We find that data augmentations techniques, such as pitch shift, improve model performance. Additionally, increasing the size of the model decreases FER and PER. Our experiments also show that adding manually-transcribed speech from non-aphasic speakers (TIMIT) improves performance when Room Impulse Response is used to augment the data. The best performing model combines aphasic and non-aphasic data and has a 21.0% PER and a 9.2% FER, a relative improvement of 9.8% compared to the baseline model on the primary outcome measurement. We show that data augmentation, larger model size, and additional non-aphasic data sources can be helpful in improving automatic phoneme recognition models for people with aphasia.

Keywords: aphasia, phoneme transcription, wav2vec 2.0, speech, phonemes, data augmentation, speech data augmentation

1. Introduction

Aphasia is a dysfunction of the ability to understand or produce language caused by damage to brain regions used for speech (Damasio, 1992). A common, broad distinction made in classifying different forms of aphasia is between fluent and non-fluent aphasia (Feyereisen et al., 1991). While those with fluent aphasias, such as Wernicke's aphasia, are typically able to produce syntactically and phonetically well-formed utterances, non-fluent aphasias such as Broca's aphasia and transcortical motor aphasia are characterized by difficulties in selecting and ordering phonemes and forming syntactically complex utterances. However, while most clinicians use fluency classifications in their diagnoses, the distinction is not well-defined (Gordon, 1998), and there is evidence that even so-called fluent aphasias involve errors in phoneme production (Blumstein et al., 1980; Kurowski and Blumstein, 2016; Vijayan and Gandour, 1995; Holloman and Drummond, 1991), possibly as a result of impaired acoustic-phonological control (Robson et al., 2012).

This phenomenon of inserting, deleting or substituting phonemes is known as phonemic paraphasia. Examples of this based on a related yet distinct clinical population with similar symptomatology include *lat* for *bat*, or *dake* for *drake*. The errors are concentrated on nouns and verbs, and occur evenly on vowels, single consonants, and consonant clusters (Dalton et al., 2018). For consonants, erroneous productions most commonly differ from the target phoneme by a single phonetic feature, though errors containing multiple phonetic feature differences occur as well. Substitution errors occur more commonly than insertion or deletion errors. These unintended phoneme substitutions are believed to be caused by a cascading activation of a target and a competitor phonetic segment with a speech output showing properties of both the target and competitor phonemes (Kurowski and Blumstein, 2016).

Several studies have shown that reliable phonemic annotation can be beneficial in the diagnosis of aphasia, and its distinction from acquired apraxia of speech (Cunningham et al., 2016), with phoneme distortion error rates being lower for patients with phonemic paraphasia. Error profiles can also be used as an indicator for the possibility of remediation of these phonological errors, as individuals displaying phonological errors display less improvement than individuals displaying motoric errors on a repetition training task (Buchwald et al., 2017). Finally, phonemic transcriptions are an important component in the development of individualized intervention plans for patients with aphasia (Abel et al., 2007). The ability to automatically transcribe the speech of aphasic patients would allow for a richer profile of data for each individual with less burden on the clinician. Automatic speech recognition (ASR) has been proposed as a valuable tool for developing effective speech therapy interventions (Jamal et al., 2017), but achieving robust, high-accuracy ASR for aphasic speech remains a challenge. Conventional ASR systems struggle with aphasic speech because of the irregularities of aphasic speech, so aphasiatic ASR systems needs to be trained specifically on aphasic speech.

In this paper we explore how speech data augmentations, data sources and model parameters can be optimized to create a robust, high accuracy phoneme transcription model for aphasic speech. We hope to give

* Equal contribution.

the reader an intuition about the steps involved in the creation of such a model with the aim of describing our work in such detail that it can be easily reproduced.

1.1. Phoneme Feature Vectors

The goal of the Post-Stroke Speech Transcription (PSST) challenge is to create accurate automatic transcriptions of phonemes produced by speakers with aphasia. To this end, we use phonemic feature vectors in order to more precisely quantify the degree to which a produced phoneme differs from a target phoneme. A phoneme feature vector maps phonemes to their articulatory correlates (Chomsky and Halle, 1968). The features correspond to aspects such as vocal tract cavity configurations, place and manner of articulation, glottal states of sounds, and tongue body positions. A value of [+] for a given feature indicates that the feature is present, [-] indicates that it is absent, and [0] indicates that a phoneme is unmarked with respect to that feature (i.e., the feature is not relevant for defining the phoneme). For example, the consonant /f/ is [- voice] while the consonant /v/ is [+ voice]. Feature error rate (FER) allows for a more fine-grained analysis of errors in aphasic speech, penalizing errors that sound more similar to the target less severely, in contrast to phoneme error rate (PER), which does not indicate how dissimilar a produced phoneme is from a target phoneme and treats all incorrect productions equally.

1.2. Models for Aphasia Prediction

Recently, Self Supervised Learning (SSL) has attracted a lot of interest in all data modalities because of the high cost of annotation of data; models like BERT (Devlin et al., 2019), SimCLR (Chen et al., 2020b) have shown the ability to learn in a self supervised setting, either by predicting the next token or by contrastive learning. SSL is especially useful in the audio modality, mainly because of the presence of an abundance of unannotated audio data on the internet. With recent advances in deep learning, architectures like HuBERT (Hsu et al., 2021) and wav2vec 2.0 (Baevski et al., 2020) have shown results on par with supervised learning methods while reducing the overhead of gathering annotated data. In this work, we explore wav2vec 2.0 Base and Large models with various data augmentation methodologies to transfer the speech recognition knowledge of the pre-trained model to speech generated by a person with aphasia.

1.3. Data Augmentation

Many deep learning pipelines incorporate data augmentation as an important technique to achieve state-of-the-art results (Chen et al., 2020a). It is known to improve generalisation and learn translation invariance, which is useful for the models to learn the underlying structure of data instead of specific aspects of the training samples, resulting in better performance (Worrall et al., 2017). It has shown-state-of-the-art results in

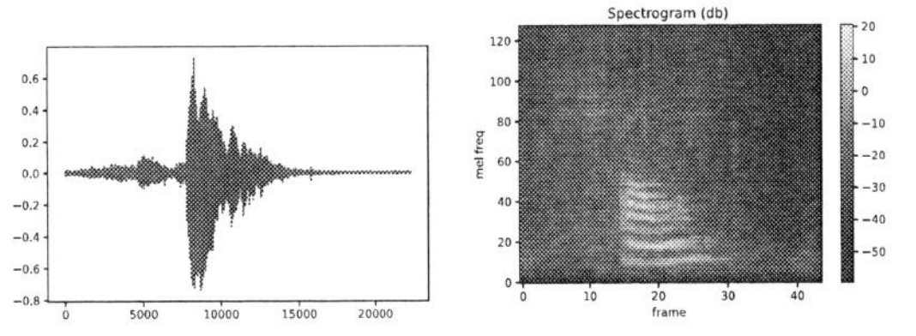

(a) Waveform (b) Mel Spectrogram

Figure 1: A sample from PSST dataset

different modalities such as images (Krizhevsky et al., 2012) and text (Feng et al., 2021). Data augmentation has also been applied successfully in the audio modality, resulting in major improvement in speech classification and speech recognition (Tak et al., 2022). In this paper we augment the audio data in the waveform domain, giving us more training samples while maintaining the i.i.d assumption of the empirical data samples.

2. Data

2.1. Datasets

In our experiments we explored how combining and augmenting data could help improve our predictions. We explored how training on the PSST, TIMIT, and Common Voice datasets affected model performance. Data statistics are summarised in Table 1.

2.1.1. PSST

The PSST challenge dataset consists of a subset of the AphasiaBank data (MacWhinney et al., 2011) annotated with manually transcribed phonemes and made available through the python package psst-data (Gale et al., 2022). The data consists of 2298 utterances in the training dataset, 341 utterances in the validation dataset and 652 utterances in the test dataset. A sample from the dataset is visualised in Figure 1. Speakers with several different types of aphasia, as categorized by the Western Aphasia Battery (WAB) (Risser and Spreen, 1985), were represented in the training dataset. Of the 73 speakers, 26 had anomic aphasia, 18 had conduction aphasia, 18 had Broca's aphasia, 8 had Wernicke's aphasia, 2 had transcortical motor aphasia, and one speaker was classified as not aphasic based on their WAB results.

2.1.2. TIMIT

TIMIT (Garofolo et al., 1993) is the most commonly used dataset for phoneme recognition, as it is one of the few datasets available with phoneme labels (Lopes and Perdigao, 2011). Although TIMIT, like the PSST data, uses a phoneme set based on ARPAbet, it is based on a revised version. While, for the most part, there is a simple mapping to the version of ARPAbet used in the PSST data, there are three items[1] that do not map exactly. To avoid introducing imprecision into the training data, we elected to choose only segments that did

[1] dx (flap), nx (nasal flap), and q (glottal stop).

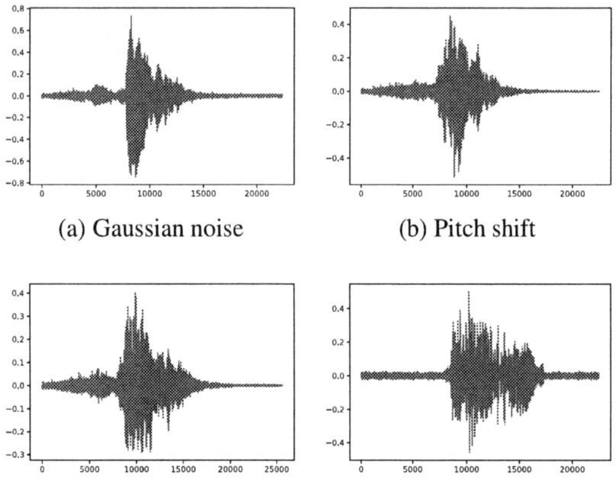

(a) Gaussian noise (b) Pitch shift

(c) Time stretch (d) Voice Conversion

Figure 2: Effect of data augmentation in the waveform

not include these three items; as the number of segments was quite low, we also drew from the test set. In total, 1414 segments were used (1016 from train, 398 from test)[2].

2.1.3. Common Voice

Common Voice is a crowdsourced dataset of speakers of different languages. We used a subset of the English Common Voice with automatically added ARPA-phonemes using the open source python g2p package.[3]

Dataset	Number of segments	Manually transcribed	Audio (mins.)
PSST	2298	Yes	166
TIMIT	1414	Yes	64
Common Voice	15777	No	1559

Table 1: Dataset overview

2.2. Data Augmentation

We used the open source audiomentations library[4] to augment the PSST data as well as other datasets used in training. In our data augmentation we strove both to augment the available samples of the PSST Dataset to increase their number still keeping the dataset balanced and similar to the original PSST dataset, and to induce the noisy artefacts of PSST dataset into TIMIT. Figure 2 shows the effect of different type of waveform augmentation on the waveform of a sample audio and Figure 3 shows the effect of the same sample in the mel spectrogram domain.

[2]A list of IDs used, along with a fine-tuned model, is included in `https://huggingface.co/jimregan/psst-partial-timit`.

[3]`https://pypi.org/project/g2p-en/`

[4]`https://github.com/iver56/audiomentations`

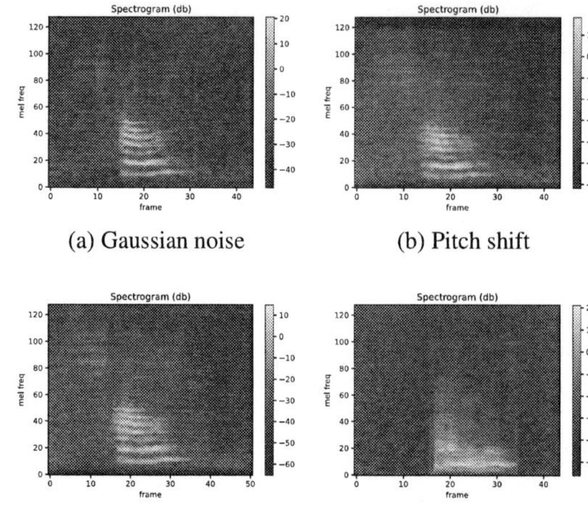

(a) Gaussian noise (b) Pitch shift

(c) Time stretch (d) Voice Conversion

Figure 3: Effect of data augmentation in mel spectrogram

2.2.1. Gaussian noise

Though seemingly paradoxical, adding noise to the data acts as regularization and improves generalization (Bishop, 1995). Gaussian noise is a common data augmentation: at each time a datapoint is exposed to the model a stochastic noise sampled from a standard Gaussian $\mathcal{N}(0, 1)$ is added to it making it different. Noise amplitude σ is a hyperparameter uniformly distributed over the range $\sigma \sim U(0.005, 0.015)$. The newly generated samples after augmentation can be represented as:

$$x(t) = x(t) + \sigma \times \mathcal{N}(0, 1)$$

The effect of this data augmentation is visible in Figure 2a for the waveform and Figure 3a for the mel spectrogram.

2.2.2. Time stretch

Time stretch is a data augmentation where the audio file is either sped up or slowed down without affecting the pitch. In theory this would improve generalization by making the model more independent of speaking rate. Generally γ is the stretch factor, if $\gamma > 1$ then the speed of the audio is increased and if $\gamma < 1$ then the speed of the audio is reduced. The stretch factor is uniformly distributed over $\gamma \sim U(0.8, 1.25)$. The augmentation results of this transformation on the original waveform can be seen in Figure 2c for the waveform and in Figure 3c for the mel spectrogram.

2.2.3. Pitch shift

We use pitch shift to vary the pitch of the signal. This improves generalization by helping learn a latent space independent of fundamental frequency. Pitch shift modifies the pitch of the audio sample either by raising or lowering the pitch while keeping the duration of the audio unchanged (Salamon and Bello, 2017). It is, in some ways, an inverse of the time stretch augmentation. We shifted individual samples by n semitones without changing the tempo where $n \sim U(-4, 4)$. Figure 2b and Figure 3b visualise the effect of this transformation in both the waveform and the mel spectrogram.

2.2.4. Voice Conversion

We used the official open source implementation[5] of (Chou et al., 2019) to do one-shot voice conversion of audio files to improve the variability in data and make the data more speaker independent. They use a Variational Auto Encoder (Kingma and Welling, 2013) as a generative model with two encoders, where one is a context encoder while the other is a speaker encoder, with the use of Instance Normalization (IN) (Ulyanov et al., 2016) and Adaptive Instance Normalization (AdaIN) (Huang and Belongie, 2017) they synthesise the text conditioned on the target speaker representation. In our experiments, for all of the audio files of each speaker, the target audio file was chosen at random from all other speakers and was augmented to their speaker characteristics. This gave us varied samples of the same utterance but with different speaker characteristics. Since this method looks for voiced segments in the mel domain, output from these are shorter than others, but for visualisation only we have padded it with Gaussian noise to make it visually similar to 2.2.1. This padding was not used while training the model. The effect of this can be seen in both the waveform Figure 2d and the mel spectrogram Figure 3d.

2.2.5. Room Impulse Response

Room Impulse Response (RIR) augmentation is a technique for simulating room acoustics (Habets, 2006) by adding artificial reverberation. Given the variability in the acoustics of the recording environments of the AphasiaBank dataset, RIR might make it possible to bridge the acoustic gap when using othe datasets. The audiomentations library uses a wave-based technique, where recordings with the reverberance qualities of a particular room have been isolated and applied to the input using a convolution operation. We used two sets of publicly available impulse responses: EchoThief[6] and the MIT McDermott dataset[7], from which a recording is selected at random for application to the utterance.

2.3. Data Processing

All data was processed to work with the fairseq (Ott et al., 2019) framework in order to standardize the training process.

2.4. Model Architecture

For training we chose to fine-tune wav2vec 2.0. We experimented with Base and Large model. Although later models like Large (LV-60k) has shown better results we wanted to focus our experiments on data augmentations and how they affect model performance.

[5]https://github.com/jjery2243542/adaptive_voice_conversion

[6]http://tulrich.com/recording/ir_capture/

[7]https://mcdermottlab.mit.edu/Reverb/IR_Survey.html

wav2vec 2.0 Model	**Base**	**Large**
Transformer blocks	12	24
Attention heads	8	16
Model dimension	768	1024
Inner dimension	3072	4096

Table 2: wav2vec 2.0 model variants and hyperparameters.

2.4.1. Wav2vec 2.0

wav2vec 2.0 (W2V2) is an architecture proposed in Baevski et al. (2020) that uses self-supervision in the audio domain to create audio vectors that can be used in training. The model consists of a multi-layer convolution feature encoder that takes as input raw audio and outputs latent speech representations. These latent representations are then fed to a Transformer to build representations that has the ability to capture information from the whole length of the sequence. This is done through a masking function in the audio domain. For our training, we chose to focus on the wav2vec 2.0 base model and the wav2vec 2.0 large model, to make a comparison of how model size affects and interacts with other techniques used while training. The model hyperparameters are mentioned in Table 2.

2.4.2. Fine-tuning

Pre-trained base models are fine-tuned for phoneme (and speech) recognition by adding a linear projection on top of the model, used to classify into the number of tokens found in the phoneme vocabulary (42).

2.4.3. Language Model

Language modelling refers to the use of various statistical and probabilistic methods to estimate the probability of a sequence of words. Formally, we can formulate the task of language modelling as

$$
\begin{aligned}
p(x_1, \ldots, x_t) &= p(x_1).p(x_2|x_1).\ldots.p(x_t|x_{<t}) \\
&= \sum_{i=1}^{i=t} p(x_i|x_{i-1}, \ldots, x_1)
\end{aligned}
$$

where x_i are the tokens in a sentence.

2.5. Evaluation

2.5.1. Phoneme Error Rate

Phoneme error rate is the number of phoneme errors (edits, insertions, and substitutions) divided by the number of phonemes in the reference transcript, calculated using the Levenshtein distance (Levenshtein, 1966).

$$PER = 100 * \frac{\#Edits}{\#Phones}$$

2.5.2. Feature Error Rate

Feature error rate is the number of phoneme feature errors where phonemes which differ by fewer features are considered more correct. Transcribed phonemes are converted into phoneme feature vectors in order to calculate the feature error rate using the Levenshtein distance.

$$FER = 100 * \frac{\#Edits}{\#Features}$$

3. Experiment

In order to improve reproducibility we kept the hyperparameters constant using the same parameters as those used in the psst-baseline training. [8] We trained in a warm state manner with 4000 warm updates keeping learning rate at 5e-05 using the Adam optimizer to train the model.

Table 3 contains a summary of the best performing models.

3.1. Base Models

Two pre-trained wav2vec 2.0 models were used as base models for all experiments: "wav2vec 2.0 Base" and "wav2vec 2.0 Large" are the "No finetuning" versions of the models, as found in the fairseq GitHub repository[9].

3.2. PSST Augmentations

We augmented the PSST dataset with augmentations defined in Section 2.2. We used Gaussian noise as a data augmentation for the base model and pitch shift and time stretch independently as augmentations for two large models. There was a 50% probability of the data being augmented, with the augmented dataset doubling in size compared to the non-augmented data with on average 25% augmented data, 25% overlapped data and 50% consisting of the original data.

3.3. PSST with Augmented TIMIT

As speech recognition models can often be sensitive to differences in acoustic conditions; it is not automatically the case that additional data will lead to an improvement when there is a difference in recording conditions. Because of the mismatch of recording conditions between TIMIT, which was recorded in clean conditions, and the PSST data, which was not, we experimented with augmenting the TIMIT data alone, to attempt to artificially match the PSST data. As well as Gaussian noise, pitch shift, and time stretch, we also added RIR to match the dry, studio conditions of TIMIT to PSST.

[8] https://github.com/PSST-Challenge/psstbaseline

[9] https://github.com/pytorch/fairseq/tree/main/examples/wav2vec/

3.4. Language Model

To explore the effect of the language model, we augmented the transcription data of the combined PSST and TIMIT datasets with the CMU Pronouncing Dictionary (CMUdict)[10], across configurations of 4-, 5-, and 6-gram models[11]. We used two versions of the PSST+TIMIT data: unmodified, and with silence tokens removed (and the spoken noise token, in the case of PSST); to emulate the silence between words with CMUdict, we used the unmodified entries, entries with a silence token added at the start, added at the end, and added at both start and end, with an additional "all silences" configuration which combined all configurations.

4. Results

The results of our experiments are summarised in Table 3 and Figure 4. While evaluating on the PSST validation dataset we found improved scores for several techniques.

While some training heuristics–such as adding an n-gram language model and using data augmentation such as Voice Cloning, Gaussian Noise and Time-stretch–had results comparable to the baseline trained on PSST dataset with wav2vec 2.0 (FER: 10.2, PER: 22.2), other configurations lead to improved results.

The wav2vec 2.0 large model trained on the PSST data had a relative improvement of 5.86% for PER (20.9 vs 22.2) and 3.92% for FER (9.8 vs 10.2).

The wav2vec 2.0 large model trained on the PSST data with pitch shift improved the scores by 4.5% for PER (21.2 vs 22.2) and 6.86% for FER (9.5 vs 10.2).

The wav2vec 2.0 large model trained on the PSST data with pitch shift + TIMIT improved the scores by 4.5% for PER (21.2 vs 22.2) and 7.3% for FER (9.7 vs 10.2).

The wav2vec 2.0 base model trained on the PSST data + TIMIT with RIR achieved the best score of the various combinations of augmentations described in section 3.3, improving the scores by 1.8% for PER (21.8 vs 22.2) and 5.88% for FER (9.6 vs 10.2).

The wav2vec 2.0 large model trained on the PSST data + TIMIT with RIR achieved the best overall score, improving the results by 5.41% for PER (21.0 vs 22.2) and 9.8% for FER (9.2 vs 10.2).

As part of our experiments we also reproduced the baseline model. Our reproduced baseline had lower scores than the PSST Baseline by 1.96% for PER (10.4 vs 10.2) and 4.05% for FER (23.1 vs 22.2). The difference could be caused by initial weight randomization. We choose to compare all our models to the original baseline model.

[10] https://github.com/cmusphinx/cmudict

[11] 6 is the maximum number of n-grams supported by the default configuration of the language model library used by the PSST Challenge scripts.

Name	Data	Model	FER	PER
PSST Baseline	PSST	Base	10.2%	22.2%
Reproduced Baseline	PSST	Base	10.4%	23.1%
Common Voice	Common Voice phonemes	Base	61.8%	91.6%
Baseline + TIMIT RIR	PSST Partial TIMIT with RIR	Base	9.6%	21.8%
Gaussian Noise (DA)	PSST with Gaussian Noise	Base	9.9%	22.9%
W2V2 Large	PSST	Large	9.8%	**20.9%**
W2V2 Large Voice Clone	PSST + Voice clone	Large	10.3%	22.7%
W2V2 Large Time-Stretch	PSST Time Stretch	Large	10.0%	21.2%
W2V2 Large Pitch-Shift	PSST Pitch Shift	Large	9.5%	21.2%
W2V2 Pitch-Shift + TIMIT RIR	PSST Pitch Shift + TIMIT RIR	Large	9.7%	21.2%
W2V2 Large + TIMIT RIR	PSST + TIMIT RIR	Large	**9.2%**	21.0%

Table 3: Experimentation results with different combinations of model and augmentations

Furthermore, we evaluated training on Common Voice and TIMIT without PSST, finding that these models were not successful at aphasic phoneme recognition without fine-tuning on aphasic speech. We also continued fine-tuning Common Voice on PSST with poor results. The poor results on Common Voice could be related to the automatic phoneme transcriptions which might not have been comparable to manually transcribed phonemes.

Several models showed improvements in PER without improvements in FER. One hypothesis is that this is due to the manner of calculation of FER versus PER per phoneme, PER has a binary outcome whereas FER is averaged over 20 features hence leading to less variation in the score for FER.

4.1. Language Models

The best performing language model, 5-gram with silences removed from PSST and TIMIT, but with CMUdict data with silence tokens added at the end, achieved PER of 22.1%, compared with the baseline of PSST and nonaugmented TIMIT without a language model (PER 22.5%). No difference in FER was observed with any language model configuration. A plot of the results of this language model and a selection of the results from section 3.3 can be viewed in figure 4.

4.2. Model Availability

The models are available for download on Huggingface[12].

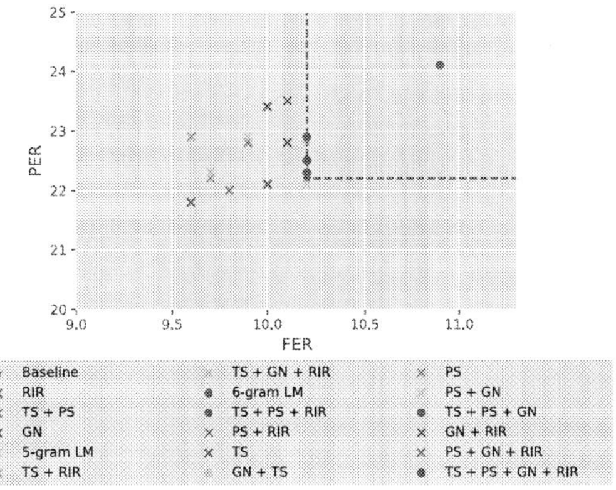

Figure 4: Sample results of TIMIT augmentation and language model experiments, using Gaussian Noise (GN), Time Stretch (TS), Pitch Shift (PS), and Room Impulse Response (RIR). LM results are on PSST/TIMIT with silences removed, augmented with CMUdict with appended silence tokens. Results to the left of the vertical line represent improvements in FER, while results below the horizontal line represent improvements in PER.

5. Discussion

In this paper, we looked at the challenges of the current Automatic Speech Recognition (ASR) techniques for the low-resource task of aphasic phoneme recognition, and devised heuristics for improving the phoneme transcriptions.

Training with a larger baseline model was one of the most straightforward ways to improve performance. In general, all the models trained with wav2vec 2.0 Large outperformed similar models trained with wav2vec 2.0 Base. This is in line with the current trend in deep learning, where larger self-supervised transformer models outperform the state of the art by keeping architecture similar while increasing model size. However, training on larger models has several drawbacks, one being increased training and inference time, another being the need for specialised GPUs that might be expensive to acquire or use. If computation is a bottleneck, it might be sensible to start by training a smaller model with different parameters and later train a larger model after good parameters have been found that improve performance.

Data augmentations on PSST was another technique that improved the performance. Pitch shift was the most useful augmentation technique when outside data sources were not used, with models using pitch shift showing good results especially on FER. Pitch shift transformation could be viewed as a transformation of

[12] https://huggingface.co/birgermoell

the vocal tract length and vocal fold of the speaker, which could help the model to generalise the difference between phonemic features and make the model more speaker independent. Given more time, experiences with pitch shift parameters might have the potential to improve accuracy further, in line with previous research (Salamon and Bello, 2017).

While working with data augmentation it is important that the underlying structure of the data is preserved, i.e., data augmentation should aim to help the model learn by augmenting features in the dataset, but not change the features so much that the underlying signal in the data gets corrupted. Voice cloning was an experiment where the data augmentation might have failed in this regard and the augmented samples had, in general, a lower pitch than the originals. When working with data augmentation, we believe that an inspection of the augmented data itself is a good first step in determining if the data will be useful for training. Here, common sense reasoning by a person knowledgeable in the field should suffice. If the data sounds reasonable, it has the potential to be helpful for improving model performance. This might seem obvious, but in the paradigm of large training sets and large models we still want to emphasize the importance of keeping a human in the loop.

A limitation in our work is the small size of the PSST dataset and the modest improvements we made compared to the baseline. The small dataset size makes it harder to determine how well our models have generalised. When working with deep learning models it is always hard to determine how parameters interact and we think it is sensible to view this work as a way to understand data augmentation in the aphasic phoneme domain rather than seeing it as a recipe for achieving state of the art.

An interesting scientific question is: to what degree do aphasic phonemic speech models improve by training on different data sources consisting of non-aphasic speech?

We found that training a model only on Common Voice or TIMIT was not sufficient to get a working model. This shows that at least in our experiment some part of the data needs to be aphasic. Furthermore, we continued fine-tuning on PSST from the model trained on Common Voice with limited results. This might be because Common Voice was automatically transcribed, but it may be related to the order of training.

In our experiment we found that the best performing model trained on TIMIT + PSST is close in performance to the best performing model trained only on PSST data. Here, data augmentations on TIMIT using RIR to make the data sound similar to PSST clearly helped performance by bringing the datasets more into alignment.

In theory, a similarly performing model that is trained on both aphasic and non-aphasic speech is preferable, as it has the potential to generalise better. Since our best performing model uses both aphasic and non-aphasic speech, a fair conclusion is that non-aphasic speech prepared in the proper format is a data source augmentation worth exploring when working with aphasic data.

A well-functioning phonetic and feature error prediction model for aphasia appears a promising way forward in order to build automated electronic tools for aphasia recovery.

Improved understanding of aphasia through automated tools for testing might also help determine which individuals are most helped by specific interventions.

6. Conclusion

In conclusion, our paper has shown that data augmentation, larger model size and additional non-aphasic data sources can be helpful in improving automatic phoneme recognition models for people with aphasia.

7. Acknowledgements

The results of this work and the tools used will be made more widely accessible through the national infrastructure Språkbanken Tal under funding from the Swedish research Council (2017-00626). We would like to thank the 509 scientific community for their support of our work. This research was also supported by the Swedish Research Council project Connected (VR-2019-05003) and partially supported by the Wallenberg AI, Autonomous Systems and Software Program (WASP) funded by the Knut and Alice Wallenberg Foundation and funded by Swedish Foundation of Strategic Research (SSF), project EACare under Grant No RIT15-0107.

8. Bibliographical References

Abel, S., Willmes, K., and Huber, W. (2007). Model-oriented naming therapy: Testing predictions of a connectionist model. *Aphasiology*, 21(5):411–447.

Baevski, A., Zhou, Y., Mohamed, A., and Auli, M. (2020). wav2vec 2.0: A framework for self-supervised learning of speech representations. *Advances in Neural Information Processing Systems*, 33:12449–12460.

Bishop, C. M. (1995). Training with Noise is Equivalent to Tikhonov Regularization. *Neural Computation*, 7(1):108–116, 01.

Blumstein, S. E., Cooper, W. E., Goodglass, H., Statlender, S., and Gottlieb, J. (1980). Production deficits in aphasia: A voice-onset time analysis. *Brain and language*, 9(2):153–170.

Buchwald, A., Gagnon, B., and Miozzo, M. (2017). Identification and remediation of phonological and motor errors in acquired sound production impairment. *Journal of Speech, Language, and Hearing Research*, 60(6S):1726–1738.

Chen, S., Dobriban, E., and Lee, J. (2020a). A group-theoretic framework for data augmentation. *Advances in Neural Information Processing Systems*, 33:21321–21333.

Chen, T., Kornblith, S., Norouzi, M., and Hinton, G. (2020b). A simple framework for contrastive learning of visual representations. In Hal Daumé III et al., editors, *Proceedings of the 37th International Conference on Machine Learning*, volume 119 of *Proceedings of Machine Learning Research*, pages 1597–1607. PMLR, 13–18 Jul.

Chomsky, N. and Halle, M. (1968). The sound pattern of english.

Chou, J.-C., chieh Yeh, C., and yi Lee, H. (2019). One-shot voice conversion by separating speaker and content representations with instance normalization. In *INTERSPEECH*.

Cunningham, K. T., Haley, K. L., and Jacks, A. (2016). Speech sound distortions in aphasia and apraxia of speech: Reliability and diagnostic significance. *Aphasiology*, 30(4):396–413.

Dalton, S. G. H., Shultz, C., Henry, M. L., Hillis, A. E., and Richardson, J. D. (2018). Describing phonological paraphasias in three variants of primary progressive aphasia. *American journal of speech-language pathology*, 27(1S):336–349.

Damasio, A. R. (1992). Aphasia. *New England Journal of Medicine*, 326(8):531–539.

Devlin, J., Chang, M.-W., Lee, K., and Toutanova, K. (2019). BERT: Pre-training of deep bidirectional transformers for language understanding. In *Proceedings of the 2019 Conference of the North American Chapter of the Association for Computational Linguistics: Human Language Technologies, Volume 1 (Long and Short Papers)*, pages 4171–4186, Minneapolis, Minnesota, June. Association for Computational Linguistics.

Feng, S. Y., Gangal, V., Wei, J., Chandar, S., Vosoughi, S., Mitamura, T., and Hovy, E. (2021). A survey of data augmentation approaches for NLP. In *Findings of the Association for Computational Linguistics: ACL-IJCNLP 2021*, pages 968–988, Online, August. Association for Computational Linguistics.

Feyereisen, P., Pillon, A., and Partz, M.-P. d. (1991). On the measures of fluency in the assessment of spontaneous speech production by aphasic subjects. *Aphasiology*, 5(1):1–21.

Gale, R., Fleegle, M., Bedrick, S., and Fergadiotis, G. (2022). Dataset and tools for the PSST Challenge on Post- Stroke Speech Transcription, March. Project funded by the National Institute on Deafness and Other Communication Disorders grant number R01DC015999-04S1.

Garofolo, J. S., Lamel, L. F., Fisher, W. M., Pallett, D. S., Dahlgren, N. L., Zue, V., and Fiscus, J. G. (1993). TIMIT Acoustic-Phonetic Continuous Speech Corpus. Type: dataset.

Gordon, J. K. (1998). The fluency dimension in aphasia. *Aphasiology*, 12(7-8):673–688.

Habets, E. A. (2006). Room impulse response generator. *Technische Universiteit Eindhoven, Tech. Rep*, 2(2.4):1.

Holloman, A. L. and Drummond, S. S. (1991). Perceptual and acoustical analyses of phonemic paraphasias in nonfluent and fluent dysphasia. *Journal of communication disorders*, 24(4):301–312.

Hsu, W.-N., Tsai, Y.-H. H., Bolte, B., Salakhutdinov, R., and Mohamed, A. (2021). Hubert: How much can a bad teacher benefit asr pre-training? In *ICASSP 2021 - 2021 IEEE International Conference on Acoustics, Speech and Signal Processing (ICASSP)*, pages 6533–6537.

Huang, X. and Belongie, S. (2017). Arbitrary style transfer in real-time with adaptive instance normalization. In *Proceedings of the IEEE International Conference on Computer Vision (ICCV)*, Oct.

Jamal, N., Shanta, S., Mahmud, F., and Sha'abani, M. (2017). Automatic speech recognition (asr) based approach for speech therapy of aphasic patients: A review. In *AIP Conference Proceedings*, volume 1883, page 020028. AIP Publishing LLC.

Kingma, D. P. and Welling, M. (2013). Auto-encoding variational bayes.

Krizhevsky, A., Sutskever, I., and Hinton, G. E. (2012). Imagenet classification with deep convolutional neural networks. In F. Pereira, et al., editors, *Advances in Neural Information Processing Systems*, volume 25. Curran Associates, Inc.

Kurowski, K. and Blumstein, S. E. (2016). Phonetic basis of phonemic paraphasias in aphasia: Evidence for cascading activation. *Cortex*, 75:193–203.

Levenshtein, V. I. (1966). Binary codes capable of correcting deletions, insertions, and reversals. In *Soviet physics doklady*, volume 10, pages 707–710. Soviet Union.

Lopes, C. and Perdigao, F. (2011). *Phoneme Recognition on the TIMIT Database*. IntechOpen, June.

MacWhinney, B., Fromm, D., Forbes, M., and Holland, A. (2011). Aphasiabank: Methods for studying discourse. *Aphasiology*, 25(11):1286–1307.

Ott, M., Edunov, S., Baevski, A., Fan, A., Gross, S., Ng, N., Grangier, D., and Auli, M. (2019). fairseq: A fast, extensible toolkit for sequence modeling. In *Proceedings of NAACL-HLT 2019: Demonstrations*.

Risser, A. H. and Spreen, O. (1985). The western aphasia battery. *Journal of clinical and experimental neuropsychology*, 7(4):463–470.

Robson, H., Sage, K., and Ralph, M. A. L. (2012). Wernicke's aphasia reflects a combination of acoustic-phonological and semantic control deficits: a case-series comparison of wernicke's aphasia, semantic dementia and semantic aphasia. *Neuropsychologia*, 50(2):266–275.

Salamon, J. and Bello, J. P. (2017). Deep convolutional neural networks and data augmentation for environmental sound classification. *IEEE Signal processing letters*, 24(3):279–283.

Tak, H., Todisco, M., Wang, X., Jung, J.-w., Yamagishi, J., and Evans, N. (2022). Automatic speaker verification spoofing and deepfake detection using wav2vec 2.0 and data augmentation. In ISCA, editor, *Submitted to ODYSSEY 2022, The Speaker Language Recognition Workshop, June 28th-July 1st, 2022, Beijing, China*, Beijing. © ISCA. Personal use of this material is permitted. The definitive version of this paper was published in Submitted to ODYSSEY 2022, The Speaker Language Recognition Workshop, June 28th-July 1st, 2022, Beijing, China and is available at :.

Ulyanov, D., Vedaldi, A., and Lempitsky, V. (2016). Instance normalization: The missing ingredient for fast stylization.

Vijayan, A. and Gandour, J. (1995). On the notion of a "subtle phonetic deficit" in fluent/posterior aphasia. *Brain and Language*, 48(1):106–119.

Worrall, D. E., Garbin, S. J., Turmukhambetov, D., and Brostow, G. J. (2017). Harmonic networks: Deep translation and rotation equivariance. In *2017 IEEE Conference on Computer Vision and Pattern Recognition (CVPR)*, pages 7168–7177, Los Alamitos, CA, USA, jul. IEEE Computer Society.

A. Experimental details

A.1. TIMIT augmentations

Table 4 contains the results of the augmentations using the 64 minutes of TIMIT (see subsection 2.1.2, above). The name of the augmentation in the table corresponds with the branch name of the git repository[13].

Augmentation	**FER**	**PER**
unaugmented	10.2%	22.5%
gaussian	10.0%	22.1%
pitchshift	9.6%	22.9%
rir	**9.6%**	**21.8%**
timestretch	10.1%	22.8%
gaussian-rir	10.0%	23.4%
pitchshift-gaussian	9.9%	22.9%
pitchshift-rir	9.9%	22.8%
timestretch-gaussian	10.2%	22.8%
timestretch-pitchshift	9.8%	22.0%
timestretch-rir	9.7%	22.2%
pitchshift-gaussian-rir	10.1%	23.5%
timestretch-gaussian-rir	9.7%	22.3%
timestretch-pitchshift-gaussian	10.2%	22.9%
timestretch-pitchshift-rir	10.2%	22.5%
timestretch-pitchshift-gaussian-rir	10.9%	24.1%

Table 4: Results of combining various augmentations of TIMIT with the unaugmented PSST data.

A.2. Language model experiments

Table 5 contains the results of all permutations of the experiments with language models (see subsection 2.4.3, above). The models are contained in the same git repository as the TIMIT augmentations; the README accompanying the repository contains a mapping of branches to the experiment.

	n-gram	**FER**	**PER**
Baseline + TIMIT	–	**10.2%**	22.5%
All silences	4	10.5%	23.0%
	5	10.5%	22.6%
	6	10.3%	22.3%
No silences	4	10.3%	22.6%
	5	**10.2%**	22.2%
	6	**10.2%**	22.4%
PSST and TIMIT without silence			
CMUdict-end	4	10.3%	22.6%
	5	**10.2%**	**22.1%**
	6	**10.2%**	22.3%
CMUdict-start	4	10.4%	22.6%
	5	10.3%	22.4%
	6	10.3%	22.3%
CMUdict-both	4	10.4%	22.7%
	5	10.4%	22.3%
	6	10.3%	22.3%
Unmodified PSST and TIMIT			
Unmodified CMUdict	4	10.3%	22.8%
	5	10.3%	22.4%
	6	**10.2%**	22.4%
CMUdict-end	4	10.3%	22.7%
	5	**10.2%**	22.2%
	6	**10.2%**	22.3%
CMUdict-start	4	10.5%	22.8%
	5	10.4%	22.5%
	6	10.3%	22.4%
CMUdict-both	4	10.5%	22.8%
	5	10.4%	22.4%
	6	10.4%	22.4%

Table 5: Results of different language model configurations.

[13] `https://huggingface.co/jimregan/psst-partial-timit`

Proceedings of the RaPID-4 @LREC 2022, pages 71–79
Marseille, 25 June 2022

Data Augmentation for the Post-Stroke Speech Transcription (PSST) Challenge: Sometimes Less is More

Jiahong Yuan, Xingyu Cai, Kenneth Church
Baidu Research USA
1195 Bordeaux Dr, Sunnyvale, CA 94089, USA
{jiahongyuan, xingyucai, kennethchurch}@baidu.com

Abstract

We employ the method of fine-tuning wav2vec2.0 for recognition of phonemes in aphasic speech. Our effort focuses on data augmentation, by supplementing data from both in-domain and out-of-domain datasets for training. We found that although a modest amount of out-of-domain data may be helpful, the performance of the model degrades significantly when the amount of out-of-domain data is much larger than in-domain data. Our hypothesis is that fine-tuning wav2vec2.0 with a CTC loss not only learns bottom-up acoustic properties but also top-down constraints. Therefore, out-of-domain data augmentation is likely to degrade performance if there is a language model mismatch between "in" and "out" domains. For in-domain audio without ground truth labels, we found that it is beneficial to exclude samples with less confident pseudo labels. Our final model achieves 16.7% PER (phoneme error rate) on the validation set, without using a language model for decoding. The result represents a relative error reduction of 14% over the baseline model trained without data augmentation. Finally, we found that "canonicalized" phonemes are much easier to recognize than manually transcribed phonemes.

Keywords: wav2vec2.0, aphasia, phoneme recognition, data augmentation

1. Introduction

The diagnosis of post-stroke language disorders, namely aphasia, depends on recognizing phonemes in speech. For example, reduced activation of lexical-semantic representations in aphasia may result in producing "dog" for the target word "cat", while reduced activation of phonological representations may result in producing "dog" for the target word "log" (Foygel and Dell, 2000). The primary task of the Post-Stroke Speech Transcription (PSST) Challenge (Task A) is to develop an automatic phoneme recognition system that accurately identifies the phonemes produced by subjects with aphasia. The phonemes they actually produce may differ in important ways from the words they intended to produce. This paper describes our effort for the task.

Recognizing phonemes in aphasic speech is a challenging task for both human judges and computers. Different types of aphasia are associated with different types of linguistic symptoms (Wilson et al., 2010). Problems such as disfluencies, mispronunciations, and articulation deficits create interesting challenges for automatic phoneme recognition. In addition, limitations in data availability introduce additional challenges. State-of-the-art models tend to be more effective when there is plenty of in-domain data with ground-truth labels (with little room for inter-annotator disagreements).

This paper fine-tunes wav2vec2.0 for Task A of the PSST Challenge. For recognition of speech from healthy speakers, the wav2vec2.0 model has recently achieved impressive results. But how well does this approach transfer to speech from the PSST challenge? Our effort focuses on data augmentation, by supplementing data from both in-domain and out-of-domain datasets for training. We found that modest amounts of out-of-domain data can improve performance, but too much of a good thing is not necessarily a good thing. In particular, performance degrades significantly when there is much more out-of-domain data than in-domain data.

Datasets vary in many respects. Some are in-domain and some are out-of-domain. Some come with better ground truth labels than others. Different annotation methods are used by different researchers. Some datasets do not provide ground truth labels.

When there are no ground truth labels, we use pseudo-labels. That is, use predictions from a trained model as if they are gold labels. Iterating the self-training process leads to improve performance, especially when utterances with low confidence are removed from the self-training process.

Less is more. That is, we found that data augmentation can be helpful, but not if there is too much out-of-domain data relative to in-domain data, or if there are too many pseudo-labels of dubious quality. Our final model achieves 16.7% PER (phoneme error rate) on the validation set, without using a language model. The result represents a relative error reduction of 14% over the baseline model trained without data augmentation.

2. Previous Work

2.1. Finetuning wav2vec2.0 for ASR

Wav2vec2.0 (Baevski et al., 2020) is a Transformer-based framework for self-supervised learning of speech representations from raw audio data. The speech signal is processed by a multilayer convolutional network to obtain latent features at every 25 ms, which are then fed into vector quantization and Transformer networks. The contextualized representations from pretrained wav2vec2.0 capture a rich amount of information about speech, demonstrated by probing experiments showing that the representations can perform well on a wide range of tasks (Ma et al., 2021; Shah et al., 2021).

Pre-trained wav2vec2.0 models can be fine-tuned for speech recognition with labeled data and a Connectionist Temporal Classification (CTC) loss (Graves et al., 2006). (Baevski et al., 2020) demonstrated that this approach achieved 1.8% word error rate on the test-clean set of Librispeech with a Transformer language model, and 8.3% phone error rate on TIMIT test set without a language model. (Yi et al., 2020) applied wav2vec 2.0 to speech recognition in low-resource languages. The paper reported more then 20% relative improvements in six languages compared with previous work. We have conducted experiments of fine-tuning wav2vec 2.0 with a CTC loss for recognition of suprasegmentals, including syllables, tones, and pitch accents (Yuan et al., 2021). Compared to previous studies, the method achieved 70% error reduction on syllable detection, 50% error reduction on Mandarin tone recognition, and 10% error reduction on pitch accent identification.

2.2. Data Augmentation

Data augmentation is widely used in computer vision (Shorten and Khoshgoftaar, 2019), NLP (Feng et al., 2021), time series (Wen et al., 2020), as well as in speech (Mena et al., 2021). Very briefly, data augmentation methods can be categorized into four different groups: data perturbation, transfer learning, semi-supervised training and generative synthesis. Without loss of generality, let $(x, y) \in \mathcal{D}$ be the input feature and corresponding label of a data sample from training set $\mathcal{D}$. **Data perturbation** does not introduce new data sources, but rather modifies the original x. Common perturbations include adding noise, random cut / crop / rotation / substitution, mixing, etc. **Transfer learning** based techniques try to bring new dataset $\hat{\mathcal{D}}$ to expand $\mathcal{D}$. Although there could be a domain shift, transfer learning methods compensate this by constructing projections from one domain to the other (e.g. adaptors). **Semi-supervised training** solves the problem that part of the y are not gold labels (e.g. closed captions) or even unlabeled. This helps when bringing new data in the same domain but lacking of gold labels. **Generative synthesis** aims to create new data samples (x', y') that is from the same distribution of $\mathcal{D}$. It relies on a generative model such as Generative Adversarial Network (GAN) (Goodfellow et al., 2014), trained on $\mathcal{D}$ or external data sources. We review some popular approaches for speech recognition, from the above 4 different categories.

Data Perturbation: Vocal Tract Length Perturbation (VTLP) (Jaitly and Hinton, 2013) changes each utterance through a warping procedure. (Thai et al., 2019) tries to alter the pitch and speaking rate of the original speech. In (Park et al., 2019), SpecAugment is proposed to mask part of the log mel spectrogram. Mixup technique (Zhang et al., 2018) is adopted in (Meng et al., 2021) to weighted sum the utterances as the augmented speech.

Transfer Learning (out-of-domain data adaption): The recent popularity of pretrain - fine-tune pipelines largely encourage domain adaption. (Hsu et al., 2021) suggests that combining data, both in-domain and out-of-domain, could improve generalization ability during wav2vec2.0 pretraining. This is also verified in an even larger setting (Chan et al., 2021), bigger model and more data. An interesting work in (Fainberg et al., 2016) uses adults' speech to enhance the children's speech recognition, via the out-of-domain stochastic feature mapping (SPF) (Cui et al., 2015) technique.

Semi-supervised Training (bootstraping): This method relies on some seed labeled data for initial supervised training, then generates pseudo labels for other noisy or unlabeled data. The pseudo labels are used to further reinforce the model. This can be done in multiple rounds, and the model can be adjusted using the seed data again (consistency regularization (Xie et al., 2020)) between those rounds. This procedure is termed as bootstraping or self-training in NLP (Yarowsky, 1995), computer vision (Reed et al., 2014) and speech (Punjabi et al., 2019; Chen et al., 2020).

Generative Synthesis: Rather than a simple combination of existing data, generative models learn joint distribution of $p(x, y)$ and sample from it. Variational Autoencoding Wasserstein GAN (VAW-GAN) is used in (Hsu et al., 2017) to build a voice conversion system. Thanks to recent advance of text-to-speech (TTS) systems, a line of works including (Laptev et al., 2020; Rossenbach et al., 2020; Rosenberg et al., 2019), leverage a popular TTS backbone model, Tacotron (Wang et al., 2017), to synthesize new training data. (Tjandra et al., 2017) named such TTS-ASR loop as "machine speech chain mechanism".

Note that the PSST challenge targets the recognition of post-stroke speech. This speech introduces new challenges, as well as opportunities to apply the literature on data augmentation (Geng et al., 2022; Jin et al., 2021; Vachhani et al., 2018) to new scenarios.

2.3. Is More Data Always Better?

In classic machine learning, when the number of data samples N, is less than model capacity (often measured by the number of parameters $|\theta|$), the model tends to overfit due to the bias-variance trade-off (Hastie et al., 2009). However, deep learning models often have a huge amount of parameters that is more than enough to overfit even random labels (Zhang et al., 2021), but such overfitting phenomenon is not commonly seen.

(Belkin et al., 2019) noticed a "double descent" curve, where test loss first becomes worse, then gets better and better, as the model capacity increases. In (Nakkiran et al., 2021), the authors analyzes double descent curve in deep learning models such as CNNs and Transformers. In particular, they found that within a critical region (the model size falls in a certain range), increasing training data size does not help on testing. But beyond this region (either under-parameterized or over-parameterized cases), more data yields better test performance. (d'Ascoli et al., 2020) even found a "tripple descent" phenomenon, and established a connection between model size $|\theta|$, training data size N, and feature dimension d. An asymptotic analysis in (Li et al., 2020) proves that infinite amount of data with infinite dimension could hurt least square estimators' performance.

Rather than simply adding more data, the model could benefit more from improving quality of the added data. For example, analyzing and compensating the domain shift is shown to be very effective in (Gong et al., 2021). In this work, we demonstrate that augmenting from the same domain can significantly improve the PSST recognition results. On the contrary, if augmenting from a different domain, more data may hurt the model's performance.

3. Phone Recognition on TIMIT, Librispeech, and PSST

3.1. Datasets and labels

3.1.1. PSST

The dataset of the PSST challenge (Gale, R., Fleegle, M., Bedrick, S. and Fergadiotis, G., 2022) consists of audio recordings and phonemic transcriptions of people with post-stroke aphasia. The audio data was sourced from the AphasiaBank database (Macwhinney, B., Fromm, D., Forbes, M. and Holland, A., 2011), from which utterances were selected, segmented, and transcribed by experts at Portland Allied Laboratories for Aphasia Technologies (PALAT). The training set contains 2,298 utterances, a total of 2.8 hours of speech. The validation set contains 341 utterances. Additional 652 audio-only utterances were provided for testing, and the results need to be submitted to the organizers for evaluation.

The dataset has 42 labels, including 39 phonemes from the CMU pronouncing dictionary[1], plus /DX/ for flaps, <sil> for long pauses, and <spn> for vocal noises. Excluding <sil> and <spn>, which will be filtered out from evaluation, the size of the label inventory is 40.

3.1.2. TIMIT

TIMIT (Garofolo, J., et al., 1993) has been used as a benchmark dataset for a number of tasks, including phoneme recognition. The corpus contains speech from 630 speakers from different dialect regions of American English, each speaking 10 phonetically balanced sentences. The 6,300 utterances were manually segmented and transcribed at the phone level. Following the literature (Lee and Hon, 1989), the 61 phone labels in the dataset were grouped into 39 categories, representing 38 phonemes plus pause. Compared to PSST, the phoneme /ZH/ does not appear in TIMIT. The corpus also contains a pronouncing dictionary, in which every word has only one canonical pronunciation. Using this dictionary, we generated "canonical" labels for every utterance by simply mapping words into canonical phonemes. The inventory of canonical labels is the same as the inventory of transcribed labels, except for flap, /DX/. Flaps are common in transcriptions (of American English), even though they do not appear in the dictionary.

The TIMIT corpus provides a standard split for training and testing. The training set contains 4,620 utterances (3.9 hours of speech). The remaining 1,680 utterances are in the test set. In our experiments below, we use the test set for validation.

Table 1: Librispeech Splits

Split	Source	Utterances	Hours
Train	train-clean + train-other	281k	960
Validation	dev-clean	2703	
Test	test-clean	2620	

3.1.3. Librispeech

Librispeech (Panayotov, V., Chen, G., Povey, D. and Khudanpur, S., 2015) is a benchmark dataset for English ASR. The corpus is derived from English audiobooks and contains 1000 hours of speech. Unlike TIMIT, LibriSpeech is not phonemically transcribed. It is standard practice to infer canonicalized phonemes. We used g2p-en[2] to convert words into phonemes. The inventory of g2p-en phonemes is the same as those in PSST except for flap, /DX/. Librispeech, when processed by g2p-en, has no flaps.

Librispeech contains subsets called train-clean, train-other, dev-clean, and test-clean. We use train-clean, train-other for training, dev-clean for validation, and test-clean for testing, as reported in Table 1.

.

3.2. PER Within and Across Datasets

We started with the pre-trained model: *wav2vec-vox-new.pt*, a large wav2vec2.0 model trained on the Libri-Light corpus of more than 60k hours of unlabeled speech. We added a linear projection layer to the top of the base model to output phoneme label tokens. The three datasets in Table 2 were used for fine-tuning. The first 10k updates apply to the projection layer, but not the base model. Updates after the first 10k are applied to both the projection layer as well as the Transformer

[1] https://github.com/cmusphinx/cmudict

[2] https://pypi.org/project/g2p-en/

Table 2: Phoneme error rate (PER) and trigram perplexity (per), computed over canonicalized (C) and transcribed (T) phonemes in validation set.

Dataset	C-PER	T-PER	C-per	T-per
TIMIT	1.37%	7.29%	10.9	13.2
Librispeech	1.05%	NA	11.1	NA
PSST	NA	19.4%	NA	10.3

in the base model. Fine-tuning uses a CTC loss. There is a limit of 800k max tokens, which corresponds to 50 seconds of speech at 16k samples per second. The learning rate was 10^{-5}. The metric of unit error rate on the validation set was used to determine the total number of updates. We used *fairseq*[3] for our experiments.

PER is reported in Table 2 for C-phonemes (canonicalized) and T-phonemes (transcribed). Note that C-PER $\ll$ T-PER. The comparison between C-PER and T-PER is easier to make in TIMIT where the gold standard provides both C-phonemes and T-phonemes. These comparisons are more challenging for the other two datasets, where we have one type of phonemes but not the other, and consequently, four cells are NA (not available) in Table 2.

Note that C-PER in Librispeech is relatively close to the C-PER for TIMIT, at about 1% (We also evaluated the Librispeech model on the test set, and the C-PER is 1.12%). The T-PER in PSST and TIMIT are well above 1%. The large differences between C-PER and T-PER are left as an intriguing topic for future research.

Why are T-phonemes so much more difficult than C-phonemes? It is possible that human transcriptions introduce inconsistencies that complicate predictions. Another hypothesis attributes the difference to fine-tuning. It is possible that fine-tuning is learning not only bottom-up acoustic properties of phonemes and contexts (coarticulation), but also top-down constraints (language model). To test this hypothesis, we trained a phoneme trigram language model on the train set, and computed the perplexity of the model on the validation set. As reported in Table 2, the perplexity is larger for transcribed phonemes (T-per > C-per), which may explain in part why recognition of transcribed phonemes is more difficult for wav2vec2.0.

The phone error rate (T-PER) is much higher for PSST. The perplexity of the phoneme language model is, however, similar for PSST, TIMIT and Librispeech. Therefore, it is unlikely that the poor T-PER performance is due to a particular distribution of phonemes in the dataset. In our opinion, factors such as data sparsity, recording conditions, acoustic characteristics of phonemes, and label quality are more likely contributors to the T-PER performance.

We also evaluated the models in a cross-dataset manner. A model trained on one dataset is evaluated on the other datasets (the validation set is used for evaluation). For TIMIT, the model of canonical phonemes was used. The results are listed in Table 3.

[3]https://github.com/pytorch/fairseq

Table 3: Within- and across-dataset PER (within-dataset: validation error; across-dataset: test error.)

	TIMIT	Librispeech	PSST
TIMIT	1.37%	8.48%	39.3%
Librispeech	8.20%	1.05%	34.8%
PSST	14.5%	14.0%	19.4%

Table 4: T-PER for out-of-domain data augmentation. The last column shows performance on PSST (validation split). 3.9 hours of TIMIT (or Librispeech) is better than too much (100+ hours) or too little (none).

Training data			T-PER
In-Domain	TIMIT	Librispeech	PSST
PSST	None	None	19.4%
PSST	3.9 hours	None	**18.0%**
PSST	None	960 hours	30.0%
PSST	None	100 hours	21.6%
PSST	None	3.9 hours	18.7%

Clearly, the models do not transfer well across datasets. The PER of the Librispeech model, for example, is 34.8% on PSST, which is much higher than its within-dataset PER of 1.05%.

Another interesting comparison is along the bottom row of Table 3. Note that $14.5 < 19.4\%$ and $14.0 < 19.4\%$. In other words, the PSST model performed better on TIMIT and Librispeech than on PSST itself.

4. Out-of-Domain Data Augmentation

In this experiment, we supplemented the training data of PSST with training data from TIMIT and Librispeech. For Librispeech, we started with the unabridged training set of 960 hours, but after receiving disappointing results, we repeated the experiment with two smaller samples of 100 hours and 3.9 hours, as shown in Table 4. The choice of 3.9 hours in the last experiment (bottom row of Table 4) was chosen to make the size of the TIMIT training set.

A modest amount of data augmentation is better than too much or too little. That is, the performance of the model was slightly improved when trained with additional data from TIMIT and 3.9 hours of Librispeech. The error rate was decreased from 19.4% of no data augmentation to 18.0% and 18.7%, respectively. On the other hand, the model trained with additional data from the entire train set of Librispeech was significantly degraded with phoneme error rate of 30.0%.

To understand why using more data from Librispeech degrades the model's performance, we plot the contextualized representations of the validation samples from

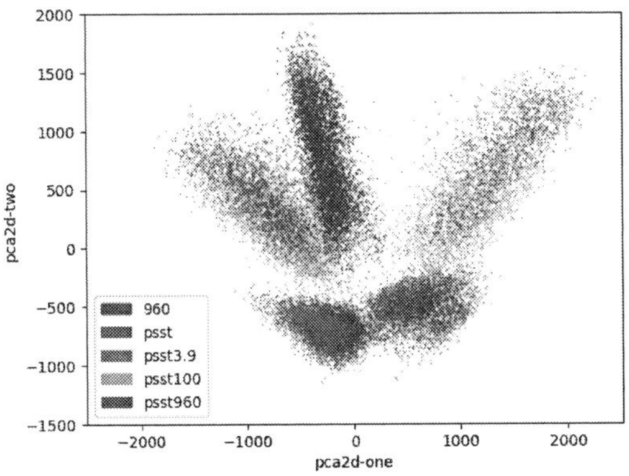

Figure 1: Contextualized representations of PSST validation samples from models trained on different amount of out-of-domain augmentation data, compared with no augmentation (*psst*).

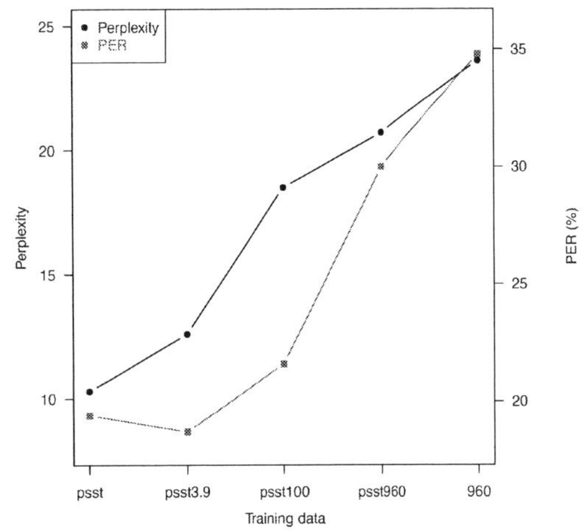

Figure 2: Perplexity of phoneme trigram language model is highly correlated with PER on the validation set of PSST, although language model is not used for decoding.

different models in Figure 1. The contextualized representations were extracted at all frames predicted as a phoneme but not <blank> (i.e., a special token used in CTC). These representations have 1024 dimensions. To make them easier to visualize, we used PCA to project the 1024 dimensions down to 2 dimensions in Figure 1.

Figure 1 shows that *psst* (**green** points) and *psst3.9* (**red** points) occupy similar regions of the plot, in contrast with the three other cases: *960, psst100 psst960.* The **green** points have no training data from Librispeech, and the **red** points have 3.9 hours. The other points have 100+ hours of Librispeech. Augmenting the training data with too much data from Librispeech shifts the representations away from the **green** and **red** points.

As discussed above, the contextualized representations form a finetuned wav2vec2.0 may contain language model information besides phonetic properties. The shift of the representations by out-of-domain data may suggest a mismatch in language model between "in" and "out" domains. To test this hypothesis, we trained a phoneme trigram language model for each amount of augmentation data, and computed the perplexity of the model on the validation set of PSST. The results are shown in Figure 2.

Figure 2 shows that perplexity increases from left to right. The large differences in perplexity indicate large differences in domains. The language model for Librispeech is very different from the language model for PSST. Increases in perplexity tend to degrade performance (in terms of PER). That is, adding too much data from Librispeech tends to increase PER.

However, *psst3.9* is an important exception. In this case, adding 3.9 hours of out-of-domain data increases perplexity by a modest amount. However, PER moves in the opposite direction. We susspect that improvements in phonetic representations are large enough to more than compensate for the modest increase in perplexity. Thus, adding 3.9 hours of Librispeech is better (in terms of PER) than too much (100+ hours) and too little (none).

5. In-Domain Data Augmentation

5.1. Extracting Utterances from AphasiaBank

The PSST dataset was derived from AphasiaBank. In this experiment we extracted 48,937 utterances (47 hours) from aphasia subjects in AphasiaBank, excluding recording sessions that include samples in the test set. Because only word transcription is available, we tried two methods to use these utterances for phoneme recognition. The first method is to use audio only for semi-supervised training. The second method is to obtain phoneme labels from word transcription through forced alignment.

In the first method we used the model trained on the train set of PSST to predict phonemes (i.e., pseudo labels). For each utterance, we also computed a confidence/probability score by averaging the probabilities of 1-best hypothesis at frames where the prediction is a phoneme but not <blank>. The distribution of the probability scores are shown in Figure 3. The probability score will be used to either select utterances or weight a CTC loss, as described below.

In the second method, we employed the Penn Phonetics Lab Forced Aligner (P2FA) to do forced alignment (Yuan and Liberman, 2008). More than half of the extracted utterances cannot be easily aligned because the transcription contains OOVs (out-of-vocabulary), e.g., "*xxx*". Only utterances with "clean" word transcription, 22,836 out of 48.937, were aligned to get phoneme labels for training.

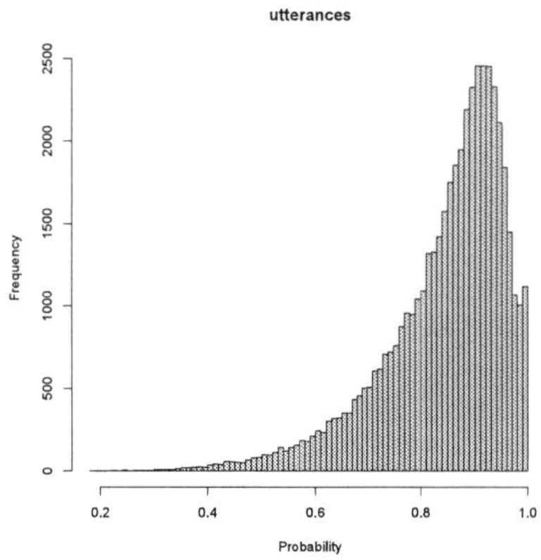

Figure 3: Distribution of AphasiaBank-utterance probability scores from a model trained on PSST.

5.2. Filtering on Confidence and Weighted/Unweighted CTC Loss

To use predicted phonemes or pseudo labels, we define a threshold to select utterances for which the model has more confidence in its prediction. We experimented with five thresholds: 0, 0.7, 0.8, 0.9, and 0.95. When the threshold is 0, all utterances are selected. Higher thresholds filter out more utterances with less confidence. The selected utterances were added to the PSST training set in one of two conditions: (1) weighted or (2) unweighted. The unweighted condition uses standard CTC loss. This condition treats AphasiaBank utterances equally with utterances in the PSST training set. In contrast, the weighted condition uses Eq. (1) to compute CTC loss in the fine-tuning process.

$$\mathcal{L}_{\text{CTC}} = \frac{1}{|\mathcal{B}|} \sum_{(x,y,s)\in\mathcal{B}} -s \log P(y|x) \qquad (1)$$

Eq. (1) computes CTC loss, $\mathcal{L}_{\text{CTC}}$, for a batch of $\mathcal{B}$ samples. Each sample consists of input frames, x, and a label, y, with a probability score, s. When training on pseudo-labels, y is a pseudo-label and s is a score from the system, where $0 \leq s \leq 1$. When training on ground truth labels from PSST, y is a label from the gold standard, and $s = 1$.

5.3. Results

Table 5 reports results on the validation set of PSST for a number of thresholds, with and without weighting. The last row reports results for forced alignment (FA). Data augmentation improves over the baseline in all conditions, with an absolute error reduction between 1.3% and 2.1%. Weighting is helpful when the threshold is small, but the differences between weighted CTC and unweighted CTC diminish for larger thresholds. PER performance improves if we exclude "bad" utterances (or downweight them). PER is 18.1% for all utterances, and reduces to 17.3% with a threshold of 0.9. This threshold selects 18k (of 48k) utterances.

Table 5: PER of in-domain data augmentation using different thresholds and CTC weighting. Baseline PER is 19.4%, and FA (forced alignment) PER is 17.9%.

Threshold	Utterances	Unweighted CTC	Weighted CTC
0	48,497	18.1%	18.0%
0.7	42,816	17.9%	17.4%
0.8	35,096	17.4%	-
0.9	18,296	17.3%	17.4%
0.95	6488	17.9%	-
FA	22,836	17.9%	-

Table 6: PER at each iteration of data augmentation, with the number of selected utterances in parentheses.

Iteration	Unweighted CTC	Weighted CTC
1	17.3% (18,296)	17.4% (42,816)
2	16.9% (28,188)	16.9% (43,793)
3	16.7% (33,554)	16.8% (46,223)

5.3.1. Results with Iteration

After a new model was trained with data augmentation, we used it to predict phonemes for utterances extracted from AphasiaBank. The predictions and probability scores are different from predictions without data augmentation. We use the new predictions and scores to select a new set of utterances. We iterated this procedure until no further improvement could be made. Table 6 reports results for a number of thresholds, with and without CTC weighting. The Table shows that our best model achieved 16.7% phone error rate on the validation set of PSST, representing a relative error reduction of 14% over the baseline model trained without data augmentation.
Figure 4 shows contextualized representations (2-D PCA projections) of the best model **red** and the baseline model **green**. Note that the **red** and **green** points occupy similar regions of the plot, unlike models of out-of-domain augmentation shown in Figure 1.

6. Conclusions

Fine-tuning wav2vec2.0 with a CTC loss not only learns bottom-up acoustic properties but also top-down constraints. In the task of phoneme recognition, a phoneme language model is implicitly learned from fine-tuning and represented in a fine-tuned model. Therefore, for the method of fine-tuning wav2vec2.0, out-of-domain data augmentation is likely to degrade performance if there is a language-model mismatch between "in" and "out" domains. Our study confirms this

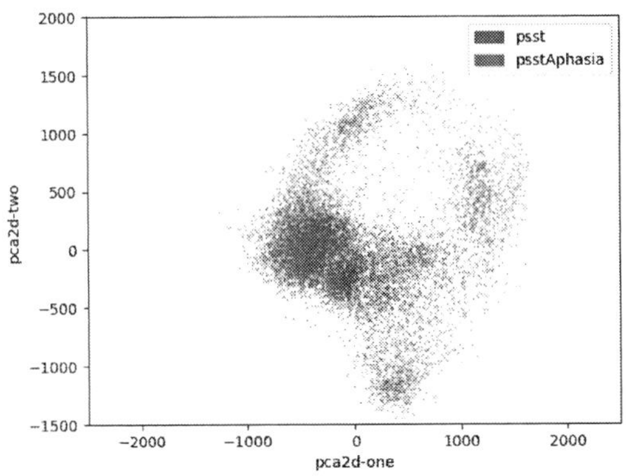

Figure 4: Contextualized representations of PSST validation samples from models trained with (*psstAphasia*) and without (*psst*) in-domain data augmentation.

hypothesis. We found that although a modest amount of out-of-domain data helps phoneme recognition from speakers with aphasia, too much out-of-domain data will degrade performance. Visualizations showed that out-of-domain data augmentation shifts the space of representations learned from fine-tuning away from the corresponding space for a baseline model. Visualizations also showed that in-domain data augmentation does not shift the space as much as out-of-domain data augmentation.

It is difficult to obtain large quantities of speech with phonemic transcriptions from subjects with aphasia. We extracted audio utterances from AphasiaBank and generated predictions (pseudo labels) from a baseline model, and used this resource for in-domain data augmentation. We found that excluding utterances with less confident predictions can lead to a better performance of the model. Therefore, for both out-of-domain and in-domain data augmentation, we found scenarios where "less is more".

We iterated the procedure of in-domain data augmentation by training a new model and updating predictions and confidence scores with the new model, until convergence. Our final model achieved 16.7% phone error rate on the PSST validation set, without using a language model for decoding. This result represents a relative error reduction of 14% over the baseline model trained without data augmentation. The results on the test set were submitted to the challenge for evaluation.

Finally, we found that with the method of fine-tuning wav2vec2.0 "canonicalized" phonemes are much easier to recognize than manually transcribed phonemes. On TIMIT, the phoneme error rate was 1.37% and 7.29% respectively for the two types of labels. On Librispeech, the phoneme error rate of "canonicalized" phonemes reached as low as 1.05%. This is an intriguing result. More research is needed, from both linguistics and machine learning, to fully understand it.

7. Bibliographical References

Baevski, A., Zhou, Y., Mohamed, A., and Auli, M. (2020). wav2vec 2.0: A framework for self-supervised learning of speech representations. *Advances in Neural Information Processing Systems*, 33:12449–12460.

Belkin, M., Hsu, D., Ma, S., and Mandal, S. (2019). Reconciling modern machine-learning practice and the classical bias–variance trade-off. *Proceedings of the National Academy of Sciences*, 116(32):15849–15854.

Chan, W., Park, D., Lee, C., Zhang, Y., Le, Q., and Norouzi, M. (2021). Speechstew: Simply mix all available speech recognition data to train one large neural network. *arXiv preprint arXiv:2104.02133*.

Chen, Y., Wang, W., and Wang, C. (2020). Semi-supervised asr by end-to-end self-training. *arXiv preprint arXiv:2001.09128*.

Cui, X., Goel, V., and Kingsbury, B. (2015). Data augmentation for deep neural network acoustic modeling. *IEEE/ACM Transactions on Audio, Speech, and Language Processing*, 23(9):1469–1477.

d'Ascoli, S., Sagun, L., and Biroli, G. (2020). Triple descent and the two kinds of overfitting: Where & why do they appear? *Advances in Neural Information Processing Systems*, 33:3058–3069.

Fainberg, J., Bell, P., Lincoln, M., and Renals, S. (2016). Improving children's speech recognition through out-of-domain data augmentation. In *Interspeech*, pages 1598–1602.

Feng, S. Y., Gangal, V., Wei, J., Chandar, S., Vosoughi, S., Mitamura, T., and Hovy, E. (2021). A survey of data augmentation approaches for nlp. *arXiv preprint arXiv:2105.03075*.

Foygel, D. and Dell, G. (2000). Models of impaired lexical access in speech production. *Journal of Memory and Language*, 43:182–216, 08.

Geng, M., Xie, X., Liu, S., Yu, J., Hu, S., Liu, X., and Meng, H. (2022). Investigation of data augmentation techniques for disordered speech recognition. *arXiv preprint arXiv:2201.05562*.

Gong, C., Wang, D., Li, M., Chandra, V., and Liu, Q. (2021). Keepaugment: A simple information-preserving data augmentation approach. In *Proceedings of the IEEE/CVF Conference on Computer Vision and Pattern Recognition*, pages 1055–1064.

Goodfellow, I., Pouget-Abadie, J., Mirza, M., Xu, B., Warde-Farley, D., Ozair, S., Courville, A., and Bengio, Y. (2014). Generative adversarial nets. *Advances in neural information processing systems*, 27.

Graves, A., Fernández, S., Gomez, F., and Schmidhuber, J. (2006). Connectionist temporal classification: labelling unsegmented sequence data with recurrent neural networks. In *Proceedings of the 23rd international conference on Machine learning*, pages 369–376.

Hastie, T., Tibshirani, R., Friedman, J. H., and Friedman, J. H. (2009). *The elements of statistical learning: data mining, inference, and prediction*, volume 2. Springer.

Hsu, C.-C., Hwang, H.-T., Wu, Y.-C., Tsao, Y., and Wang, H.-M. (2017). Voice conversion from unaligned corpora using variational autoencoding wasserstein generative adversarial networks. *arXiv preprint arXiv:1704.00849*.

Hsu, W.-N., Sriram, A., Baevski, A., Likhomanenko, T., Xu, Q., Pratap, V., Kahn, J., Lee, A., Collobert, R., Synnaeve, G., et al. (2021). Robust wav2vec 2.0: Analyzing domain shift in self-supervised pre-training. *arXiv preprint arXiv:2104.01027*.

Jaitly, N. and Hinton, G. E. (2013). Vocal tract length perturbation (vtlp) improves speech recognition. In *Proc. ICML Workshop on Deep Learning for Audio, Speech and Language*, volume 117, page 21.

Jin, Z., Geng, M., Xie, X., Yu, J., Liu, S., Liu, X., and Meng, H. (2021). Adversarial data augmentation for disordered speech recognition. *arXiv preprint arXiv:2108.00899*.

Laptev, A., Korostik, R., Svischev, A., Andrusenko, A., Medennikov, I., and Rybin, S. (2020). You do not need more data: Improving end-to-end speech recognition by text-to-speech data augmentation. In *2020 13th International Congress on Image and Signal Processing, BioMedical Engineering and Informatics (CISP-BMEI)*, pages 439–444. IEEE.

Lee, K.-F. and Hon, H.-W. (1989). Speaker-independent phone recognition using hidden markov models. *IEEE Trans. Acoust. Speech Signal Process.*, 37:1641–1648.

Li, Z., Xie, C., and Wang, Q. (2020). Provable more data hurt in high dimensional least squares estimator. *arXiv preprint arXiv:2008.06296*.

Ma, D., Ryant, N., and Liberman, M. (2021). Probing acoustic representations for phonetic properties. *Proceedings of ICASSP 2021*.

Mena, C., DeMarco, A., Borg, C., van der Plas, L., and Gatt, A. (2021). Data augmentation for speech recognition in maltese: A low-resource perspective. *arXiv preprint arXiv:2111.07793*.

Meng, L., Xu, J., Tan, X., Wang, J., Qin, T., and Xu, B. (2021). Mixspeech: Data augmentation for low-resource automatic speech recognition. In *ICASSP 2021-2021 IEEE International Conference on Acoustics, Speech and Signal Processing (ICASSP)*, pages 7008–7012. IEEE.

Nakkiran, P., Kaplun, G., Bansal, Y., Yang, T., Barak, B., and Sutskever, I. (2021). Deep double descent: Where bigger models and more data hurt. *Journal of Statistical Mechanics: Theory and Experiment*, 2021(12):124003.

Park, D. S., Chan, W., Zhang, Y., Chiu, C.-C., Zoph, B., Cubuk, E. D., and Le, Q. V. (2019). Specaugment: A simple data augmentation method for automatic speech recognition. *arXiv preprint arXiv:1904.08779*.

Punjabi, S., Arsikere, H., and Garimella, S. (2019). Language model bootstrapping using neural machine translation for conversational speech recognition. In *2019 IEEE Automatic Speech Recognition and Understanding Workshop (ASRU)*, pages 487–493. IEEE.

Reed, S., Lee, H., Anguelov, D., Szegedy, C., Erhan, D., and Rabinovich, A. (2014). Training deep neural networks on noisy labels with bootstrapping. *arXiv preprint arXiv:1412.6596*.

Rosenberg, A., Zhang, Y., Ramabhadran, B., Jia, Y., Moreno, P., Wu, Y., and Wu, Z. (2019). Speech recognition with augmented synthesized speech. In *2019 IEEE automatic speech recognition and understanding workshop (ASRU)*, pages 996–1002. IEEE.

Rossenbach, N., Zeyer, A., Schlüter, R., and Ney, H. (2020). Generating synthetic audio data for attention-based speech recognition systems. In *ICASSP 2020-2020 IEEE International Conference on Acoustics, Speech and Signal Processing (ICASSP)*, pages 7069–7073. IEEE.

Shah, J., Singla, Y. K., Chen, C., and Shah, R. R. (2021). What all do audio transformer models hear? probing acoustic representations for language delivery and its structure. *ArXiv:2101.00387*.

Shorten, C. and Khoshgoftaar, T. M. (2019). A survey on image data augmentation for deep learning. *Journal of big data*, 6(1):1–48.

Thai, B., Jimerson, R., Arcoraci, D., Prud'hommeaux, E., and Ptucha, R. (2019). Synthetic data augmentation for improving low-resource asr. In *2019 IEEE Western New York Image and Signal Processing Workshop (WNYISPW)*, pages 1–9. IEEE.

Tjandra, A., Sakti, S., and Nakamura, S. (2017). Listening while speaking: Speech chain by deep learning. In *2017 IEEE Automatic Speech Recognition and Understanding Workshop (ASRU)*, pages 301–308. IEEE.

Vachhani, B., Bhat, C., and Kopparapu, S. K. (2018). Data augmentation using healthy speech for dysarthric speech recognition. In *Interspeech*, pages 471–475.

Wang, Y., Skerry-Ryan, R., Stanton, D., Wu, Y., Weiss, R. J., Jaitly, N., Yang, Z., Xiao, Y., Chen, Z., Bengio, S., et al. (2017). Tacotron: Towards end-to-end speech synthesis. *Proc. Interspeech 2017*, pages 4006–4010.

Wen, Q., Sun, L., Yang, F., Song, X., Gao, J., Wang, X., and Xu, H. (2020). Time series data augmentation for deep learning: A survey. *arXiv preprint arXiv:2002.12478*.

Wilson, S., Henry, M., Besbris, M., Ogar, J., Dronkers, N., Jarrold, W., Miller, B., and Gorno-Tempini, M. L. (2010). Connected speech production in three variants of primary progressive aphasia. *Brain : a journal of neurology*, 133:2069–88, 07.

Xie, Q., Dai, Z., Hovy, E., Luong, T., and Le, Q. (2020). Unsupervised data augmentation for consistency training. *Advances in Neural Information Processing Systems*, 33:6256–6268.

Yarowsky, D. (1995). Unsupervised word sense disambiguation rivaling supervised methods. In *33rd annual meeting of the association for computational linguistics*, pages 189–196.

Yi, C., Wang, J., Cheng, N., Zhou, S., and Xu, B. (2020). Applying wav2vec2.0 to speech recognition in various low-resource languages. *ArXiv:2012.12121*.

Yuan, J. and Liberman, M. (2008). Speaker identification on the scotus corpus. *ournal of the Acoustical Society of America*, 123:3878.

Yuan, J., Ryant, N., Cai, X., Church, K., and Liberman, M. (2021). Automatic recognition of suprasegmentals in speech. *ArXiv:2108.01122*.

Zhang, H., Cisse, M., Dauphin, Y. N., and Lopez-Paz, D. (2018). mixup: Beyond empirical risk minimization. In *International Conference on Learning Representations*.

Zhang, C., Bengio, S., Hardt, M., Recht, B., and Vinyals, O. (2021). Understanding deep learning (still) requires rethinking generalization. *Communications of the ACM*, 64(3):107–115.

8. Language Resource References

Gale, R., Fleegle, M., Bedrick, S. and Fergadiotis, G. (2022). *Dataset and tools for the PSST Challenge on Post-Stroke Speech Transcription*. https://doi.org/10.5281/zenodo.6326002.

Garofolo, J., et al. (1993). *TIMIT Acoustic-Phonetic Continuous Speech Corpus (LDC93S1)*. https://catalog.ldc.upenn.edu/LDC93s1.

Macwhinney, B., Fromm, D., Forbes, M. and Holland, A. (2011). *AphasiaBank: Methods for Studying Discourse*. https://doi.org/10.1080/02687038.2011.589893.

Panayotov, V., Chen, G., Povey, D. and Khudanpur, S. (2015). *Librispeech: an ASR corpus based on public domain audio books*. https://www.openslr.org/12.

Proceedings of the RaPID-4 @LREC 2022, pages 80–85
Marseille, 25 June 2022

CorEDs: a Corpus on Eating Disorders

Melissa Donati, Carlo Strapparava
University of Trento, FBK-IRST
melissa.donati@studenti.unitn.it, strappa@fbk.eu

Abstract

Eating disorders (EDs) constitute a widespread group of mental illnesses affecting the everyday life of many individuals in all age groups. One of the main difficulties in the diagnosis and treatment of these disorders is the interpersonal variability of symptoms and the variety of underlying psychological states that are not considered in traditional approaches. In order to gain a better understanding of these disorders, many studies have collected data from social media and analysed them from a computational perspective, but the resulting dataset were very limited and task-specific. Aiming to address this shortage by providing a dataset that could be easily adapted to different tasks, we built a corpus collecting ED-related and ED-unrelated comments from *Reddit* focusing on a limited number of topics (fitness, nutrition, etc.). To validate the effectiveness of the dataset, we evaluated the performance of two classifiers in distinguishing between ED-related and unrelated comments. The high-level accuracy of both classifiers indicates that ED-related texts are separable from texts on similar topics that do not address EDs. For explorative purposes, we also carried out a linguistic analysis of word class dominance in ED-related texts, whose results are consistent with the findings of psychological research on EDs.

Keywords: Corpus Linguistics, Text Classification, Eating Disorders

1. Introduction and motivation

The term Eating Disorders (EDs) groups a number of mental illnesses characterized by abnormal or disturbed eating habits that have an adverse effect on both mental and physical health. Despite the commonality of these health issues that constitute one of the prevalent types of psychological disorders nowadays, EDs are still underdiagnosed and interventions are oftentimes ineffective because traditional "one-size-fits-all" approaches in treatment do not allow to target the specific psychological variables for each individual (Zhou et al., 2020). The self-protective nature of EDs represents an additional obstacle for researchers that are willing to investigate deeper the factors that promote EDs, because people suffering from these disorders are not likely to communicate their experiences and emotions with physicians and doctors (Zhou et al., 2020). However, the increasing engagement of social media users in health-related conversations and discussions (Lenhart et al., 2010) could constitute a potential solution to such problems. Indeed, given the community-building nature of social media, individuals with an ED tend to engage more and more openly in discourse about their disorders with users sharing similar experiences (Kenny et al., 2020), thus making available large amount of ED-related linguistic data. As a consequence, applying data mining techniques to extract and analyse data from social media has become a popular methodological approach in health care research. So far, however, the investigations that where conducted involving EDs led to the collection of small datasets created *ad hoc* for single studies. Besides not being representative and therefore not allowing to generalise the observed trends, the small size of such datasets constitutes also an issue for the implementation of machine learning approaches. Given the need for a larger collection of ED-related data, in this paper we present an English corpus of ED-related posts extracted from *Reddit*. The aim of this work is to create a dataset that can be used for different purposes, from linguistic and content analysis of ED-related discourse in order to gain crucial insights into the factors that can motivate and trigger EDs behaviours, to the development of classifiers that could detect ED-relevant contents on social media. The paper is organized as follows: Section 2 describes the related works; Section 3 is devoted to the dataset creation process; Section 4 presents some statistics on the dataset; Section 5 shows our evaluation of the dataset based on a machine learning approach and a short linguistic analysis; finally Section 6 presents our conclusions and future directions of the work.

2. Related work

The extraction and analysis of health-related data from social networks is now a well-established methodology in different areas of healthcare research (Mullany et al., 2015) The main advantage of electronic communication is that it allows to discuss medical concerns in a less direct way, making users feel less vulnerable and thus allowing them to express their opinions and emotions more openly (Suler, 2004). This is particularly true for people (especially teenagers and adolescents) suffering from EDs. Indeed, researchers have observed that, due to a desire for anonymity, a significant portion of information seeking and discussion with respect to EDs takes place on the Internet and through social media (Oh et al., 2013). For this reason, recently many studies in the field of psychology and medicine have investigated EDs adopting a corpus-based approach to analyse linguistic data extracted from social media (Lukač and others, 2011;

Malson et al., 2011; Leonidas and Dos Santos, 2014; Hunt and Harvey, 2015; Mullany et al., 2015). In particular, the analysis of ED-related forums using linguistic inquiry tools such as term frequency analysis, part of speech (POS) analysis and sentiment analysis allowed to uncover some specific linguistic properties that characterize ED-related discourse and that could be useful for clinicians to understand the underlying needs and emotions of individuals suffering from these disorders (Oh et al., 2013). All previous works, however, share a relevant limitation: the linguistic analyses were carried out on small datasets created ad hoc for single studies and they were often focused on a limited number of keywords. This is the case, for example, for Bohrer's work (Bohrer et al., 2020), that analysed online ED-related forums targeting the process of recovery; but also for McCaig and colleagues' works (McCaig et al., 2018; McCaig et al., 2019; McCaig et al., 2020), whose thematic analysis of ED-related forums was centred on calorie counting apps and fitness tracking technology; as well as for Moessner's study (Moessner et al., 2018), that focused on identifying topics related to social support in EDs treatment. Besides reducing the generalizability of the observed trends to the population, the small dataset size does not allow to implement machine learning algorithms for ED-relevant contents identification and recognition tasks. So far, there has been only a single attempt to develop a machine learning-based classifier to identify tweets related to EDs (Zhou et al., 2020). In this case the authors did manage to collect a quite large dataset, but the nature of the texts they collected, that are short, often convoluted and difficult to analyse because of the presence of hashtags and abbreviations, does not allow to adapt the dataset to different tasks, thus limiting its applications.

3. Methods

Our goal was to create a corpus on EDs that could be used for various types of analyses, being at the same time easily adaptable for different machine learning tasks. In order to accomplish this, we focused on the American social news website and forum *Reddit*, a discussion website where registered members submit contents such as links, text posts, images, and videos, which are then voted up or down by other members. Registrations is free and posts are organized by subject into user-created boards called "communities" or "subreddits", which cover a wide variety of topics and can be accessed via keyword search. The reason why we selected this platform is twofold: on the one hand, not imposing any limitation in the length of the posts, *Reddit* makes available longer and more complex texts (compared for example with the largely investigated *Twitter*, where the maximum length of a post is 280 characters); on the other hand, the discussion-oriented nature of the website also naturally leads to more articulated and linguistically rich comments. For these reasons, the type of linguistic data that can be extracted from *Reddit* appears to be suitable for the task at hand, that is building a multi-purpose corpus on EDs. Indeed, it has been shown that performance of NLP methods increase with the length of the documents being analyzed (Curiskis et al., 2020). In addition, as suggested by Shen & Rudzicz (2017), the lenght of *Reddit*'s posts, together with the website organization, constitute a "considerable potential for sophisticated methods of feature extraction as well as qualitative analysis" (Shen and Rudzicz, 2017, pag.63).

3.1. Keyword-based search on *Reddit*

In order to get access to the relevant comments we performed a keyword-based search using the Python Reddit API Wrapper[1] (PRAW), a Python package that allows for simple access to Reddit's API[2]. As keywords we used the list of names of the most prevalent EDs that was obtained from a dedicated website[3]. For each ED name we obtained the related subreddits titles and collected all the posts classified under each subreddit (see Table 1 for the complete list). Each text was then annotated according to the ED it describes using an abbreviation of the corresponding ED name (ex. BU for Bulimia). The abbreviations are reported below the ED names in the first column of Table 1. Given that we aimed to build a corpus that could be used for EDs classification purposes, we needed to collect an equally extensive sample of EDs-unrelated comments that would constitute the negative class. Following the same procedure that was described above, we performed a keyword-based search on *Reddit*, and we extracted all the posts classified under each subreddit related to the keywords. One of the most common ways of building negative class dataset is via random selection, however, in this case the comments were extracted starting from a list of manually selected keywords that refer to frequently occurring topics in EDs discourse (i.e. *food, fitness*). In doing so, we could hypothesize that the main feature(s) distinguishing the positive class (ED-related posts) from the negative class (ED-unrelated posts) are exactly the features that characterize EDs discourse. Table 2 reports the list of selected topics, the corresponding subreddit titles and the number of posts extracted for each subreddit.

3.2. Comments selection and cleaning

In the cleaning step we cleared each comment from emoticons, hyperlinks and hashtags, but we did not remove punctuation marks because they have often been shown to provide a crucial contribution for understanding the psychological state of the speaker (Say and Akman, 1996; Oh et al., 2013). In order to standardise the texts and to maximize the quantity and quality of linguistic information, we replaced contractions (i.e.

[1]https://github.com/praw-dev/praw

[2]https://www.reddit.com/dev/api

[3]https://www.freedeatingdisorders.org/patient-family-support/types-of-eating-disorders/

ED names	subreddit titles	posts
Eating Disorder(s) ED	*EatingDisorders', 'eating_disorders', 'EatingDisorderHope', 'edsupport', 'EDAnonymous', 'EdAnonymousAdults', 'EDRecovery_public', 'EDRecovery'*	5089
Anorexia AN	*'AnorexiaNervosa', 'AnorexiaRecovery', 'ProAnaBuddies', 'anorexiaflareuphelp'*	3957
Bulimia BU	*'bulimia',' BulimiaAndAnaSupport'*	685
Binge Eating BE	*'BingeEatingDisorder', 'bingeeating'*	811
Purging PU	*'PurgingDisorder'*	6
Not Otherwise Specified NOS	*'NotOtherwiseSpecified', 'Ednos*	23

Table 1: List of ED-related word included in the search, corresponding subreddit titles and total number of posts retrieved for each subreddit

Common EDs topics	subreddit titles	posts
Nutrition	*'nutrition', 'EatCheapAndHealthy', 'ketogains', 'SportNutrition', 'EatingHealthy', 'EatHealthy', 'intuitiveeating'*	2332
Food	*'HealthFoodChat', 'FitnessFood', 'Macrofoodients'*	17
Fitness	*'xxfitness', 'veganfitness', 'runmeals', 'workout', 'bodyweightfitness'*	1833
Diet	*'Dietandhealth', 'diet', ' dieting', 'PlantBasedDiet', 'Pescetarian'*	1351

Table 2: List of frequently occurring topics in EDs discourse included in the search, corresponding subreddit titles and total number of posts retrieved for each subreddit

don't), abbreviations and slang forms (i.e. *asap*), and medical acronyms (i.e. *AN*) with the corresponding extended forms (respectively: *do not, as soon as possible* and *Anorexia Nervosa*). Finally, given the already discussed potential of longer texts for both quantitative and qualitative analysis (see Section 3), we decided to exclude from the cleaned dataset comments that were shorter than the maximum length of a tweet (280 char.).

4. Corpus statistics

In this section we highlight some additional statistics regarding CorEDs. These statistics refer to the total number of posts that were collected, the total number of words and the average post length for each of the two datasets. As shown in Table 3, the ED-related dataset contains 7662 posts (more than 1.4 million of words) whose average length is 194 words, while in the ED-unrelated dataset there are 6538 posts (around 1.2 million of words) whose average length is 184 words. The whole corpus contains 14200 posts for a total of almost 2.7 million of words and is available for research purposes on request from the corresponding author [CS].

Dataset	ED-rel	ED-unrel	Total
# of posts	7662	6538	14200
# of words	1 486 325	1 210 495	2 696 820
Av.len.	194	184	189

Table 3: Statistics of the two datasets and of the whole corpus: total number of posts, total number of words and average length of posts (in number of words).

5. Experiments and Results

In this section we describe, the different experiments we carried out to test the validity of the datasets. In particular, we trained two machine learning classifiers and compared their performances. We also performed a short linguistic analysis of the datasets by identifying the dominant word classes.

5.1. Classification

The two classifiers selected for the task were the Multinomial Naive Bayes (MNB) and the Support Vector Machine (SVM). Both are well known machine learning algorithms that have been shown to be accurate and highly effective in binary classification tasks. The dataset was split 80% for training and 20% for testing.

5.2. Results

In this subsection we report on and discuss the performance of the two classifiers on our corpus. In order to evaluate and compare their results we used the usual metrics in text classification: Precision (*P*), Recall (*R*), F-score (F_1) and Accuracy (*Acc*). The results achieved with the two classifiers are reported in Table 4. The high classification performance of both classifiers indicates that good separation between ED-related and unrelated posts can be obtained by using automatic classifiers. As can be seen, overall the SVM performed better than the MNB and this might be due to the fact that the nature of the SVM is probabilistic and it takes into account the interaction between features, while the MNB is geometric and based on the assumption that the features are independent. For explorative purposes, we decided to extract from the MNB the most informative features that the classifier selected to distinguish between ED-related and ED-unrelated texts. We reported in Table 5 the 20 most informative features for the positive (ED-related) and negative (ED-unrelated) datasets. Interestingly, many features are shared between the two datasets, indicating a high level of similarity between the texts they contain. This is probably due to the fact that the ED-unrelated dataset was specifically built using texts covering topics that overlap with those in the ED-related dataset, such as dieting, fitness and healthy eating, with the only difference that in the ED-related texts these topics are discussed from the perspective of individual suffering from EDs. Indeed, features like 'food', 'eat/eating', 'weight' are shared by the two datasets, while distinguishing features (highlighted in bold in Table 5) are strongly ED-related in the positive dataset ('recovery', 'binge', 'help') and connected to fitness and fitness dieting in the negative one ('protein', 'workout', 'good').

Classifier	*P*	*R*	F_1	*Acc*
MNB	0.91	0.91	0.90	0.904
SVM	0.93	0.93	0.93	**0.935**

Table 4: Results obtained with the Multinomial Naive Bayes (MNB) and the Support Vector Machine (SVM), reported in terms of Precision (*P*), Recall (*R*), F-score (F_1) and Accuracy (*Acc*).

5.3. Identifying dominant word classes in ED-related text

In order to gain a better understanding of the characteristics of ED-related text, we performed an analysis to identify the dominant word classes in the ED-related dataset. The adopted methodology was inspired by the work of (Mihalcea and Strapparava, 2009), to calculate the saliency *(dominance)* of a word class in a target collection of texts (for a precise description of the methodology see Mihalcea & Strapparava, 2009). The dominance score obtained with such methodology (Mihalcea and Strapparava, 2009) should be interpreted as follows: if the dominance score takes on a value that is close to 1 this means that the target word class is similarly distributed in both datasets; if the value is significantly higher than 1, then the target word class is dominant in the ED-related dataset; and vice-versa, if the value is significantly lower than 1, this indicates that the word class is dominant in the ED-unrelated dataset. The word classes were extracted from the 2007 version of the Linguistic Inquiry and Word Count (LIWC) lexicon, a resource developed for psycholinguistic analysis that has been largely validated (Pennebaker et al., 2001). LIWC 2007 includes 4482 words and word

Positive		Negative	
coefficient	feature	coefficient	feature
-5.9344	eating	-5.9675	**diet**
-5.4386	just	-5.9924	like
-5.4889	like	-6.0296	eat
-5.5006	feel	-6.0308	weight
-5.6289	eat	-6.0453	just
-5.6370	weight	-6.1417	eating
-5.7025	know	-6.2835	food
-5.7844	want	-6.2852	body
-5.8613	really	-6.3035	day
-5.8731	food	-6.3171	**protein**
-6.0693	time	-6.3339	want
-6.1010	**recovery**	-6.3871	feel
-6.1958	body	-6.3876	really
-6.2067	**going**	-6.4113	**fat**
-6.2152	**did**	-6.4349	**workout**
-6.2329	day	-6.4497	**have**
-6.2649	**binge**	-6.4557	know
-6.2677	**help**	-6.5064	week
-6.2823	**think**	-6.5317	time
-6.3845	does	-6.5494	**good**

Table 5: Most informative features and corresponding coefficients for the positive (ED-related) and the negative (ED-unrelated) datasets.

stems grouped into 64 word classes that are considered relevant for analysing psychological processes. Table 6 and 7 report the top ranked classes for both datasets along with their dominance score and a few sample words belonging to the class and also appearing in the texts. In the direction of a clearer discussion of the results, we divided the word classes into two groups using LIWC categories as reference. More specifically, Table 6 shows the "standard function words categories" (Chung and Pennebaker, 2007, pg.344), i.e. *function words, verbs, pronouns, relatives, prepositions* etc., that are useful to analyse the morphosyntactic structure of the texts, in other words to analyze *how* the content is expressed. On the other hand, Table 7 displays content and emotion words (Chung and Pennebaker, 2007), that are needed to analyse the semantics of the texts, that is to say *what* the text is about. As we can see, focusing on the morphosyntactic structure of discourse (Table 6), ED-related texts appear to be characterized by the large presence of negations, first-person narrative, extensive use of pronouns and preponderance of past tense. This is coherent with the literature, as it has been shown that the use of the first person singular pronoun (Oh et al., 2013), as well as of negations (Leis et al., 2019), is often linked to depression, isolation and mental distress, all conditions strongly related to EDs. In addition, the large use of past tense and/or reference to the past is also in line with the psychological and emotional condition of both people suffering from EDs, who often use the web to talk about events in the past that might have triggered the onset of the

Class	Score	Sample words
ED-related texts		
negate	1.48	*no, never*
i	1.35	*i, mine, my*
ppron	1.34	*his, our, oneself*
pronoun	1.27	*this, which*
past	1.26	*was, were*
ED-unrelated texts		
you	0.79	*you, yours*
assent	0.84	*absolutely,awesome*
quant	0.85	*any, less*

Table 6: Dominant morphosyntactic word classes in ED-related and ED-unrelated texts along with sample words.

Class	Score	Sample words
ED-related texts		
family	2.10	*mum, dad, family*
swear	1.98	*shit, suck*
friend	1.75	*friend, roomate*
anx	1.75	*scared, guilty*
anger	1.63	*angry, fucked*
negemo	1.46	*alone, hate*
excl	1.26	*without, rather*
ED-unrelated texts		
leisure	0.52	*relax, party*
work	0.72	*duty, hardwork*
body	0.75	*abdomen, hips*
money	0.81	*cheap, discount*
posemo	0.86	strong, amazing

Table 7: Dominant semantic word classes in ED-related and ED-unrelated texts along with sample words.

disorder, and people recovering or already recovered who tell their story and share the steps of their healing process (Wolf et al., 2007). Interestingly, at the content level (Table 7) we can see that words indicating personal relationships (*family* and *friends*) appear to be dominant in ED-related texts. This observation does not conflict with the self-protective nature of EDs and it can be explained in different ways. In some cases the comments that we collected were written by people expressing their concern for a loved one struggling with an ED, but in most cases the comments are produced by the people suffering from EDs themselves, who talk about how the disorder affected their social relationships or, unfortunately just as often, describe what role their relatives played in the onset of the ED. Other dominant word classes that emerged are those connected to negative emotions (*anx*, *anger* and *negemo*) and exclusion (*excl*), that describe emotional and psychological conditions typically shared by people suffering from EDs. It is also worth noticing the high dominance score obtained by the class grouping swear words, that are often associated either broadly with the ED (ex. *"fucking anorexia"*) or more specifically with its symptoms (ex. *"purging is shit"*), indicating the "friend and foe" relationship that pulls individuals towards and against their ED (Serpell et al., 1999). By contrast, word classes relating to entertainment (*leisure*), wealth and income (*money*) and positive emotions (*posemo*) are less likely to be found in ED-related texts and resulted dominant in ED-unrelated texts. The high presence of words related to body parts (*body*) and work (*work*) in the dataset that we collected as negative for the classification, is due to the fact that the texts were extracted from subreddits on fitness, diet and healthy eating, where one of the main topics of discussion is the *work*out routine of users and how exercising benefits the physical appearance.

6. Conclusions and future directions

In this paper, we have described an English corpus on EDs, containing comments extracted from *Reddit* covering a limited number of topics (*diet, healthy eating, fitness, nutrition* etc.). The texts are labeled as ED-related or ED-unrelated depending on whether they were extracted from a subreddit on EDs or not. Within the ED-related dataset, the texts are further annotated with an abbreviation referring to the type of ED the text is about. The corpus contains a total of 14200 comments (2 696 820 words), whose average length is 189 words. Since our aim was to build a corpus that could be easily adapted to different tasks and used to perform various types of analysis, while normalizing the text we did not remove punctuation nor stop words and we did not add Part-of-Speech (POS) tags. Moreover, in order to validate the effectiveness of the dataset, we also proposed a machine learning approach for automatically detecting ED-related comments in texts. Our preliminary results are promising, as they show that ED-related texts are separable from texts covering very similar topics but not addressing EDs. However, given the complexity of automatic EDs detection and classification, further experiments need to be carried out to test the soundness of our dataset on different tasks. Finally, the linguistic analysis performed to explore the word classes that characterize ED-related discourse revealed some interesting patterns of word usage –such as the prevalence of first-person narratives, the predominance of negations and a vocabulary that emphasizes the sense of exclusion and negative emotions– that are in line with the related findings in psychology and psychotherapy. As future work we plan to perform more experiments on the datasets, applying other techniques and testing different classifiers with the purpose of understanding how the corpus could be improved and refined. We would also like to extract the most informative features from the SVM classifier in order to compare them with those extracted from the MNB. At the level of linguistic analysis, we would like to implement more fine-grained investigations on the ED-related texts, in particular trying to better handle the fact that words in LIWC can exist within more than one category and can have more than one meaning, which could have skewed the current results to some degree. In conclusion, we consider this corpus as a first attempt to build a flexible tool that could be used to investigate more extensively possible automatic approaches to EDs detection and discourse analysis and we look forward to further work that could address, from a computational perspective, the main issues in diagnosis and treatment of these pervasive disorders.

7. Bibliographical References

Bohrer, B. K., Foye, U., and Jewell, T. (2020). Recovery as a process: Exploring definitions of recovery in the context of eating-disorder-related social media forums. *International Journal of Eating Disorders*, 53(8):1219–1223.

Chung, C. and Pennebaker, J. W. (2007). The psychological functions of function words. *Social communication*, 1:343–359.

Curiskis, S. A., Drake, B., Osborn, T. R., and Kennedy, P. J. (2020). An evaluation of document clustering and topic modelling in two online social networks: Twitter and reddit. *Information Processing & Management*, 57(2):102034.

Hunt, D. and Harvey, K. (2015). Health communication and corpus linguistics: Using corpus tools to analyse eating disorder discourse online. In *Corpora and Discourse Studies*, pages 134–154. Springer.

Kenny, T. E., Boyle, S. L., and Lewis, S. P. (2020). # recovery: Understanding recovery from the lens of recovery-focused blogs posted by individuals with lived experience. *International Journal of Eating Disorders*, 53(8):1234–1243.

Leis, A., Ronzano, F., Mayer, M. A., Furlong, L. I., Sanz, F., et al. (2019). Detecting signs of depression in tweets in spanish: behavioral and linguistic analysis. *Journal of medical Internet research*, 21(6):e14199.

Lenhart, A., Purcell, K., Smith, A., and Zickuhr, K. (2010). Social media & mobile internet use among teens and young adults. millennials. *Pew internet & American life project*.

Leonidas, C. and Dos Santos, M. A. (2014). Social support networks and eating disorders: An integrative review of the literature. *Neuropsychiatric Disease and Treatment*, 10:915.

Lukač, M. et al. (2011). Down to the bone: A corpus-based critical discourse analysis of pro-eating disorder blogs. *Jezikoslovlje*, 12(2):187–209.

Malson, H., Bailey, L., Clarke, S., Treasure, J., Anderson, G., and Kohn, M. (2011). Un/imaginable future selves: A discourse analysis of in-patients' talk about recovery from an 'eating disorder'. *European Eating Disorders Review*, 19(1):25–36.

McCaig, D., Bhatia, S., Elliott, M. T., Walasek, L., and Meyer, C. (2018). Text-mining as a methodology to assess eating disorder-relevant factors: Comparing mentions of fitness tracking technology across online communities. *International Journal of Eating Disorders*, 51(7):647–655.

McCaig, D., Elliott, M. T., Siew, C. S., Walasek, L., and Meyer, C. (2019). Profiling commenters on mental health–related online forums: A methodological example focusing on eating disorder–related commenters. *JMIR mental health*, 6(4):e12555.

McCaig, D., Elliott, M. T., Prnjak, K., Walasek, L., and Meyer, C. (2020). Engagement with myfitnesspal in eating disorders: Qualitative insights from online forums. *International Journal of Eating Disorders*, 53(3):404–411.

Mihalcea, R. and Strapparava, C. (2009). The lie detector: Explorations in the automatic recognition of deceptive language. In *Proceedings of the ACL-IJCNLP 2009 conference short papers*, pages 309–312.

Moessner, M., Feldhege, J., Wolf, M., and Bauer, S. (2018). Analyzing big data in social media: Text and network analyses of an eating disorder forum. *International Journal of Eating Disorders*, 51(7):656–667.

Mullany, L., Smith, C., Harvey, K., and Adolphs, S. (2015). 'am i anorexic?'weight, eating and discourses of the body in online adolescent health communication. *Communication & medicine*, 12(2-3):211–223.

Oh, J. S., He, D., Jeng, W., Mattern, E., and Bowler, L. (2013). Linguistic characteristics of eating disorder questions on yahoo! answers–content, style, and emotion. *Proceedings of the American Society for Information Science and Technology*, 50(1):1–10.

Pennebaker, J. W., Francis, M. E., and Booth, R. J. (2001). Linguistic inquiry and word count: Liwc 2001. *Mahway: Lawrence Erlbaum Associates*, 71(2001):2001.

Say, B. and Akman, V. (1996). Current approaches to punctuation in computational linguistics. *Computers and the Humanities*, 30(6):457–469.

Serpell, L., Treasure, J., Teasdale, J., and Sullivan, V. (1999). Anorexia nervosa: friend or foe? *International Journal of Eating Disorders*, 25(2):177–186.

Shen, J. H. and Rudzicz, F. (2017). Detecting anxiety through reddit. In *Proceedings of the Fourth Workshop on Computational Linguistics and Clinical Psychology—From Linguistic Signal to Clinical Reality*, pages 58–65.

Suler, J. (2004). The online disinhibition effect. *Cyberpsychology & behavior*, 7(3):321–326.

Wolf, M., Sedway, J., Bulik, C. M., and Kordy, H. (2007). Linguistic analyses of natural written language: Unobtrusive assessment of cognitive style in eating disorders. *International journal of eating disorders*, 40(8):711–717.

Zhou, S., Zhao, Y., Bian, J., Haynos, A. F., and Zhang, R. (2020). Exploring eating disorder topics on twitter: Machine learning approach. *JMIR Medical Informatics*, 8(10):e18273.

Proceedings of the RaPID-4 @LREC 2022, pages 86–93
Marseille, 25 June 2022

A Database of Multimodal Data to Construct a Simulated Dialogue Partner with Varying Degrees of Cognitive Health

Ruihao Pan*, Ziming Liu, Fengpei Yuan**, Maryam Zare*, Xiaopeng Zhao**, Rebecca J. Passonneau***
*Penn State University, **University of Tennessee
State College, PA, **Knoxville, TN
{rvp5555, muz50, rjp49}@psu.edu, **{zliu68, fyuan6}@vols.utk.edu,
**xzhao9@utk.edu

Abstract

An assistive robot that could communicate with dementia patients would have great social benefit. An assistive robot Pepper has been designed to administer Referential Communication Tasks (RCTs) to human subjects without dementia as a step towards an agent to administer RCTs to dementia patients, potentially for earlier diagnosis. Currently, Pepper follows a rigid RCT script, which affects the user experience. We aim to replace Pepper's RCT script with a dialogue management approach, to generate more natural interactions with RCT subjects. A Partially Observable Markov Decision Process (POMDP) dialogue policy will be trained using reinforcement learning, using simulated dialogue partners. This paper describes two RCT datasets and a methodology for their use in creating a database that the simulators can access for training the POMDP policies.

Keywords: dementia care, referential communication task, dialogue data

1. Introduction

An assistive robot for dementia care that could communicate with dementia patients would have great social benefit, given the high incidence of Alzheimer's disease and similar kinds of cognitive decline in the elderly (AA, 2020), in combination with the scarcity of caregivers to provide one-on-one companionship and assistance (GCOA, 2021). The ultimate goal of our work is to develop a Partially Observable Markov Decision Process (POMDP) policy for an artificial agent to engage in dialogues with elderly patients at different stages of cognitive decline, to provide assistance, companionship or facilitate early detection. As an initial step towards our larger goal, we aim to develop a POMDP policy that can engage in Referential Communication Tasks (RCTs; see below) with Alzheimer's patients. The POMDP dialogue policy will be trained using Reinforcement learning (RL), which requires many thousands of training episodes (trial dialogues). RL of policies for dialogue systems, as well as for robotics and other applications, typically utilizes simulators in place of interactions with the real world. This paper describes two datasets we will harvest to populate a simulator database for training a variety of RCT dialogue policies.

Referential Communication Tasks (RCTs), which have many applications, pertain to referential skills, meaning the way people introduce and refer back to concrete or abstract objects, and the way they interpret others' referring expressions. When humans engage in a dialogue, they can mention and then refer back to different people, objects, locations, plans, complex ideas, and so on. Referring expressions are the noun phrase descriptions, pronouns, and other linguistic devices we use to indicate what entities we are talking about. RCTs have been used to study how people choose referen-

Figure 1: Pepper administering an RCT; inset shows Pepper's screen in detail. The subject describes one of the four unfamiliar images that appear in the four corners. Pepper must infer the correct image from the subject's verbal description. For the selected image, identified in the inset with a blue box around it, the subject said "the picture looks like some bent over grass."

tial expressions, e.g., for navigating a map (HCRC, 1993), or as part of studies of turn-taking behavior (Hirschberg et al., 2021), complex scene discrimination (Manuvinakurike et al., 2016), or to identify countries on the world map (Paetzel et al., 2020). RCTs have also been used to investigate communication impairments in children (Bishop and Adams, 1991) or dementia patients (Feyereisen et al., 2007). Typically, an RCT involves a visual stimulus that is fully visible only to one participant, who must describe it to the other dialogue participant in a way that leads to the identification of the correct object. RCTs is used to assess the ability to provide and understand specific information of both ordinary people and people with dementia in our experiment.

To illustrate an RCT from one of our two datasets, Figure 1 shows a Pepper robot administering an RCT to a subject with no cognitive deficit. Pepper's screen presents four unfamiliar images to the subject (see inset), while Pepper instructs the subject to provide a ver-

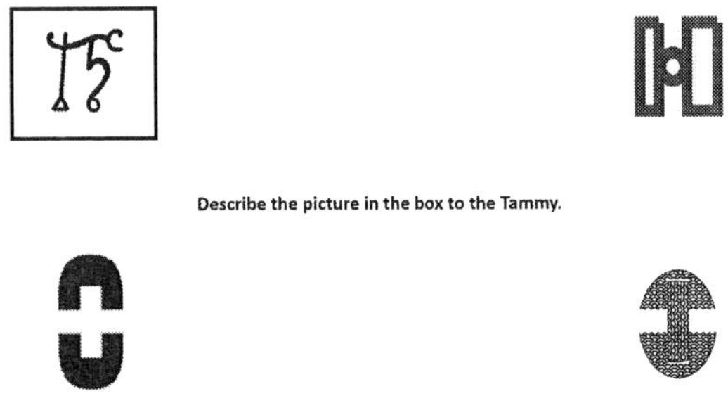

Scripted Pepper

Pepper_1 *Pepper shows four images on its screen to the subject, one of which is boxed.*
Student_1: There are three lines, there is a triangle, a circle and a C at the end of the line.
Pepper_2: Give me a second to figure it out.
Pepper_3: Can you give me more details?
Student_3: It looks like fifteen.
Pepper_4: Give me a second to figure it out.
Pepper_5: Can you give me more details?
Student_5: One has a triangle at the bottom, five has a C at the top and a circle at the bottom.
Pepper_4: Give me a second to figure it out.
Pepper_5: I think I know the one you are trying to describe. I'm ready for the next one.

Future POMDP Version

Pepper_1 *Pepper shows four images on its screen to the subject, one of which is boxed.*
Student_1: There are three lines, there is a triangle, a circle and a C at the end of the line.
Pepper_2: Give me a second to figure it out.
Pepper_3: Does it have any other features?
Student_3: It looks like fifteen.
Pepper_4: It's between the two at the top.
Pepper_5: Can you describe it again?
Student_5: It almost looks like cave art of an animal, with one round hoof and one triangular hoof.
Pepper_4: Give me a second.
Pepper_5: Got it. Thanks for your patient explanation. Let us move on to the next one.

Figure 2: The current scripted version of Pepper administering an RCT, and the envisioned dialogue-enabled version of Pepper administering an RCT.

bal description of one of the four images. The main purpose of this first data collection is to study how use of Pepper to administer an RCT affects subjects' attitudes about robots and the RCT. For this data collection, Pepper followed a rigid script, as in Figure 2. In future work, we aim to carry out a similar RCT where we replace Pepper's script with a POMDP dialogue policy, for more natural interactions with subjects. This dataset and a second one are described in section 3. Briefly, the second dataset consists of RCTs administered by a human researcher to elderly patients, including patients with dementia. We will utilize these two datasets to construct a database of simulator turns-at-talk from three populations engaging in similar RCTs: young individuals with no known cognitive decline, elderly patients with no known dementia, and elderly patients with Alzheimer's.

POMDP dialogue policies can be used for dialogue agents where there is a defined goal to achieve during the dialogue, such as to complete an RCT interview, and where dialogue states are not fully observable. The interpretations of the dialogue partners' intents are only partially observable from the actual words used, and any other relevant behavior, given that human language is highly ambiguous. In reinforcement learning of a POMDP dialogue policy, a fully trained policy will choose each next communicative action a given its current belief state s, based on its expectation of how an action taken in a given state progresses the dialogue towards the agent's goal.

Construction of a simulator for reinforcement learning of a dialogue policy requires a method to sample different outcomes (successor states of s) for agent's communicative actions a taken in s. For example, to simulate the way subjects might respond to Pepper when Pepper displays the image shown in the inset of Figure 1, the initial state s would include a representation of the full display, a set of available actions for Pepper to choose among $\{a_1, \ldots, a_n\}$, and candidate simulator responses to each action. For example, assume we want to test the hypothesis that a policy could be learned for Pepper to respond to a dialogue partner who seems to experience a moment of confusion by selecting an encouragement utterance (e.g., "`You seem a bit tired, let me know when you are ready for the next picture`") instead of immediately moving to the next RCT item (e.g., "`Okay, let's do the next picture`"). During the policy training, the simulator could be designed to choose between a relevant response, such as the one illustrated in Figure 1, or a response that suggests a moment of confusion, such as "*I forgot what I'm supposed to say now.*" Our method for providing a simulated dialogue partner with this type of functionality involves creation of a database of response types where the values of the

attributes of entries in a response table make it possible to control for different response types, during policy training.
The remainder of the paper presents related work, describes the two RCT datasets, and presents our methodology for constructing simulated dialogue partners so that we can train a range of RCT dialogue policies.

2. Related Work

Simulation has been utilized for training dialogue policies for well over two decades (Schatzmann et al., 2006) Eckert et al. (1997) proposed a statistical simulator permitting off-line testing and evaluation in an automated fashion. Scheffler and Young (2000) proposed a graph-based model which produce a probabilistic simulation of mixed initiative dialogue with recognition and understanding errors. Georgila et al. (2005) designed a Markov Model for use with Information State Update dialogue systems. Cuayáhuitl et al. (2005) used a network of hidden Markov models (HMMs) to predict system and dialogue partner intentions, where a statistical language model predicts sequences of goals, and the component HMMs predict sequences of intentions. For robustness to imperfect automatic speech recognition, Schatzmann et al. (2007b) simulated speech recognition errors at random levels, using generative models that conditioned words on the sets of dialogue actions expected from people, with conditioning probabilities estimated from corpora (Schatzmann et al., 2007b). Later work demonstrated bootstrapped policy learning in the absence of domain-specific corpora, using more complex simulators to maintain a dialogue state tuple across simulator turns, consisting of the dialogue goal plus a stack-based agenda to track progress towards the goal (Schatzmann et al., 2007a). Georgila et al. (2010) used simulated users to train dialogue policies for older adults, even though older adults have more complex and diverse interaction. Agenda-based simulators are still used, e.g., in the movie domain (Li et al., 2016). Asri et al. (2016) proposed a sequence-to-sequence model in the restaurant search domain which takes into account the entire dialogue history. Shah et al. (2018) used end-to-end neural models to build an agenda-based simulator. Kreyssig et al. (2018) introduced the Neural User Simulator which trains on corpora to learn how to generate natural language. Shi et al. (2019) developed a rule-based simulator in training reinforcement learning based dialog systems. An alternative to simulation has been explored in incremental dialogue policy learning in the context of fast-paced dialogue games (Manuvinakurike et al., 2017).
We have experience training an adaptive POMDP policy for learning through communication using a simulated dialogue partner that accesses a multi-modal database to look up answers to questions about games, including visual demonstrations of board moves or ways to win (Zare et al., 2022). We refer to this policy as 3GA because it has 3-way grounding in world knowledge, game knowledge, and the discourse context, and it is adaptive. Because the partners answer the agent's questions, rather than asking the agent for help to complete a task, there is no need for an agenda, or an HMM to predict the dialogue partner's intentions. During training, we controlled for the completeness of information in the simulator's answers, so that the trained policy could adapt to different individuals who provide more or less complete information.

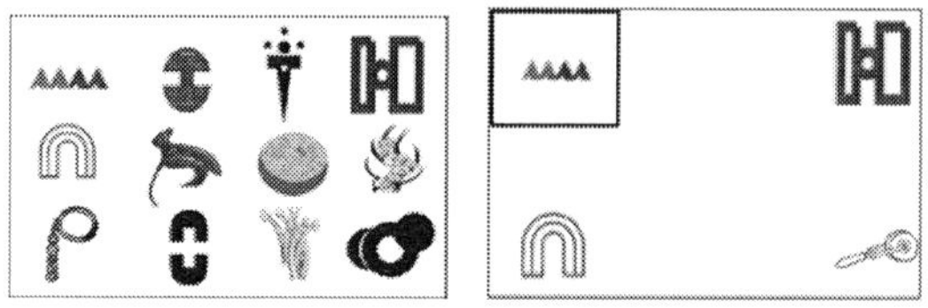

(a) Sorting phase. (b) Testing phase.

Figure 3: RCT Stimuli.

3. Two Datasets of RCT Interactions

The two datasets discussed here are from human-robot RCTs with student participants (HR_RCT_St), as illustrated in Figure 1, and from human-human RCTs with elderly patients (HH_RCT_EP). Initially, we will use the human-robot dataset (HR_RCT_St) to construct a simulator for training a dialogue policy $\pi_{\text{HRI\_RCT}}$ to invest the Pepper robot illustrated in Figure 1 with more natural dialogue capabilities, and eliminate the rigidity of a script. The HH_RCT_EP data dataset will be used to train a dialogue policy $\pi_{\text{HRI\_EP}}$ for interaction with elderly patients. The purpose of this policy is to adapt to the cognitive state of the patient, analogous to (Yuan et al., 2021a; Yuan et al., 2021b), as described in section 5. Based on insights from these initial policies, we will later train a dialogue policy $\pi_{\text{HRI\_RCT\_EP}}$ that can administer RCTs to elderly patients with and without dementia. In short, access to different RCT datasets provides us with the means to design and populate a database for multiple simulators.
The human-robot dataset (HR_RCT_St) was collected to assess how comfortable humans would be with a Pepper-based RCT. The data consists of 98 interactions between Pepper and human subjects, where each RCT interaction consisted of a sorting phase to help participants acclimate to Pepper and orient to the RCT, followed by a testing phase. Each interaction was approximately 15-20 minutes in length. The subjects' audio was recorded for each interaction. The audio has been transcribed using automatic speech recognition (ASR), and will later be manually corrected.[1]
During an initial sorting phase to familiarize the subjects with the task, Pepper's screen displayed 12 unfamiliar images to the subject, as in Figure 3a. Pep-

[1]The HR_RCT_St dataset can be made public once the transcriptions have been corrected.

per would describe one of the images for the subject to select. The subject had three chances to pick the correct image, where each next description from Pepper would have more detail, before Pepper would move on to the next image. During the testing phase it was Pepper's turn to guess a target image from four that would be displayed to the subject, as in Figure 3b, with the subject providing a spoken description. CLIP, a pre-trained image captioning model (Radford et al., 2021), was used to compute probabilities for the four images on the screen, given the subject's description. If one image probability was sufficiently high, Pepper would instruct the subject to move to the next display. Otherwise, Pepper would prompt the subject to give more details. After three failed tries, Pepper would move to the next display. The testing phase had 24 trials, with different target images on each trial.

The human-human (HH_RCT_EP) dataset comprised manual transcripts from 12 older adults with mild-to-moderate AD and 16 cognitively healthy older adults (Liu et al., 2022).[2] The experiment also included a sorting phase and a testing phase. Each subject's interaction had an approximate duration of two hours. In the sorting phase, the subject was given a set of 12 abstract images (Figure 3a) in a random order and the experimenter was given the same 12 images in a certain order. The experimenter described each of the 12 images to the subject and the subject rearranged the image cards accordingly. The sorting task was repeated at least four rounds. If subjects made errors, they repeated the task up to nine rounds until successfully sorting the images without errors for two consecutive rounds. Two experimenters carried out the testing phase together. One was the same experimenter from the sorting phase (A), and the other one was a new experimenter (B). The two experimenters and the subject were all shown the same four images, three that had been included in the sorting phase and one new image. For the subject only, one of the four images was highlighted by a black box, as in Figure 3b. The subject was instructed to describe the target image to the knowledgeable experimenter (A) or the naive experimenter (B). The appointed experimenter marked the targeted image and the other experimenter proceeded to the next trial. The testing phase had 24 trials in a set: 12 trials referred to the familiar images and 12 trials referred to the unfamiliar new images.

4. POMDP Dialogue Policies

A Markov Decision Process (MDP) models an agent's step-by-step decision making for situations where each decision can have different outcomes with different probabilities. MDPs and their variants simplify the decision making task by adopting the Markov assumption that each action is conditioned only on the current state, not on any prior states. Formally, an MDP is a 5-tuple $< S, A, T, R, s_0 >$, where $\boldsymbol{S}$ is the set of states, $\boldsymbol{A}$ is the set of agent actions, $\boldsymbol{T}$ is the transition model consisting of a probability distribution over successor states $\boldsymbol{s_{i+1}}$ given an action $\boldsymbol{a_i}$ taken in $\boldsymbol{s_i}$, $\boldsymbol{R}$ is a reward function for the outcome of each action, and $\boldsymbol{s_0}$ is the initial state. An MDP dialogue agent's communicative actions are chosen by a trained policy π that maps dialogue states to optimal actions. In a Partially Observable MDP (POMDP), states are not fully observed. For dialogue policies, $\boldsymbol{S}$ consists of the agent's belief states that represent the agent's uncertain interpretations of a human dialogue partner's utterances, $\boldsymbol{A}$ represents communicative actions available to the agent, and the reward function $\boldsymbol{R}$ depends on the application. In our recent work, it is a trade-off between a small cost per turn and metrics that encourage the agent to achieve its dialogue goal, such as to learn a board game, using a measure of the inrease in the total game knowledge (Zare et al., 2022). The turn cost leads to policies where the agent ends the dialogue when the expected penalty outweighs the potential gain. This contrasts with a small turn reward used in (Manuvinakurike et al., 2017), where the goal was for the agent to find an image described by the user, and therefore to give the agent more time. For the RCT task, we will experiment with different reward functions, such as number of RCT steps completed, and possibly signs of fatigue from the human subject.

We apply Q-learning to learn the policy. The Bellman equation shown below illustrates that a Q function from a state s to the optimal action a sums over the cumulative reward of all possible outcomes s' of a, where the cumulative reward is a product of the probability of each outcome s' with the sum of the immediate reward R for that action, and the discounted Q function applied to each successive state, using the discount γ. The best action is the one with the maximum Q value.

$$Q(s,a) = \sum_{s'} P(s'|s,a)[R(s,a,s') + \gamma \max_{a'} Q(s',a')]$$

The role of a simulated dialogue partner in training a dialogue policy is to simulate a wide range of partner turns that might ever occur, so that during training, the policy can explore many possible communicative action choices, to learn a good Q function. The policy cannot be learned from static transcripts: any one transcript represents actual turn sequences that occurred, rather than all possible turn sequences that might occur. In contrast, simulator databases can be constructed by harvesting transcripts.

To illustrate using the π_{HRI_RCT} policy, the immediate reward for a communicative action a taken by Pepper in state s would be computed after the simulator responds to the agent, which in turn would contribute to the discounted cumulative sum for the entire dialogue. Say we assume that a human subject will tend towards

[2]The experimental protocol was approved by the Internal Review Board at UTK under the number: UTK IRB-21-06631-XM.

more helpful descriptions if Pepper thanks the subject each time a single description is sufficiently clear for the CLIP model to disambiguate, and if Pepper expresses confusion otherwise. At every turn exchange, the reward includes a small penalty to encourage efficiency. After Pepper picks a correct image, there would be also be a positive reward. The simulator can be used to train the policy when to use a "thank you" communicative action versus a "confusion" communicative action through thousands of trials that use the full array of images in the experiment. Note that simulator turns do not need to be identical to turns humans might take, or even realistic. Ai and Litman (2011) showed that given a simulator constrained to a range of behaviors, generating those behaviors randomly leads to better performance. Rather, they need representations that human turns might be mapped to, say by a natural language understanding module.

3GA-Q1 *RequestNewWinCondition()*
NL: Can you show me an example of a way to win?
A1
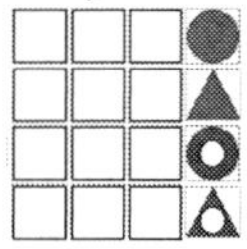
3GA-Q2 *SameContext(D_1), Confirm(translate(col0))*
NL: Would it still count if the pieces were placed down column one instead of column four?
A2 *Affirm()*
NL: Yeah, it would.

Figure 4: Excerpt of a dialogue where 3GA is learning Quarto, a 4-in-a-row game, showing the natural language (NL) below each MRL expression. These answers are produced by a simulator, but 3GA also communicates well with people, using a text-based interface.

5. Simulated Dialogue Partners

The preceding sections have explained how a Pepper robot can administer an RCT (section 1), described two datasets of RCT sessions (section 3), and outlined Q-learning for POMDP dialogue policies to illustrate the need for simulating many trial dialogues (section 4). In section 2, we have also seen that a wide range of simulator architectures have been used, from those that maintain a stack-based agenda based on the simulator goal for task-oriented systems (Schatzmann et al., 2007a; Li et al., 2016), use of HMMs to predict sequences of dialogue-partner intentions, and turn-by-turn look-up of response sets for our 3GA agent that asks questions. Here we put it all together with a discussion of how to design and populate a database to simulate dialogue partners for the RCT tasks. We first present our previous work on a database for simulators to train an adaptive POMDP that can learn board games through multi-modal communication with people (Zare et al., 2022). Then we describe how we will construct an RCT database by analogy with this prior work.

5.1. The 3GA Simulator Database

We previously developed an adaptive POMDP dialogue policy called 3GA, for learning board games from people through multimodal communication. Figure 4 illustrates an excerpt of a 3GA dialogue to learn the Quarto board game, which is played on a 4-by-4 grid, using 24 pieces in two colors (12 each), differentiated by two heights, two shapes, and hollow or solid. The 3GA policy was trained on three n-in-a-row board games, so it could adapt to the game. It was also trained to adapt to how informative the dialogue partner's answers tended to be. A dialogue partner who responds to questions with *"I don't know"*, or with only partial information, has lower rates of information sharing. The fully trained 3GA policy would ask more open-ended questions (e.g., *"where else can I put this piece?"*) with partners who had high degrees of information sharing. With partners who shared less information, 3GA asked more yes-no questions, as in question 3GA-Q2 in Figure 4. Our experiments showed that the strategy of adapting to partner's information sharing led to more knowledge gain about a game (Zare et al., 2022).

The dialogue excerpt in Figure 4 shows a sequence of two questions from the policy (3GA-Q1 and 3GA-Q2) and the corresponding answers (A1 and A2), the first of which is a demonstration of a way to win the Quarto game. To win, four pieces in a row must share at least one property; here all pieces are tall, represented as solid colors rather than hashed. Apart from the first answer (A1), where the dialogue partner displays a game board to 3GA, each turn from 3GA or the dialogue partner is shown both in a meaning representation language (MRL) that we developed for communicating in unambiguous expressions about board games (e.g., `RequestNewWinCondition()`), and in natural language. For natural language understanding and generation, we trained encoder-decoder models on a corpus of dialogues where the MRL had English translations. We collected a corpus of 960 dialogues where students trained in our MRL added colloquial English translations of all MRL turns to simulated dialogues.

During training, the 3GA policy was exposed to any of the three games, and to different levels of information sharing.[3] A simulator would randomly select the game, and a level of information sharing. To answer questions generated by the policy, the simulator accessed a database. For the simulator to generate responses to the questions shown in Figure 4, it accessed a static database that stored all MRL questions associated with a given game, an exhaustive set of possible MRL answers to each question (including `Unknown`), and for each MRL answer, multiple possible translations of the

[3]We refer the reader to our previous work for further details.

Action	Script
`elicit_next_description`	Press record when you are ready.
`inform_processing_description`	Give me a second to figure it out.
`inform_understood`	I think I know the one you are trying to describe.
`inform_move_on`	Let us move on to the next one.
`request_more_detail`	Can you give me more details?
`end_session`	Thank you for completing the test!

Figure 5: Pepper's scripted communicative actions.

MRL into English text. Requests for demonstrations of game boards were indexed with images showing all possible game boards. In addition, the simulator accessed a dynamic database in which it stored answers it had used already within a given dialogue.

Initial versions of 3GA were MDP policies, in which the entire simulated dialogue would be carried out in MRL. To train POMDP policies, after the simulator accessed an MRL answer, it would also randomly select an English text version. To interpret the English answer, 3GA utilized an encoder-decoder natural language understanding module that produces a probability distribution over possible MRLs (see above). The MRL with the highest probability translation and its probability would then be used.

5.2. RCT Databases

The preceding section described a database we used for a simulator to train MDP and POMDP dialogue policies in which the dialogue policy goal was for the agent to learn board games from people. To train dialogue policies for our Pepper robot in RCTs with different subjects, we will construct an analogous database. As discussed in section 3, we aim to develop simulators to train RCT policies with different behaviors. Here we discuss the database formats required for simulators for two types of policies.

The current Pepper script for the first dataset described above (HR_RCT_St) has the six atomic actions shown in Figure 5. A POMDP dialogue policy to replace this script could be trained that could use a natural language generation sequence-to-sequence model, as in our previous work (Zare et al., 2022), to produce alternative verbalizations for the same dialogue action. The advantage of a policy instead of a script would be to extend the range of communicative actions, and the states in which they could be selected, so as to influence subjects to produce better descriptions. As noted in an earlier section, subjects could be thanked when the first description leads Pepper (via the CLIP model) to pick the correct image. Another way to influence subjects descriptions would be to replace the single action `request_more_detail` with a larger range of actions, given an initial description that is not understood, depending on different dialogue states, such as different probability distributions from CLIP over the four possibilities. If two images were equally probable, Pepper could say *That rules two out, but I'm still unsure.* During training, the input to the simulator would consist of a representation of the current state of the dialogue, and the dialogue action chosen by the policy. The database for generating the simulator responses would require tables for each image that contain alternative natural language descriptions harvested from the previous data collection. We would develop an automated procedure to sort each set of descriptions by various criteria, such as length in words and concreteness of the vocabulary, as well as ability of CLIP to discriminate the image from the various combinations of other images, so that the simulator could select new descriptions based on the dialogue state. To continue our example, if Pepper is confused between two images, one of which is the target image, the input to the simulator could include this information, and the simulator could be designed to produce a description that is highly ranked as a descriptor of the target and very improbable as a descriptor of the confounding image.

Difficulty	Example
Easy	Would you like some tea?
Moderate	What would you like to drink?
Difficult	What do you think about this tea?

Figure 6: Question difficulty

In our previous work to apply Q-learning for interactions in patients with dementia (Yuan et al., 2021a), we investigated a simulator to encourage a policy to adaptively respond to the simulator with easy, moderate or difficult questions, depending on different simulator settings to reflect different degrees of dementia. The simulator could be set to have different rates of producing relevant versus irrelevant versus non-responses to questions from the agent. We found that an adaptive policy could be trained to follow up with difficult, moderate and easy questions. Figure 6 illustrates three categories of question difficulty. *Yes/No* questions tend to be very specific, can be answered in the affirmative, negative, or unknown. The moderate question is open-ended, thus more difficult, but elicits a response that is very concrete. In contrast, the difficult open-ended question elicits an opinion that requires reflection and reasoning. The data we collected from the dementia patients in RCT tasks can be used test whether a similar policy could be trained that utilizes a database of actual responses to RCT questions from elderly and dementia patients, categorized by relevance, and other properties of the utterance, such as coherence.

6. Conclusion

The development of artificial agents to interact with dementia patients is a challenging task. Referential communication tasks (RCTs) have been used to assess dementia, but in practice, administering these such tasks is labor intensive. Our work addresses how to develop an agent that can administer RCT tasks to human subjects from youthful versus elderly populations, the latter includes individuals with dementia. Many techniques are available to create simulated dialogue partners that can be used to train MDP and POMDP dialogue policies. We have illustrated how two data from our RCT datasets could be used to train a range of dialogue policies to enhance an existing robot that administers RCTs using a scripted dialogue, and replace the script with more naturalistic RCT interviews. Our future work will test a range of simulators, investigate policy performance, and ultimately test the trained policies with humans.

7. Acknowledgements

This work was partly funded by the National Institute on Aging under the grant number R01AG077003. The experimental protocol was approved by the Internal Review Board at UTK under the number: UTK IRB-21-06631-XM."

8. Bibliographical References

AA. (2020). 2020 Alzheimer's disease facts and figures. *Alzheimer's and Dementia*, 16(3):391–481. Alzheimer's Association (AA).

Ai, H. and Litman, D. (2011). Comparing user simulations for dialogue strategy learning. *ACM Transactions on Speech and Language Processing*, 7(3):1–18, May.

Asri, L. E., He, J., and Suleman, K. (2016). A sequence-to-sequence model for user simulation in spoken dialogue systems. *arXiv preprint arXiv:1607.00070*.

Bishop, D. V. M. and Adams, C. (1991). What do referential communication tasks measure? A study of children with specific language impairment. *Applied Psycholinguistics*, 12(2):199–215.

Cuayáhuitl, H., Renals, S., Lemon, O., and Shimodaira, H. (2005). Human-computer dialogue simulation using hidden markov models. In *IEEE Workshop on Automatic Speech Recognition and Understanding, 2005.*, pages 290–295. IEEE.

Eckert, W., Levin, E., and Pieraccini, R. (1997). User modeling for spoken dialogue system evaluation. In *1997 IEEE Workshop on Automatic Speech Recognition and Understanding Proceedings*, pages 80–87. IEEE.

Feyereisen, P., Berrewaerts, J., and Hupet, M. (2007). Pragmatic skills in the early stages of Alzheimer's disease: an analysis by means of a referential communication task. *International Journal of Language & Communication Disorders*, 42(1):1–17.

GCOA. (2021). Building the caregiving workforce our aging world needs. Global Coalition on Aging (GCOA).

Georgila, K., Henderson, J., and Lemon, O. (2005). Learning user simulations for information state update dialogue systems. In *Ninth European Conference on Speech Communication and Technology*.

Georgila, K., Wolters, M., and Moore, J. (2010). Learning dialogue strategies from older and younger simulated users. In *Proceedings of the SIGDIAL 2010 Conference*, pages 103–106, Tokyo, Japan, September. Association for Computational Linguistics.

HCRC. (1993). Map task corpus. LDC Catalogue number LDC93S12, University of Edinburgh, Human Communication Research Center (HCRC).

Hirschberg, J., Gravano, A., Benus, S., Ward, G., and German, E. S. (2021). Columbia games corpus. LDC Catalogue number LDC2021S02.

Kreyssig, F., Casanueva, I., Budzianowski, P., and Gasic, M. (2018). Neural user simulation for corpus-based policy optimisation for spoken dialogue systems. *arXiv preprint arXiv:1805.06966*.

Li, X., Lipton, Z. C., Dhingra, B., Li, L., Gao, J., and Chen, Y.-N. (2016). A user simulator for task-completion dialogues. *arXiv preprint arXiv:1612.05688*.

Liu, Z., Paek, E. J., Yoon, S. O., Casenhiser, D., Zhou, W., and Zhao, X. (2022). Detecting Alzheimer's disease using natural language processing of referential communication task transcripts. *Journal of Alzheimer's Disease*, Preprint.

Manuvinakurike, R., Kennington, C., DeVault, D., and Schlangen, D. (2016). Real-time understanding of complex discriminative scene descriptions. In *Proceedings of the 17th Annual Meeting of the Special Interest Group on Discourse and Dialogue*, pages 232–241, Los Angeles, September. Association for Computational Linguistics.

Manuvinakurike, R., DeVault, D., and Georgila, K. (2017). Using reinforcement learning to model incrementality in a fast-paced dialogue game. In *Proceedings of the 18th Annual SIGdial Meeting on Discourse and Dialogue*, pages 331–341, Saarbrücken, Germany, August. Association for Computational Linguistics.

Paetzel, M., Karkada, D., and Manuvinakurike, R. (2020). RDG-map: A multimodal corpus of pedagogical human-agent spoken interactions. In *Proceedings of the 12th Language Resources and Evaluation Conference*, pages 600–609, Marseille, France, May. European Language Resources Association.

Radford, A., Kim, J. W., Hallacy, C., Ramesh, A., Goh, G., Agarwal, S., Sastry, G., Askell, A., Mishkin, P., Clark, J., et al. (2021). Learning transferable visual models from natural language supervision. In *International Conference on Machine Learning*, pages 8748–8763. PMLR.

Schatzmann, J., Weilhammer, K., Stuttle, M., and Young, S. (2006). A survey of statistical user simulation techniques for reinforcement-learning of dialogue management strategies. *The Knowledge Engineering Review*, 21(2):97–126.

Schatzmann, J., Thomson, B., Weilhammer, K., Ye, H., and Young, S. (2007a). Agenda-Based User Simulation for Bootstrapping a POMDP Dialogue System. In *Human Language Technologies 2007: The Conference of the North American Chapter of the Association for Computational Linguistics; Companion Volume, Short Papers*, pages 149–152, Rochester, New York, April. Association for Computational Linguistics.

Schatzmann, J., Thomson, B., and Young, S. (2007b). Error simulation for training statistical dialogue systems. In *2007 IEEE Workshop on Automatic Speech Recognition & Understanding (ASRU)*, pages 526–531, The Westin Miyako Kyoto. IEEE.

Scheffler, K. and Young, S. (2000). Probabilistic simulation of human-machine dialogues. In *2000 IEEE International Conference on Acoustics, Speech, and Signal Processing. Proceedings (Cat. No. 00CH37100)*, volume 2, pages II1217–II1220. IEEE.

Shah, P., Hakkani-Tur, D., Liu, B., and Tür, G. (2018). Bootstrapping a neural conversational agent with dialogue self-play, crowdsourcing and on-line reinforcement learning. In *Proceedings of the 2018 Conference of the North American Chapter of the Association for Computational Linguistics: Human Language Technologies, Volume 3 (Industry Papers)*, pages 41–51.

Shi, W., Qian, K., Wang, X., and Yu, Z. (2019). How to build user simulators to train RL-based dialog systems. In *Proceedings of the 2019 Conference on Empirical Methods in Natural Language Processing and the 9th International Joint Conference on Natural Language Processing (EMNLP-IJCNLP)*, pages 1990–2000, Hong Kong, China, November. Association for Computational Linguistics.

Yuan, F., Sadovnik, A., Zhang, R., Casenhiser, D., Paek, E. J., Yoon, S. O., and Zhao, X. (2021a). A simulated experiment to explore robotic dialogue strategies for people with dementia. *CoRR*, abs/2104.08940.

Yuan, F., Zhang, R., Bilal, D., and Zhao, X. (2021b). Learning-based strategy design for robot-assisted reminiscence therapy based on a developed model for people with dementia. In *International Conference on Social Robotics*, pages 432–442. Springer.

Zare, M., Wagner, A., and Passonneau, R. J. (2022). A POMDP dialogue policy with 3-way grounding and adaptive sensing for learning through communication. In *Submission*.

Proceedings of the RaPID-4 @LREC 2022, pages 94–99
Marseille, 25 June 2022

Segmentation of the Speech Flow for the Evaluation of Spontaneous Productions in Pathologies Affecting the Language Capacity. 4 Case Studies of Schizophrenia

Valentina Saccone, Simona Trillocco
University of Florence

valentina.saccone@unifi.ti, simona.trillocco@unifi.ti

Abstract

This paper aims to present a multi-level analysis of spoken language, which is carried out through Praat software for the analysis of speech in its prosodic aspects. The main object of analysis is the pathological speech of schizophrenic patients with a focus on pausing and its information structure. Spoken data (audio recordings in clinical settings; 4 case studies from CIPPS corpus) has been processed to create an implementable layer grid. The grid is an incremental annotation with layers dedicated to silent/sounding detection; orthographic transcription with the annotation of different vocal phenomena; Utterance segmentation; Information Units segmentation. The theoretical framework we are dealing with is the Language into Act Theory and its pragmatic and empirical studies on spontaneous spoken language. The core of the analysis is the study of pauses (signaled in the silent/sounding tier) starting from their automatic detection, then manually validated, and their classification based on duration and position inter/intra Turn and Utterance. In this respect, an interesting point arises: beyond the expected result of longer pauses in pathological schizophrenic than non-pathological, aside from the type of pause, analysis shows that pauses after Utterances are specific to pathological speech when >500 ms.

Keywords: spontaneous speech, segmentation, schizophrenic speech

1. Introduction

Our main purpose is to broaden the pragmatic knowledge of pathological speech, starting from the observation of the prosodic profile of 4 patients with schizophrenia and highlighting their atypia in contrast to non-pathological speech. This work focuses on a functional and structural method, creating a standard to analyze and describe pathological spontaneous spoken language. For this reason, we present the elaboration of a visual structure of segmentation with Praat software (Boersma and Weenink, 2021), on which it is possible to develop different and parallel linguistic levels of analysis for the study of spoken language. We organized a layer grid, starting from an early distinction between sounding and silent, firstly using an automatic script and then manually validating the resulted segmentation. Further annotations have been added at different levels of analysis that are interconnected and allowed cross-layer observation of spoken data.
In more detail, we report here 4 case studies on schizophrenic patients based on the analysis of the Italian CIPPS corpus (Dovetto and Gemelli, 2013) compared to non-pathological spoken language of the Italian section of C-ORAL-ROM corpus (Moneglia, 2005).
Our theoretical framework is L-AcT, Language into Act Theory for the information structure of speech (Cresti, 2000; Cresti and Moneglia, 2010; Moneglia and Raso, 2014) in the reference point of pragmatics. In this perspective, the speech is naturally divided into linguistic units – easily identified by perception – that are called *utterances*. The Utterance[1] carries the meaning expressed by the speaker, is autonomous and independent (Cresti, 2000): it must necessarily have an illocutionary force (Moneglia and Raso, 2014). Its identification as the linguistic counterpart of a speech act (Austin, 1962; Cresti, 2000) allows us to make important observations on the prosodic characteristics of pathological patients and their strategies for the information articulation of speech.
The analysis of Information Units in schizophrenic speech is a continuation of works of Dovetto, Cresti and Rocha (2015) and Cresti and Moneglia (2017).

2. CIPPS Corpus

The CIPPS Corpus (Corpus of Italian Spoken Pathological/Schizophrenic)[2] is a collection of psychiatric interviews with 4 schizophrenic patients, anonymized with the letters A, B, C, and D. They experience different stages of the disease: A is in a pre-delusional condition of *Wahnstimmung* without hallucination; B suffers from paranoid schizophrenia with unstructured delirium without hallucinations; C has paranoid schizophrenia with structured delirium and hallucinations; D corresponds to the diagnosis of paranoid schizophrenia with delirium.
The corpus currently consists of 17 hours of recordings in an ordinary environment without any elicitation: three medical sessions for A (150 min), four sessions for B (238 min), two sessions for B (128 min), and one session for D (28 min). The four subjects are all males from Naples, with an age ranging from 35 to 45, and report standard Italian speech with some dialect inflections (more consistently pronounced in D). The corpus is currently being updated with new acquisitions of drug-resistant schizophrenic speech, in collaboration with the AOU of Naples Federico II[3]. The project is edited and coordinated by Dovetto and dedicated to "Non-standard Dialogic Speech Corpora" which also includes an innovative PhD scholarship (Dovetto et al., 2021).

---

[1] In this work, we use Utterance with capital letter because it is considered a unit of measurement for speech and segmentation on PRAAT. The same applies for Information Units.

[2] The CIPPS corpus results from the collaboration between the Scuola Sperimentale per la Formazione alla Psicoterapia (ASL NA1) and CIRASS - Centro Interdipartimentale di Ricerca per l'Analisi e la Sintesi dei Segnali of the University of Naples "Federico II".

[3] The contact person for the AOU is Prof. De Bartolomeis.

The recording sessions are in the form of dialogues/medical interviews between the patients and their doctor, and mainly consist of monological excerpts due to the low presence of the doctor's turns.

The recordings were manually transcribed (the transcription is available for the first 10 hours) with orthographic criteria based on Savy (2007), then implemented in Dovetto and Gemelli (2015) reporting different types of phenomena: vocal non-verbal phenomena, such as laugh, tough, breath, inspiration, tongue click and throat clearing; vocal non-lexical phenomena, as vowel or consonant lengthening, vocalizations and nasalization; and empty pauses, initially divided into small <sp> and large <lp>, then more finely classified in relation to specific thresholds.

3. Methods

The first step of spoken data processing has been analyzing the recording sessions through WinPitch software (Martin, 2004) for the text-sound alignment, and then through Praat software, to identify Utterances and, within them, Information Units and their exact prosodic boundaries.

More specifically, through Praat TextGrids, the audio files have been processed with a multi-level analysis, obtaining an incremental annotation with one information per tier:

- silent/sounding detection;
- Utterance identification with orthographic transcription, with the annotation of different vocal phenomena;
- Information Units identification;
- Tag of Information Units.

This annotation can be implemented with other and potentially unlimited levels, from phonetic and phonological phenomena (vowel lengthening, different types of vocalizations or nasalizations) to paralinguistic annotations (breathing/empty silences; tongue-clicks; cough, laugh, throat clearing, etc.).

After annotating, we differentiated between spontaneous speaking and other peculiar parts[4] of the clinical sessions, such as reading (for patients C and D) or drawing (for patient C).

3.1 Silent detection

The first tier is named "silences" in addition to a code that includes the letter identification of the patient and the number of the recording session[5]. The tier reports a distinction between sounding and silent stretch of the recordings. The method for the data processing is divided into three steps:

- noise removal, if necessary;
- automatic segmentation of the recording sessions in sounding and silent segments, with a preparatory adjustment of the dedicated Praat script based on the minimum intensity value per speaker;
- manual control of the automatic procedure by two evaluators.

To generate denoised audio files, we adopted a Praat tool that automatically elaborates a noise profile on the base of a selected time range inside the recording, and operates a spectral subtraction[6].

Regarding the segmentation in sounding and silent segments, the clearer the sound, the more the automatic procedure is reliable. However, due to the type of recording, the manual operation was still pervasive[7]. To assess the reliability, reproducibility and consistency of the segmentation, we carried out an agreement test between annotators, resulting in a rate of 0.85[8].

After the detection of pauses, we individuated a minimal threshold for silence in the value of 150 ms[9], according to the average duration of stop consonants (cf. Giannini, 2008; Dovetto and Gemelli 2013), and then we operated two different classifications: one on duration and the other on position criteria.

Concerning the duration, we operated a preliminary analysis based on the literature (references listed below in this paragraph) to identify significant thresholds; then, we considered equidistant thresholds in order to observe objective differences in the distribution of pauses. For this reason, we created two groupings related to intervals with different thresholds. In the first, the thresholds are distributed according to the following non-regular distances: 200 ms (Lea and Kloker, 1975; Duez, 1985); 250 ms, (Moneglia, 2005; Dovetto et al., 2021); 500 ms (Dovetto et al., 2021); 1000 ms and 5000 ms (Dovetto and Gemelli, 2013). Lastly, we added a 20000 ms threshold, which allowed us to identify very long pauses in patients with schizophrenia. In the second, the grouping follows regular intervals of duration to evaluate the distribution trend of pauses.

Regarding their position, and according to the literature, pauses have been tagged considering inter/intra Turns placement, and a further classification was adopted for the silences within the same turn (cf. *inter-tours* and *intra-tours* in Dodane and Hirsch, 2018; gaps and pauses in Heldner and Edlund, 2010; Fors, 2011). The resulting typology distinguishes between:

- T-pauses: inter Turns pauses;
- UT-pauses: inter Utterances pauses (inside the same Turn);

[4] In the medical interviews, patients (except for patient B) sometimes read texts previously written at home and discuss them with the doctor. In two cases (C and D), there is a description of a drawing; in one case (C), there is a dermatological examination describing a physical state, showing body parts to the doctor.

[5] The code consists of PZ, an abbreviation for "patient", plus an identification letter for each of the 4 patients (A, B, C, and D) and the number of the recording. The second recording of patient D, for example, is indicated by the PZD2 code.

[6] The method of spectral subtraction was defined in Boll (1979). The variant implemented in Praat is modeled after a script by Ton Wempe.

[7] Only the 11% of boundaries of the automatic detection remains unaffected.

[8] The test agreement has been made on a sample of PZD. On the base of the silent/sounding detection, we observed the manually verified boundaries comparing starting (t-min) and ending (t-max) times of silences. We adopted a fluctuation range of 150 ms, based on the minimum chosen threshold.

[9] For what concerns pauses under 150 ms, they are unlikely to seem relevant in monologues. Note that in Duez (1982) pauses were considered significant within the speech flow when <180 ms. The same threshold has been selected by CMU Open Source Speech in speech analysis (https://cmusphinx.github.io/).

- IU-pauses: intra Utterances pauses (between Information Units inside the same Utterance).

The observation of the two scales and mainly their interaction reveal important details about the behavior of pauses in schizophrenics. Among the various possible developments of the pauses analysis, there is the differentiation between empty silences and silences with paralinguistic annotations (cf. *respiratoires* and *non respiratoires* pauses in Fauth and Trouvain, 2018).

3.2 Utterance identification

The second tier is labeled "utterances" with the code of the patient. It reports the orthographic transcription of the speech flow with the annotation of specific vocal phenomena; the speech is here segmented into Utterances according to L-AcT.
Based on perception, it is possible to identify terminal breaks inside the speech flow that function as boundaries of interpretable units of the language. The theoretical framework we are dealing with has its core in the correspondence between pragmatic and prosodic units in speech, based on the empirical observation of linguistic corpora and tonal contour analysis (Cresti and Moneglia, 2010).
Each Utterance is filled with its transcription. Thanks to this, we can observe the presence or the absence of specific linguistic characteristics such as disfluency or retracting phenomena, and verify their percentage in schizophrenic speech Utterances. We can also calculate the number of Utterances and their length in terms of word numbers. Furthermore, it is possible to measure the stretch of speech[10] of each patient by correlating this tier to the sounding/silent value of the first one.
The orthographic transcription of the Utterances is internally segmented into Information Units, separated with non-terminal breaks.

3.3 Information Units identification

The third tier is labeled "words" with the code of the patient; it is used to segment the transcription of each Utterance in the corresponding Information Units (Moneglia and Raso, 2014)[11].
Inside Utterances, non-terminal boundaries show the information structure of speech underlining different strategies of language architecture. With the support of the prosodic configuration, we segmented the Utterances in non-autonomous units, i.e. the Information Units. The most significant clue to validate this phase is the pitch contour, both analyzed with Praat and WinPitch. Non-terminal boundaries can occur not only in the presence of pauses, but also concurrently with an f0 reset, intensity variations, or the change of the voice quality.
Below the "words" tier, a fourth tier indicates the tag of the Information Units according to L-AcT. It is named "info.units" together with the code of the patient. This layer of annotation allows us to link a word (or a series of words) to its pragmatic function, and easily identify the more recurring types of Informative Units used by speakers. This analysis permits the elaboration of precise statistics for schizophrenic speech, also and above all in comparison with non-pathological speech.
Figure 1 shows an example of the multi-level annotation described so far.

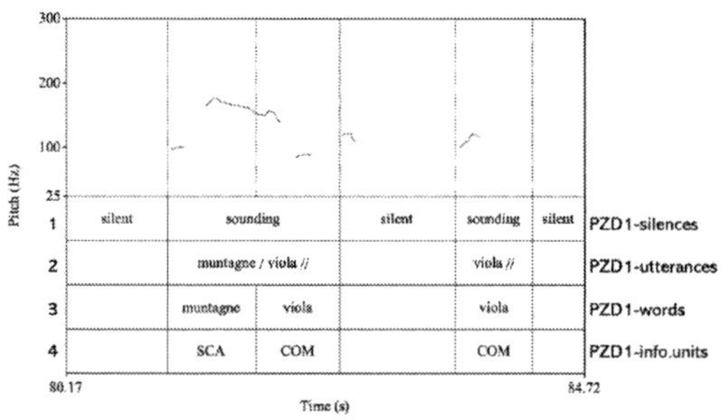

Figure 1. Example of the multi-level annotation in PZD1

4. Analysis

Based on the 3 levels of segmentation it is possible to extract data and information about: silent analysis; information structure of the language; comparison with non-pathological data and its measurements.
Thanks to the transcription, it is also possible to obtain measurements about lexical density, part of speech analysis (automatic PoS tagging), verbal/non-verbal utterances; disfluencies such as retracting phenomena.
We will discuss here in-depth data and results of silent analysis of CIPPS and its comparison with non-

---

[10] The stretch of speech includes silent/sounding only intra-turns, net of T pauses (see 4.1).

[11] As above (see 1.), the Utterance must necessarily have an illocutionary unit (= unit of Comment), the only one that can be interpreted as such in isolation. If the illocutionary unit is not accompanied by other elements, it is called *simple utterance*, otherwise *compound utterance*. The Information Units can be *textual* or *dialogic*. The first ones, of which the illocutionary unit is also part, constitute the semantic part of the Utterance, while the second ones (AUX = dialogic auxiliary) do not participate in the construction of the meaning of an Utterance but perform functions for its pragmatic success.
The textual units, in addition to the Comment, are the Topic (the identification domain of the Comment, and generally identified by three specific prosodic profiles, of which the most common in Italian presents ascending contour on the tonic and descending on the post-tonic), the Appendix of Comment and the Appendix of Topic (additions, often negligible, with descending or flat prosodic profile and low intensity), the Parenthesis (a secondary textual level, generally with a lower intensity and higher rate) and the Locutive Introducer (which introduces meta-illocutions, the most frequent of which is the reported speech).
The dialogic units, on the other hand, are the Incipit (with short duration, high intensity, and variable profile, marks a contrast with the previous Utterance or a turn taking), the Conative (with short duration, high intensity, and descending profile, has the function of pushing the listener to take part in the dialogues, or stopping his uncollaborative behavior), the Allocutive (with short duration, low intensity and descending profile, identifies the interlocutor and establishes social cohesion), the Phatic (with short duration, low intensity, variable profile, keeps the communication channel open), the Expressive (prosodically variable, represents emotional support for the illocution) and the Discursive Connector (long duration, medium intensity, and variable profile, establishes a bond without contrast between two statements or subpatterns).

pathological data. All the measurements have been calculated on the patients, excluding the doctor's speech.

4.1 Silent analysis

Pause duration and collocation inside/between turns of conversation have been analyzed, thanks to the interaction between the different layers of segmentation. Pauses have been marked in a dedicated layer as described in 3.1 per type and divided into groups based on their durations.
First of all, it is interesting to notice the relation between the duration of pauses (silences) and the duration of the stretch of speech (silences+soundings inside the turns) per patient.

	Pauses	Stretch of speech	P/SoS
A	1582.3 ms	2669.2 ms	59.3%
B	3158.3 ms	13205.1 ms	23.9%
C	1381.9 ms	4810.1 ms	28.7%
D	235.8 ms	908.4 ms	25.9%

Table 1: Pause/Stretch of Speech

Data show that A's behavior stands out from the other patients and reflects his effort in communicating and keeping the turn (almost 60% "filled" with silences). This measurement increases its importance when evaluated in comparison with other data (such as non-pathological data) because it eliminates the T-pause influence on data, that is the most affected by the context in which the communication takes place. Even if the percentage of silence is exaggeratedly high just for A, there is a stronger presence of pauses also in the other patients than in non-pathological speech (Goldman-Eisler, 1961; Banfi, 1999; Heldner and Edlund, 2010).
Inside the turn, measurements of the four patients show a different trend for the two types IU and UT:

- IU-pauses follow 15.1% of IU and are mostly <1000 ms;
- UT-pauses follow 41.6% of UT and show a relevant peak of occurrence in the duration of 500-1000 ms.

A unique behavior is observed in patient B concerning UT-pauses: in his case, the percentage of UT followed by a pause raises to 61.1%, strongly influencing the mean percentage (35.1% without D's measurements) and prolonging his time of building turns.
For what concerns T-pauses, they follow 73.9% of T and are mostly <1000 ms. In this case, the behavior of patient B strongly influences the mean percentage, because 70.9% of his silence is made only by T-pauses >1000 ms.
Moreover, our analysis shows that talking about pauses >1000 ms for CIPPS is likely to be reductive; above this threshold, we find pauses with duration >5 s or even >20 s. For a general overview of the frequency of pauses Table 2[12] shows the absolute number and the percentage (in brackets):

	IU Pauses	UT Pauses	T Pauses
A	312 (39%)	217 (27%)	273 (34%)
B	2289 (44%)	2656 (50%)	334 (6%)
C	739 (42%)	574 (32%)	455 (26%)
D	159 (40%)	113 (28%)	126 (32%)

Table 2: Frequency of pauses

4.2 Information structure analysis

Ongoing analysis shows that the four patients' speech has a clear attitude for simple Utterances; in fact, nearly 50.7% of the CIPPS utterances are filled by a single Information Unit. More precisely, the percentage differences between the four patients are minimal: 54.3% for A, 57.7% for B, 45.2% for C, and 47.9% for D. Even if in two cases (C and D) the speakers produce more compound utterances, their number is still low.
This means that the schizophrenic internal structure of the Utterance is usually poor, and the autonomous illocutions are mainly not accompanied by other textual or dialogic units, as in the following example (where the double slash // indicates the terminal boundary, i.e. the perceivable end of the utterance):

(1) PZA1: questa è la domanda //

[this is the question//]

Further analysis will show new characteristics of the schizophrenic speech concerning the Information structure after completing the annotation of the units following L-AcT (Moneglia and Raso, 2014).

4.3 Comparison with non-pathological data

CIPPs data have been compared with non-pathological spoken data collected through previous linguistic analysis of spontaneous speech, namely on the Italian section of C-ORAL-ROM corpus within L-AcT theoretical framework, selecting a subset of male speakers[13].

[12] Preparatory statistical analysis (Kruskal-Wallis and Dunn tests) regarding pause duration per type (IU, UT, T) highlight the lack of homogeneity in the corpus; the only non-significant difference appears in A, C, and D measurements of IU-pauses. The analysis has been carried out by Lorenzo Gregori.

[13] The subset was chosen in particular to have gender homogeneity with the schizophrenic corpus, where the subjects are all males.

As already mentioned, the doctor-patient relationship conditions the speech properties. More specifically, one of the main differences between medical interviews and spontaneous dialogues is the turn-taking rate. In spontaneous spoken language, the hearer tends to answer before the very end of another speaker's turn, as soon as he/she understands the interlocutor's intent. Non-pathological conversation often appears to be characterized by overlaps, while in psychiatric sessions the doctor limits himself to a few backchannels and lets the patient speak.
To avoid this asymmetry, the distinction between different types of pauses results relevant and permits to compare only the two sets of IU- and UT-pauses of pathological and non-pathological.
The two plots below (Figures 2 and 3) compare schizophrenic and non-pathological speech concerning the types of pauses divided by their duration.

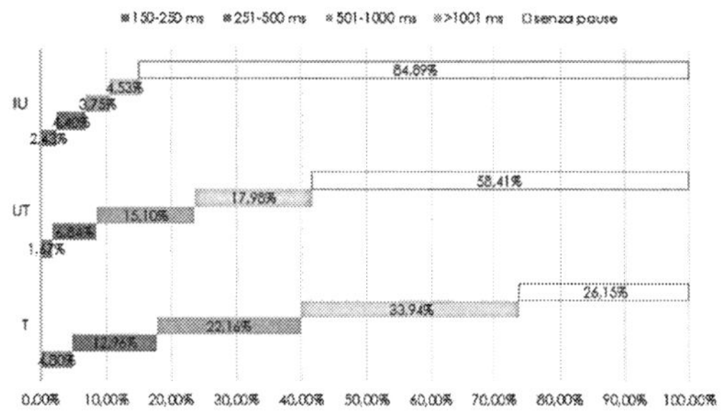

Figure 2. CIPPS mean duration of pauses (frequencies)

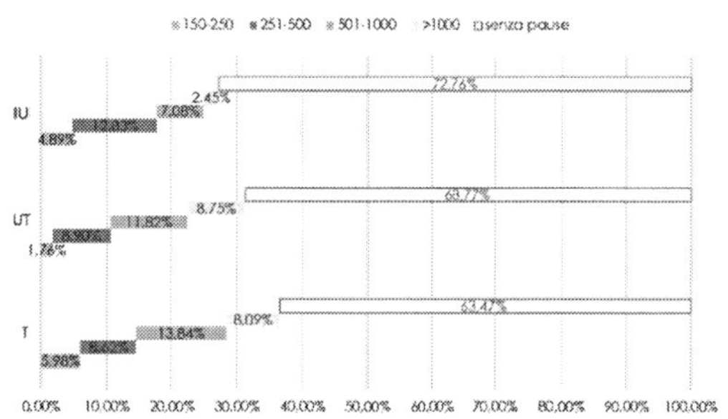

Figure 3. non-pathological mean duration of pauses (frequencies)

Regarding the Information structure analysis, the presence of simple and compound utterances in non-pathological speech reveal interesting observations. In fact, the percentage of complex utterances in non-pathological speech is nearly 68% (see also Cresti and Moneglia, 2005), that is greater than in the four patients.

5. First results

Even if we are dealing with 4 case studies and the research is ongoing, our analysis already revealed interesting and coherent pieces of information on schizophrenic speech, which immediately suggest the characteristic atypia of this type of speech. In fact, the trend of pauses in CIPPS is clearly perceived as different from the non-pathological speech and, despite the non-homogeneity in data collection, highlights a particular mental organization about the *position*, and therefore the *function*, of pauses within the Utterance.
Expected result, consistent with the literature (among the others, see Banfi, 1999), is that pauses of pathological schizophrenic speech are generically longer than non-pathological aside from the type (IU, UT or T).
A distinction between IU- and UT-pauses can be stated: IU-pauses match the non-pathological trend for what concerns their durations; UT-pauses >500 ms are rather more numerous than the non-pathological pauses. More in detail, for the control group: with increasing duration i. the incidence of IU pauses significantly decreases (from 70% with 937 pauses in the range 250-500 ms to 36% with 214 pauses in the range 1000-5000 ms); ii. the UT pauses increase (from 22% to 55% in the two considered ranges). Instead, the trend for schizophrenic subjects is different: i. IU pauses are quite more than UT pauses for the duration between 250 and 500 ms (53% with 1055 IU pauses vs 35% with 700 UT pauses); ii. IU pauses significantly decrease in the range 500-1000 ms with a clear preponderance of UT pauses (57% of UT pauses vs 30% of IU pauses i.e. 1450 vs 779 occurrences), similarly to the trend between 1000 and 5000 ms.
This means that a greater presence of pauses inside the Stretch of Speech in CIPPS underlines the difficulty of these patients in speech processing. The silence is a symptom not only of lexical retrieval (Dovetto and Gemelli, 2013), but also of a weak Information structure.
Finally, we remark that all the observations are made thanks to the visual structure of Praat. In fact, the cross layers interaction allows an in-depth analysis of schizophrenic speech, and it is easily implemented according to the linguistic aspect of interest (lexical, morphological, etc).

6. Bibliographical References

Banfi, E. (1999). Pause, interruzioni, silenzi. Un percorso interdisciplinare. In *Labirinti*, 36, Trento, Dipartimento di Scienze Filologiche e Storiche.

Boersma, P. and Weenink, D. (2021). Praat: doing phonetics by computer [Computer program]. Version 6.1.50, retrieved 20 June 2021 from http://www.praat.org/

Boll, S.F. (1979). Suppression of acoustic noise in speech using spectral subtraction. In *IEEE Transactions on ASSP* 27:113-120.

CMUSphinx, Open source speech recognition toolkit, https://cmusphinx.github.io/

Cresti, E. (2000). Corpus di italiano parlato. In *Studi di grammatica italiana pubblicati dall'Accademia della Crusca*. Firenze: presso l'Accademia della Crusca.

Cresti, E. and Moneglia, M. (2010). Informational Patterning Theory and the Corpus based description of Spoken language. The compositionality issue in the Topic Comment pattern. In M. Moneglia. and A. Panunzi (Eds), *Bootstrapping Information from Corpora in a Cross Linguistic Perspective*, Firenze: Firenze University Press, 13-46.

Cresti, E. and Moneglia, M. (2017). Prosodic Monotony and Schizophrenia. In *Lingua e patologia*. Napoli, Aracne:147-197.

Dodane, C. & Hirsch, F. (2018). L'organisation spatiale et temporelle de la pause en parole et en discours. In *Langages*, 211:5-12.

Dovetto, F.M. and Gemelli, M. (2013). Il parlar matto. Schizofrenia tra fenomenologia e linguistica. Il corpus CIPPS. Napoli, Aracne.

Dovetto, F.M., Cresti, E., and Rocha, B. (2015). Schizofrenia tra prosodia e lessico. Prime analisi. In *Studi Italiani di Linguistica Teorica e Applicata*, XLIV. Pacini Editore:486-507.

Dovetto, F.M., Guida, A., Pagliaro, A. C., Guarasci, R., Trillocco, S., Sorrentino, A. and Raggio, L., (forthcoming). Corpora di italiano parlato patologico dell'età adulta e senile: CIPPS, CIPP-ma, CIPP-mci. In *Congresso Internazionale della Società di Linguistica Italiana*, LIV, online, 8-10 settembre 2021.

Dovetto, F.M., Guida, A., Pagliaro, A. C. and Guarasci, R., (forthcoming). Silences and disfluencies in a corpus of patients with Alzheimer's Disease (CIPP-ma). In R. L. Rose and R. Eklund, *Proceedings of DISS 2021*, Saint Denis, Université Paris VIII Vincennes:121-124.

Duez, D. (1982). Silent and non-silent pauses in three speech styles. In *Language and Speech* 25(1):11-28.

Duez, D. (1985). Perception of Silent Pauses in Continuous Speech. In *Language and Speech*, 28:377-389.

Fauth, C. and Trouvain, J. (2018). Détails phonétiques dans la réalisation des pauses en français: étude de parole lue en langue maternelle vs en langue étrangère. In *Langages*, 211:81-95.

Fors, K.L. (2011). Pause length variations within and between speakers over time. In *Proceedings of the 15th Workshop on the Semantics and Pragmatics of Dialogue*, Los Angeles:198-199.

Giannini, A. (2008). I silenzi del telegiornale. In M. Pettorino, A. Giannini, M. Vallone and R. Savy (eds), *La comunicazione parlata (I), Atti del Congresso Internazionale (Napoli 23-25 febbraio 2006).* Napoli, Liguori:97-108.

Goldman-Eisler, F. (1961). The Rate of Changes in the Rate of Articulation. In *Language and Speech*, 4:171-174.

Heldner, M. and Edlund, J. (2010). Pauses, gaps and overlaps in conversations. In *Phonetics*, 38:555-568.

Izre'el, S., Mello, H., Panunzi, A. & Raso, T. (2020). *In Search of Basic Units of Spoken Language. A corpus-driven approach*. Amsterdam: John Benjamin.

Lea, W.A. (1976). Prosodic Aids to Speech Recognition: 9. Acoustic Patterns in Selected English Phrase Structures

Martin, P. (2004). WinPitch Corpus: A text to Speech Alignment Tool for Multimodal Corpora. In *Proceedings of the 4th International Conference on Language Resources and Evaluation (LREC'04)*, Lisboa.

Moneglia, M. (2005). The C-Oral-Rom resource. In E. Cresti and M. Moneglia (Eds), *C-ORAL-ROM. Integrated reference corpora for spoken romance languages*. Amsterdam, John Benjamins:1-70.

Moneglia, M. and Raso, T. (2014). Notes on Language into Act Theory (L-AcT). In T. Raso and H. Mello (Eds), *Spoken corpora and linguistic studies*. Amsterdam: John Benjamins:468-495.

Moneglia, M. and Cresti. E. (2015). The cross-linguistic comparison of information patterning in spontaneous speech corpora: Data from C-ORAL-ROM ITALIAN and C-ORAL-BRASIL. In Klaeger, S. and Thörle (Eds.), *International Linguistics: Grammar and interaction in Romance Languages from a Contrasting Point of View*. Tübingen: Stauffenburg: 107-128.

Savy, R. (2005). Specifiche per la trascrizione ortografica annotata dei testi. In F. Albano Leoni and R. Giordano (Eds), *Italiano Parlato. Analisi di un dialogo*, Napoli, Liguori.

Author Index

Association for Computational Linguistics
209 N. Eighth Street
Stroudsburg, Pennsylvania 18360

ISBN 978-1-7138-6112-6